# JEZEL

# SPIRIT

# EXPOSED

# &

# DEFEATED

## "Unleashing Heaven's Army in the Battle Against Jezebel"

## TIMOTHY ATUNNISE

Glovim Publishing House
Atlanta, Georgia

Jezebel Spirit Exposed & Defeated

Copyright © 2023 by Timothy Atunnise

Unless otherwise specified, all Scripture quotations in this book are from The Holy Bible, King James Version. KJV is Public domain in the United States printed in 1987.

Glovim Publishing House
1078 Citizens Pkwy
Suite A
Morrow, Georgia 30260

glovimbooks@gmail.com
www.glovimonline.org

Printed in the United States of America

# Table of Contents

Introduction..................................................7

Unmasking Jezebel ....................................10

Arming yourself for spiritual warfare................21

Decoding Jezebel's tactics..............................30

Breaking free from manipulation......................39

The power of prayer......................................48

Decreeing victory........................................58

Burning away Jezebel's stronghold....................65

Jezebel in disguise ......................................71

Sword of truth against Jezebel..........................83

Walking in spiritual purity..............................93

Confronting Jezebel's familiar spirits ................104

Destroying the altars of Jezebel......................115

Prophetic warfare......................................126

Breaking free from Jezebel's influence................137

Defeating Jezebel's assassins ........................146

Jezebel in the church..................................157

The Jezebel-Ahab connection........................168

Breaking the curse of control..........................180

Stepping into boldness against Jezebel................191

Jezebel's influence of gender roles ..................202

Partnering with Elijah to confront Jezebel............213

The Jehu Anointing....................................222

Silencing Jezebel's false prophets....................231

Demolishing Jezebel's Baal worship ................240

Warrior bride............................................249

Jezebel in politics......................................258

The spirit of Elijah ....................................269

The Blood of Jesus....................................280

Breaking Jezebel's generational curses..............290

Dethroning the queen of control ....................299

The mantle of authority................................................307

Jezebel's spirit of rebellion.........................................318

Supernatural strategies..............................................326

Jezebel's effect on mental health.................................337

Crushing Jezebel's intimidation...................................346

The spirit of Esther....................................................357

Jezebel's destruction.................................................366

Discerning Jezebel's jealousy......................................376

Jezebel's seductive manipulation................................385

Worship warfare against Jezebel..................................394

Exposing Jezebel's false doctrines...............................403

Jezebel's assault on the family....................................412

Overcoming Jezebel's jealousy...................................421

Jezebel's control in the workplace...............................430

Jezebel's fear of the prophetic....................................439

Jezebel's false accusations.........................................449

The roar of intercession.............................................458

Jezebel's grip on the entertainment industry.................468

Triumph over Jezebel.................................................478

Other bestselling books from the author.......................488

# Introduction

In the realm of spiritual warfare, there is one adversary that has wreaked havoc throughout history, leaving a trail of destruction and broken lives in its wake. This relentless foe is none other than the Jezebel spirit—a deceptive and manipulative force that seeks to control, dominate, and ultimately destroy all who come under its influence. But fear not, for this book is your guide to unmasking, confronting, and ultimately defeating the Jezebel spirit.

The Jezebel spirit derives its name from the infamous Queen Jezebel of ancient Israel, who epitomized the characteristics and tactics of this spirit. Just as she seduced and manipulated the people of Israel into idolatry and immorality, the Jezebel spirit continues its assault on individuals, families, churches, and even nations in our present time. It operates through both men and women, using seduction, manipulation, intimidation, and control to establish its dominion.

However, the purpose of this book is not to instill fear or highlight the power of the Jezebel spirit, but rather to equip and empower you to expose and defeat it. Through the pages that follow, you will embark on a journey of spiritual enlightenment, gaining insights, strategies, and powerful tools to wage war against this ancient enemy.

Chapter by chapter, we will dive deep into the nature of the Jezebel spirit, uncovering its deceptive tactics and shedding light on its various expressions in today's world. We will explore the signs of Jezebel's presence, both within individuals and within the broader cultural landscape. Armed with this knowledge, you will learn to discern the subtle workings of this spirit and recognize its destructive influence.

But knowledge alone is not enough. To effectively confront and overcome the Jezebel spirit, you must engage in spiritual warfare. Throughout this book, you will discover powerful prayers, decrees, and declarations that will ignite a fire within you, empowering you to take a stand against this formidable enemy. These prayers are not mere words on a page; they carry the authority of heaven, and as you release them, they will unleash divine power to break the chains of Jezebel's influence.

Furthermore, you will learn how to partner with the Holy Spirit and embrace the spiritual gifts and anointing that God has bestowed upon you. As you step into your identity as a warrior in God's kingdom, you will walk in boldness, unafraid to confront Jezebel and reclaim the territory that rightfully belongs to you.

It is important to note that this book is not a condemnation of individuals who may exhibit Jezebel-like traits. Instead, it is a call to intercession, restoration, and healing. It is a clarion call to the Body of Christ to rise up, united against this common enemy, and bring freedom and deliverance to those ensnared by the Jezebel spirit.

So, are you ready to embark on this journey of discovery, empowerment, and victory? Are you ready to expose and defeat the Jezebel spirit in your own life and in the world around you? If your heart is resounding with a resolute "yes," then let us press forward together, armed with the truth, the power of prayer, and the unshakeable authority of Christ. Together, we will expose the Jezebel spirit and see it utterly defeated in the name of Jesus.

## Chapter 1

# Unmasking Jezebel: Understanding the Deceptive Spirit

In the realm of spiritual warfare, few adversaries have captured the collective imagination quite like the Jezebel spirit. This cunning and manipulative force has left a trail of destruction throughout history, and its influence continues to permeate our lives today. But who is Jezebel? What are her characteristics, tactics, and motivations? In this chapter, we will embark on a journey of unmasking the Jezebel spirit, peeling back the layers of deception to gain a deeper understanding of this formidable enemy.

Jezebel: A Historical Figure and Symbolic Archetype

To truly grasp the nature of the Jezebel spirit, it is essential to examine its historical roots. Jezebel, the infamous Queen of Israel, is the archetype from which the spirit takes its name. Her story, recorded in the pages of the Bible, serves as a cautionary tale and a timeless warning about the destructive power of this spirit.

Jezebel was a Phoenician princess who married Ahab, the King of Israel. From the moment she entered the royal court, she sought to establish her influence and introduce her foreign gods and pagan practices to the nation of Israel. She was an embodiment of idolatry, immorality, and witchcraft—a force that sought to subvert the worship of the one true God and replace it with her own agenda.

The Characteristics of the Jezebel Spirit

To effectively identify and confront the Jezebel spirit, we must understand its distinctive characteristics. While it is important to remember that the Jezebel spirit can manifest in both men and women, there are certain traits that are commonly associated with its presence.

1. Manipulation and Control: The Jezebel spirit operates through manipulation, using charm, flattery, and seduction to gain control over individuals and situations. It seeks to dominate and manipulate others to fulfill its own desires and agendas.

2. Deception and Seduction: Jezebel is a master of deception, cloaking her true intentions behind a facade of false spirituality and charisma. She preys on vulnerable individuals, appealing to their weaknesses and exploiting their trust for her own gain.

3. Intimidation and Fear: The Jezebel spirit thrives on intimidation, employing tactics of fear, threats, and coercion to silence opposition and maintain its dominance. It seeks to instill fear in those who would dare to challenge its authority.

4. Jealousy and Competition: Jezebel is driven by an insatiable desire for power and recognition. She cannot tolerate anyone else receiving attention or authority, and she will go to great lengths to undermine and destroy those who pose a threat to her position.

5. Control of Information: Jezebel seeks to control information flow, distorting the truth and spreading lies to maintain her influence. She manipulates narratives and creates an atmosphere of confusion and doubt.

The Jezebel Spirit in Today's World

While the historical Jezebel serves as a foundation for understanding the spirit, it is vital to recognize that the Jezebel spirit is not confined to ancient history. Its influence extends into our modern-day society, infiltrating various arenas of life.

1. The Church: The Jezebel spirit has found its way into the Church, masquerading as spiritual authority while promoting false teachings and doctrines. It seeks to undermine the true worship of God and derail the purposes of the Church.

2. Relationships and Families: The Jezebel spirit wreaks havoc on relationships and families, sowing discord, division, and strife. It targets marriages, seeking to undermine the God-ordained roles and destroy the unity of the family unit.

3. Workplace and Leadership: The Jezebel spirit is prevalent in workplaces and leadership structures, promoting unhealthy competition, manipulation, and abuse of power. It thrives on control and will stop at nothing to maintain its authority.

4. Culture and Society: The Jezebel spirit operates on a broader scale, influencing societal norms, values, and beliefs. It promotes a culture of immorality, idolatry, and rebellion against God's principles.

Unmasking Jezebel's Endgame

To fully grasp the gravity of the Jezebel spirit's influence, it is important to understand its ultimate goals. Jezebel's primary objective is to undermine the worship and authority of the true God and replace it with idolatry and self-centeredness. She seeks to exert control over individuals, families, churches, and nations, diverting them from God's divine purposes.

Unveiling the Jezebel spirit's endgame allows us to recognize the urgency of confronting and defeating it. We cannot afford to underestimate its power or dismiss its presence. Instead, we must arm ourselves with knowledge, discernment, and spiritual weapons to expose and overcome the Jezebel spirit's deceptive schemes.

In the chapters that follow, we will delve deeper into the strategies and tools necessary to confront and defeat the Jezebel spirit. We will explore the power of prayer, divine discernment, spiritual authority, and the anointing of the Holy Spirit. Together, we will rise up as warriors in the kingdom of God, ready to expose, dismantle, and utterly defeat the Jezebel spirit in the name of Jesus.

---

The Jezebel spirit is not a foe to be taken lightly. Its cunning and destructive nature have left countless lives shattered and communities in ruins. But armed with understanding, discernment, and the power of God, we can expose and defeat this deceptive spirit.

In the chapters that follow, we will equip ourselves with the necessary spiritual tools to confront and overcome the Jezebel spirit. We will dive deep into the strategies of spiritual warfare, explore the role of prayer and intercession, and learn how to walk in the authority and anointing of Christ. Together, we will reclaim territory that has been lost, bring healing and restoration to those affected by the Jezebel spirit, and see the Kingdom of God advance in power.

Now is the time to unmask Jezebel, to expose her tactics, and to rise up as victorious warriors in Christ. Are you ready to embark on this journey of understanding, empowerment, and triumph? If so, let us press forward together, arming ourselves with the truth and stepping into the destiny God has prepared for us. The battle has begun, and victory is assured in the name of Jesus.

# Deliverance Prayer

1. Heavenly Father, I come before you in the name of Jesus, and I take authority over the Jezebel spirit that has been operating in my life and in the lives of those around me. I declare that its power is broken, and its influence is nullified by the blood of Jesus.

2. I decree and declare that the deceptive tactics of Jezebel are exposed and brought into the light. Every hidden agenda, manipulation, and control is revealed and rendered powerless in the name of Jesus.

3. I renounce and reject any agreement or alliance I may have made with the Jezebel spirit knowingly or unknowingly. I break every soul tie and sever every connection to its influence. I declare my allegiance to Jesus Christ alone.

4. I release the fire of the Holy Spirit to consume every stronghold and foothold of the Jezebel spirit in my life. I command every chain of bondage to be shattered, and every door it has opened to be closed permanently.

5. I declare that the spirit of Jezebel has no authority over my relationships. I break every curse of division, strife, and manipulation that it has released. I release a spirit of unity, love, and godly order into my relationships.

6. Heavenly Father, I ask for your divine discernment to recognize the Jezebel spirit's presence in my surroundings. Grant me wisdom and insight to identify its deceptive tactics and protect me from its influence.

7. I decree and declare that I am not a victim but a victorious warrior in Christ. I am clothed with the armor of God, and I stand firm against every scheme of the enemy, including the Jezebel spirit.

8. I release the power of forgiveness and choose to forgive those who have operated under the influence of the Jezebel spirit. I release them into your hands, Lord, trusting that justice will prevail.

9. I declare that my mind is renewed by the Word of God, and I reject every lie and deception of the Jezebel spirit. I embrace the truth of God's Word and align my thoughts with His divine perspective.

10. I declare that I am a vessel of honor for God's purposes. I reject any counterfeit anointing and submit myself fully to the Holy Spirit's leading and guidance.

11. I command every Jezebel's stronghold in my life to crumble and fall. I release the power of the Holy Spirit to demolish every high place and false altar erected by the Jezebel spirit.

12. I decree and declare that my worship and devotion belong to God alone. I break free from every form of idolatry and rebellion, and I yield my heart completely to the Lord.

13. I release the spirit of Elijah into my life, which carries the anointing to confront and overcome the Jezebel spirit. I walk in boldness, prophetic authority, and uncompromising obedience to God's Word.

14. I declare that the Jezebel spirit's power to intimidate and instill fear is broken in my life. I receive a spirit of boldness, courage, and holy confidence to stand against its schemes.

15. I decree and declare that the Jezebel spirit's plans to silence the prophetic voice are thwarted. I release the fire of God's Word through my mouth, and I speak forth His truth with authority and conviction.

16. I break every generational curse of the Jezebel spirit that has been passed down through my family line. I declare freedom, healing, and restoration in every area affected by its influence.

17. I decree and declare that my mind is protected by the helmet of salvation, guarding against the infiltration of Jezebelic thoughts, doubts, and fears. I am rooted in the truth of God's Word.

18. I release the power of divine separation from any environment or association that fosters the Jezebel spirit. I am set apart for God's purposes, and I refuse to compromise my convictions or values.

19. I decree and declare that my emotions are stable and anchored in the peace of God. I reject the emotional manipulation and instability caused by the Jezebel spirit, and I embrace the fruit of the Spirit in my life.

20. I release the fire of God's love to consume every trace of Jezebel's jealousy and competition within me. I celebrate the success and achievements of others, walking in humility and unity.

21. I declare that the Jezebel spirit's attacks on my identity and worth are defeated. I am fearfully and wonderfully made by God, and I embrace my true identity as a child of the Most High.

22. I decree and declare that my spiritual authority is restored and strengthened. I exercise the authority of Jesus Christ to bind and cast out the Jezebel spirit and its demons from my life and sphere of influence.

23. I release the power of God's healing and deliverance to those who have been wounded and oppressed by the Jezebel spirit. I declare freedom, restoration, and wholeness in Jesus' name.

24. I declare that the Jezebel spirit's attempts to sabotage and hinder God's purposes in my life are nullified. I am empowered by the Holy Spirit to fulfill my divine destiny and walk in the fullness of God's calling.

25. I release the spirit of discernment to recognize Jezebel influences in the media, entertainment, and cultural spheres. I am vigilant and discerning, refusing to partake in anything that promotes Jezebel's agenda.

26. I decree and declare that the Jezebel spirit's attacks on my faith and trust in God are futile. I stand firm in the promises of God, unshaken by doubt or unbelief, and I declare that my faith is unwavering.

27. I release the power of God's grace to those who have been ensnared by the Jezebel spirit. I declare a season of restoration, healing, and transformation, as they encounter the love and mercy of God.

28. I declare that my spiritual senses are sharpened to discern the subtle workings of the Jezebel spirit. I am alert and sensitive to the leading of the Holy Spirit, refusing to be deceived or swayed by its tactics.

29. I decree and declare that my prayers are potent and effective against the Jezebel spirit. I release the fire of intercession, dismantling its strongholds and establishing God's kingdom authority in every area of my life.

30. I declare that the Jezebel spirit is defeated in my life, my relationships, my church, and my community. I walk in victory, knowing that greater is He who is in me than he who is in the world. In Jesus' mighty name, Amen.

## Chapter 2

## Arming Yourself for Spiritual Warfare: The Battle Begins

Spiritual warfare is an unavoidable reality for every believer. As we journey through life, we encounter unseen forces of darkness that seek to hinder, distract, and destroy us. The battle is real, and the enemy is relentless. But fear not, for in this chapter, we will explore how to arm ourselves for spiritual warfare, equipping ourselves with the weapons and strategies necessary to stand firm and emerge victorious.

Understanding the Nature of Spiritual Warfare:

Before we delve into the specifics of arming ourselves for spiritual warfare, it is crucial to understand the nature of the battle we face. We are engaged in a spiritual conflict that extends beyond the physical realm. The Apostle Paul reminds us in Ephesians 6:12, "For we do not wrestle against flesh and blood, but against principalities, against powers, against the rulers of the darkness of this age, against spiritual hosts of wickedness in the heavenly places."

Our enemy, Satan, and his demonic forces are relentless in their attempts to steal, kill, and destroy (John 10:10). They wage war against our minds, emotions, relationships, health, and even our faith. But the good news is that Jesus has already secured the victory through His death and resurrection. As believers, we have been given the authority and power to overcome the enemy and walk in victory.

Equipping Yourself with Spiritual Weapons:

In order to effectively engage in spiritual warfare, we must arm ourselves with the weapons that God has provided. These weapons are not physical but spiritual in nature, and they carry immense power to demolish strongholds and thwart the enemy's attacks.

1. The Word of God: The Bible is our ultimate weapon in spiritual warfare. It is the living and powerful Word of God that exposes the lies of the enemy, brings truth, and releases faith. Through the diligent study, meditation, and application of God's Word, we gain wisdom, discernment, and the ability to speak truth into every situation.

2. Prayer and Intercession: Prayer is a vital weapon in our spiritual arsenal. It is through prayer that we commune with God, align ourselves with His will, and engage in warfare against the enemy. By interceding on behalf of ourselves and others, we release the power of God to break strongholds, release healing, and bring about supernatural breakthroughs.

3. The Name of Jesus: The name of Jesus carries extraordinary authority in the spiritual realm. When we invoke the name of Jesus, demons tremble,

and strongholds crumble. It is through His name that we have access to the power and victory of God.

4. The Blood of Jesus: The blood of Jesus is a powerful weapon against the enemy. It not only cleanses us from sin but also serves as a constant reminder of the victory that was won on the cross. By applying the blood of Jesus through faith, we can overcome the accusations of the enemy and walk in the freedom and authority that Christ has secured for us.

5. The Armor of God: Ephesians 6:13-18 describes the spiritual armor that God has provided for us. Each piece of the armor—the belt of truth, the breastplate of righteousness, the shoes of the gospel of peace, the shield of faith, the helmet of salvation, and the sword of the Spirit—plays a crucial role in our spiritual defense and offense. When we put on the armor of God, we are equipped to withstand the enemy's attacks and stand firm in the truth.

Strategies for Spiritual Warfare:

Alongside our spiritual weapons, we must employ strategic and tactical approaches to engage effectively in spiritual warfare. Here are some key strategies to consider:

1. Know Your Enemy: Understanding the enemy's tactics, strategies, and

areas of influence is essential. The enemy often operates through deception, distractions, and temptations. By studying the Word of God and seeking the discernment of the Holy Spirit, we can identify the enemy's schemes and counter them with the truth.

2. Stay Connected to God: Maintaining a vibrant and intimate relationship with God is crucial in spiritual warfare. Spending time in prayer, worship, and meditation on His Word keeps us aligned with His will and strengthens our spiritual discernment. It is in His presence that we find strength, guidance, and strategy for battle.

3. Walk in Holiness: Living a life of holiness and righteousness is a powerful weapon against the enemy. By maintaining purity in our thoughts, actions, and relationships, we close the doors to the enemy's access points in our lives. Walking in obedience to God's commands fortifies our spiritual defenses and ensures that we are aligned with His purposes.

4. Stand on God's Promises: The promises of God are sure and unchanging. In times of battle, we must stand on the promises found in His Word. Promises of protection, provision, healing, and victory are weapons of assurance and faith. By declaring and meditating on these promises, we fortify our hearts and minds against the attacks of the enemy.

5. Engage in Corporate Warfare: While personal spiritual warfare is crucial, there is also power in corporate intercession and warfare.

Partnering with other believers in united prayer and intercession amplifies our effectiveness and releases greater spiritual breakthrough. In times of intense warfare, seeking the support and agreement of other strong believers can provide strength, encouragement, and spiritual covering.

---

Spiritual warfare is not a battle we can afford to ignore or underestimate. As believers, we are called to stand firm, armed with the weapons and strategies that God has provided. By understanding the nature of spiritual warfare, equipping ourselves with spiritual weapons, and employing strategic approaches, we can navigate the battlefield with confidence and emerge victorious.

Remember, the battle is not ours alone; it belongs to the Lord. As we rely on His strength, walk in obedience, and engage in prayerful warfare, we can be assured that the enemy's schemes will be exposed, his strongholds demolished, and his power rendered powerless. The journey of spiritual warfare is not without challenges, but in Christ, we are more than conquerors. So, arise, fellow warrior, for the battle begins, and victory is assured in Jesus' mighty name.

## Deliverance Prayer

1. Heavenly Father, I come before you in the name of Jesus, and I take authority over every spiritual force of darkness that opposes

me. I declare that I am armed and equipped with your spiritual weapons to stand firm in the battle.

2. I declare that I am covered by the precious blood of Jesus. By the power of His blood, I am redeemed, cleansed, and protected from the attacks of the enemy. I walk in the victory that His blood provides.

3. I take hold of the sword of the Spirit, which is the Word of God. I declare that every lie, deception, and scheme of the enemy is exposed and rendered powerless by the truth of God's Word.

4. I put on the full armor of God. I fasten the belt of truth around my waist, wearing the breastplate of righteousness, and having my feet fitted with the readiness that comes from the gospel of peace.

5. I take up the shield of faith to extinguish all the fiery arrows of the enemy. I declare that my faith is strong, unwavering, and rooted in the promises of God.

6. I put on the helmet of salvation to protect my mind from the enemy's attacks. I declare that my thoughts are aligned with God's truth, and I am filled with the mind of Christ.

7. I lift up the shield of faith, and I declare that no weapon formed against me shall prosper. Every attack, accusation, or curse directed towards me is nullified by the power of the blood of Jesus.

8. I declare that the enemy's plans to distract, discourage, and hinder me are foiled. I am focused, determined, and unwavering in my pursuit of God's purposes for my life.

9. I release the fire of the Holy Spirit to consume every demonic stronghold and fortress that has been erected against me. I declare that no weapon formed against me shall prevail, for I am anointed and empowered by the Holy Spirit.

10. I break every generational curse and soul tie that has given the enemy a legal right to operate in my life. I declare my freedom and deliverance in the name of Jesus.

11. I declare that every door of access the enemy has used to infiltrate my life is closed and sealed by the blood of Jesus. I am protected, and no weapon formed against me shall prosper.

12. I release the power of God's love to penetrate every area of my life that has been wounded or affected by the enemy's attacks. I receive His healing, restoration, and wholeness.

13. I take authority over every spirit of fear, doubt, and unbelief. I declare that I walk in the confidence and boldness that comes from knowing who I am in Christ.

14. I release the fire of God's presence to consume every demonic assignment and plot against me. I declare that the enemy's plans are exposed, and his power is broken in Jesus' name.

15. I declare that I am a vessel of honor, set apart for God's purposes. I reject every counterfeit anointing and declare that I am filled with the power and anointing of the Holy Spirit.

16. I command every stronghold of addiction, bondage, and oppression to crumble and fall. I walk in the freedom and liberty that Christ has secured for me.

17. I release the power of God's angels to surround me and protect me from the attacks of the enemy. I am under the divine covering and angelic assistance in all my ways.

18. I decree and declare that every plan, plot, and scheme of the enemy is exposed and frustrated. I am victorious, for the battle is not mine but the Lord's.

19. I declare that every demonic assignment against my health, relationships, and destiny is cancelled and rendered powerless. I

walk in divine health, restoration, and the fullness of God's blessings.

20. I declare that my prayers are effective and powerful. I release the fire of intercession, tearing down strongholds and releasing breakthrough in every area of my life. In Jesus' name, Amen.

## Chapter 3

## Decoding Jezebel's Tactics: Exposing the Snare

In our battle against the Jezebel spirit, it is essential to understand the tactics and strategies employed by this deceptive force. Jezebel operates through manipulation, control, and seduction, seeking to establish her dominion and subvert the purposes of God. In this chapter, we will decode Jezebel's tactics, shedding light on her schemes and exposing the snare that she sets for unsuspecting individuals. Through this understanding, we can navigate the battlefield with wisdom and discernment, avoiding the traps that Jezebel sets.

1. Manipulation and Charisma:

Jezebel is a master manipulator, using charm, flattery, and charisma to gain control over individuals. She seeks to captivate and influence others, appealing to their desires, emotions, and vulnerabilities. Her manipulation is often subtle and disguised as care or concern, making it difficult to recognize her true intentions.

2. Seduction and Sexual Immorality:

One of Jezebel's primary tools is seduction. She seeks to ensnare individuals through sexual immorality and illicit relationships. Jezebel exploits the God-given gift of sexuality, twisting it for her own purposes, and using it as a means of control and manipulation. She entices individuals into compromising situations, leading them away from purity and righteousness.

## 3. Division and Strife:

Jezebel thrives in an atmosphere of division and strife. She works to create discord among individuals, families, churches, and communities. Jezebel's goal is to break down unity, trust, and relationships, sowing seeds of discord and conflict. By fostering division, she weakens the body of Christ and hinders the advancement of God's kingdom.

## 4. Intimidation and Fear:

Jezebel operates through intimidation and fear, seeking to silence opposition and maintain her control. She uses threats, manipulation, and emotional manipulation to instill fear in those who would dare to challenge her authority. Jezebel's goal is to paralyze individuals with fear, preventing them from rising up and fulfilling their God-given purposes.

## 5. False Spirituality and Counterfeit Authority:

Jezebel presents herself as spiritual, often masquerading as a prophetess or spiritual leader. She twists and distorts the truth, promoting false doctrines and practices. Jezebel seeks to establish a counterfeit authority, claiming spiritual superiority while leading others away from the true worship of God.

6. Witchcraft and Control:

Jezebel employs witchcraft and control to manipulate and dominate others. She uses occult practices, spells, and rituals to exert her influence and maintain control over individuals. Jezebel seeks to bind and control others, stifling their freedom and preventing them from walking in the fullness of their God-given destinies.

7. Jealousy and Competition:

Jezebel is driven by jealousy and an insatiable desire for power and recognition. She cannot tolerate anyone else receiving attention or authority. Jezebel's jealousy fuels her competitive nature, leading her to undermine and destroy those who pose a threat to her position or influence.

Recognizing the Snare:

In order to effectively combat Jezebel's tactics, we must be able to recognize the snare that she sets. The following signs indicate the presence of the Jezebel spirit:

1. Manipulative behavior: Jezebel operates through manipulation, seeking to control and dominate others.

2. Sexual immorality and seduction: Jezebel entices individuals into compromising situations, leading them away from purity and righteousness.

3. Division and strife: Jezebel fosters discord and conflict, sowing seeds of division and breaking down unity.

4. Intimidation and fear: Jezebel uses threats and emotional manipulation to instill fear and maintain control.

5. False spirituality and counterfeit authority: Jezebel presents herself as spiritual, promoting false doctrines and practices.

6. Witchcraft and control: Jezebel employs occult practices to manipulate and dominate others.

7. Jealousy and competition: Jezebel is driven by jealousy and seeks to undermine and destroy those who pose a threat to her authority.

Navigating the Snare:

While Jezebel's tactics are cunning and destructive, we can navigate the snare by:

1. Seeking God's discernment: By staying close to God and relying on His discernment, we can recognize Jezebel's tactics and avoid falling into her traps.

2. Walking in purity and righteousness: By maintaining a lifestyle of purity and righteousness, we close the doors to Jezebel's seduction and control.

3. Cultivating unity and healthy relationships: By fostering unity, trust, and healthy relationships, we create an environment that is resistant to Jezebel's divisive tactics.

4. Standing firm in the truth: By grounding ourselves in the truth of God's Word, we are able to discern and reject Jezebel's false doctrines and counterfeit authority.

5. Rejecting fear and intimidation: By standing firm in faith and rejecting fear, we neutralize Jezebel's attempts to intimidate and control us.

6. Walking in humility and godly authority: By embracing humility and godly authority, we resist the spirit of competition and jealousy that Jezebel promotes.

---

Jezebel's tactics are designed to deceive, manipulate, and control. By understanding her strategies and recognizing the snare she sets, we can navigate the battlefield of spiritual warfare with wisdom and discernment. Through prayer, reliance on God's Word, and walking in the power and authority of the Holy Spirit, we can overcome Jezebel's deceptive schemes and emerge victorious. Let us stand firm, exposing the snare of Jezebel, and walk in the freedom and victory that Christ has secured for us.

## Deliverance Prayer

1. Heavenly Father, I come before you in the name of Jesus, and I take authority over every tactic and scheme of the Jezebel spirit. I declare that its power is broken, and its influence is nullified in my life and in the lives of those around me.

2. I renounce and reject every form of manipulation and control that the Jezebel spirit has used against me. I break every chain and stronghold of manipulation, and I declare my freedom in Christ.

3. I declare that I am covered by the blood of Jesus, and no seductive or immoral influence of the Jezebel spirit has power over me. I walk in purity, righteousness, and sexual integrity, honoring God with my thoughts, words, and actions.

4. I reject division and strife in every area of my life. I release forgiveness and reconciliation where there has been discord, and I declare unity, love, and peace to prevail.

5. I refuse to be intimidated or controlled by the Jezebel spirit. I release the spirit of courage and boldness, knowing that God has not given me a spirit of fear, but of power, love, and a sound mind.

6. I break every false spiritual influence and counterfeit authority of the Jezebel spirit. I declare that I am guided by the true Holy Spirit and the Word of God, discerning between truth and deception.

7. I renounce and reject every form of witchcraft and occult influence associated with the Jezebel spirit. I break every curse and demonic assignment that has been released against me or my loved ones.

8. I declare that I am secure in my identity and purpose in Christ. I am not threatened by jealousy or competition, for my worth and significance are found in Him alone.

9. I release the fire of God to consume every Jezebel stronghold in my life and in my sphere of influence. I command every chain of bondage to be shattered, and I walk in the freedom and liberty that Christ has secured for me.

10. I refuse to be deceived by false spirituality and twisted doctrines. I declare that I have a hunger for the truth of God's Word, and I am anchored in His unchanging truth.

11. I break every spirit of control, domination, and manipulation that the Jezebel spirit has used against me. I declare that I am led by the Holy Spirit and empowered to make godly decisions in alignment with God's will.

12. I release the power of forgiveness to those who have been influenced by the Jezebel spirit. I forgive them, and I release them into your hands, Lord, knowing that vengeance belongs to you.

13. I declare that every snare and trap set by the Jezebel spirit is exposed and dismantled. I walk in discernment and wisdom, avoiding the strategies and pitfalls of the enemy.

14. I resist every spirit of fear and intimidation that the Jezebel spirit attempts to impose upon me. I declare that I am strong, courageous, and filled with the confidence that comes from knowing who I am in Christ.

15. I declare that every false spiritual authority and counterfeit anointing is brought down in the name of Jesus. I submit only to the authority of Jesus Christ and the leading of the Holy Spirit.

16. I break every generational curse and soul tie associated with the Jezebel spirit. I declare my freedom and deliverance, and I walk in the fullness of God's blessings for my life.

17. I release the fire of God's love to penetrate every area of my life that has been wounded or affected by the Jezebel spirit. I receive healing, restoration, and wholeness in Jesus' name.

18. I declare that my mind is renewed by the truth of God's Word. I reject every lie and deception of the Jezebel spirit, and I embrace the mind of Christ.

19. I release the power of God's angels to surround me and protect me from the attacks of the Jezebel spirit. I am under the divine covering and angelic assistance in all my ways.

20. I declare that the Jezebel spirit is defeated in my life and in the lives of those around me. I walk in victory, knowing that greater is He who is in me than he who is in the world. In Jesus' mighty name, Amen.

## Chapter 4

# Breaking Free from Manipulation:
# Unleashing Divine Discernment

Manipulation is a powerful tactic employed by the enemy to deceive and control. It is a snare that binds individuals, relationships, and even entire communities. In this chapter, we will explore the destructive nature of manipulation and the key to breaking free from its grip—divine discernment. By cultivating a keen sense of discernment, guided by the Holy Spirit, we can navigate through the web of manipulation and walk in the freedom and truth that Christ offers.

Understanding Manipulation:

Manipulation is the art of subtly influencing others to act or think in a way that benefits the manipulator. It involves deceptive tactics, emotional control, and the exploitation of vulnerabilities. The manipulator seeks to gain power, control, and personal advantage, often at the expense of others' well-being and autonomy. Manipulation operates in various spheres of life, including relationships, work environments, and even spiritual settings.

The Destructive Effects of Manipulation:

Manipulation leaves a trail of destruction in its wake. It undermines trust, distorts communication, and erodes healthy boundaries. Its impact can be devastating, leading to damaged relationships, emotional turmoil, and a loss of personal identity and autonomy. Manipulation hinders personal growth, stifles individuality, and prevents healthy decision-making. It robs individuals of their voice and prevents them from walking in the fullness of their God-given potential.

Cultivating Divine Discernment:

Divine discernment is a gift from God that enables us to perceive and understand the true motives and intentions behind actions and words. It is through divine discernment that we can identify manipulation and navigate through its snares. Here are key principles to cultivate divine discernment:

1. Intimacy with God: Developing a deep and intimate relationship with God is the foundation of divine discernment. Spending time in His presence, studying His Word, and seeking His guidance through prayer allows us to align our hearts and minds with His truth and wisdom.

2. Renewing the Mind: The transformation of our minds through the power of the Holy Spirit is crucial for discernment. Romans 12:2 urges us to "be transformed by the renewing of our minds." By immersing ourselves in God's Word and meditating on His truth, we align our thought patterns with His ways and are better equipped to recognize manipulation.

3. Seeking the Holy Spirit's Guidance: The Holy Spirit is our ultimate guide and teacher. Inviting the Holy Spirit to lead us, teach us, and reveal truth enables us to discern the manipulative tactics of the enemy. The Spirit imparts wisdom, knowledge, and understanding beyond our human capabilities.

4. Testing the Spirits: 1 John 4:1 encourages us to test every spirit, to discern whether they are of God. We must evaluate the fruit, character, and motives of individuals and their actions against the truth of God's Word. Discernment helps us distinguish between genuine love, wisdom, and guidance, and deceptive manipulation.

5. Cultivating Emotional Intelligence: Emotional intelligence is crucial for discernment. Understanding and managing our emotions, as well as recognizing the emotions of others, helps us detect manipulation. Emotional intelligence enables us to assess situations objectively and respond appropriately.

6. Seeking Wise Counsel: Proverbs 15:22 reminds us that plans fail for lack of counsel, but with many advisers, they succeed. Seeking wise counsel from godly mentors and trusted individuals can provide valuable insights and perspectives in discerning manipulation.

Breaking Free from Manipulation:

Breaking free from manipulation requires intentional steps and unwavering commitment to truth and freedom. Here are essential actions to take:

1. Recognize Manipulative Tactics: Educate yourself about common manipulative tactics, such as guilt-tripping, gaslighting, love-bombing, and selective truth-telling. Understanding these tactics helps in identifying manipulation.

2. Set and Maintain Healthy Boundaries: Establishing healthy boundaries is crucial in resisting manipulation. Clearly define your personal limits, values, and expectations, and communicate them assertively. Boundaries empower us to protect our well-being and maintain healthy relationships.

3. Trust Your Intuition: Pay attention to your instincts and gut feelings. God often speaks to us through our intuition. If something feels off or inconsistent, it may be a sign of manipulation. Trust the promptings of the Holy Spirit within you.

4. Seek Accountability: Share your experiences and concerns with trusted individuals who can provide support and hold you accountable. They can offer outside perspectives and help identify manipulation when it may be difficult for you to see.

5. Practice Assertiveness and Self-Advocacy: Develop assertiveness skills to express your needs, opinions, and boundaries confidently.

Communicate honestly and respectfully, standing firm in your convictions. Self-advocacy empowers you to resist manipulation and assert your autonomy.

6. Take Responsibility for Personal Growth: Invest in personal growth and development. Strengthen your self-esteem, emotional resilience, and self-awareness. Cultivate a strong sense of identity rooted in Christ, enabling you to resist manipulation and embrace your God-given potential.

7. Walk in Truth and Transparency: Commit to living a life of truth and authenticity. Be transparent in your interactions and communication, promoting openness and trust. Honesty and integrity are powerful antidotes to manipulation.

---

Manipulation is a destructive force that seeks to control and deceive. However, through cultivating divine discernment and walking in the truth, we can break free from its grip. By developing intimacy with God, renewing our minds, seeking the Holy Spirit's guidance, and practicing emotional intelligence, we sharpen our discernment. Breaking free from manipulation requires recognizing manipulative tactics, setting healthy boundaries, trusting our intuition, seeking accountability, practicing assertiveness, taking responsibility for personal growth, and walking in truth and transparency. With divine discernment as our compass, we can navigate through the snares of manipulation and walk in the freedom, authenticity, and truth that Christ offers.

# Deliverance Prayer

1. Heavenly Father, I come before you in the name of Jesus, and I take authority over every spirit of manipulation that has operated in my life and in the lives of those around me. I declare that its power is broken, and its influence is nullified by the power of the Holy Spirit.

2. I renounce and reject every form of manipulation that has hindered my growth, distorted my relationships, and undermined my identity. I break every chain and stronghold of manipulation, and I declare my freedom in Christ.

3. I release the fire of the Holy Spirit to expose every manipulative tactic that has been employed against me. I ask for divine discernment to recognize the schemes and strategies of the enemy.

4. I declare that I am rooted in the truth of God's Word, and I reject every lie and deception that has been used to manipulate and control me. I embrace the truth that sets me free.

5. I break every soul tie and ungodly attachment that has been formed through manipulation. I declare my independence and autonomy in Christ, and I sever any unhealthy connections that have been used to manipulate and control me.

6. I release the power of forgiveness to those who have manipulated and deceived me. I choose to forgive them, releasing them into your hands, Lord, knowing that vengeance belongs to you.

7. I declare that I am filled with the wisdom and discernment of the Holy Spirit. I am guided by His leading, and I can discern the motives and intentions behind manipulative actions and words.

8. I declare that I walk in emotional intelligence, recognizing and managing my own emotions. I am sensitive to the emotions of others, discerning when manipulation is being used to exploit or control.

9. I take hold of the authority given to me by Jesus Christ, and I command every manipulative spirit to leave my life and the lives of those connected to me. I release the power of the Holy Spirit to expose and defeat the manipulative tactics of the enemy.

10. I break every generational curse of manipulation that has been passed down through my family line. I declare freedom and deliverance, breaking the cycle of manipulation in the name of Jesus.

11. I declare that I am equipped with divine discernment to see through the deceptive tactics of the enemy. I am not easily swayed or deceived by manipulative words or actions.

12. I release the power of God's truth into every area of my life that has been affected by manipulation. I declare that the truth of God's Word exposes and dismantles every lie and deception.

13. I declare that my mind is renewed by the truth of God's Word. I reject every manipulative thought pattern or belief system, and I embrace the renewing power of the Holy Spirit.

14. I release the fire of God's love to heal and restore any wounds or brokenness caused by manipulation. I receive His healing, comfort, and restoration in those areas of my life.

15. I break the power of fear and intimidation that has been used to manipulate and control me. I declare that I walk in the boldness and courage of the Holy Spirit, refusing to be swayed or silenced by the enemy's tactics.

16. I declare that I walk in the freedom and autonomy that Christ has secured for me. I am not bound by the opinions or expectations of others, but I am free to be who God has created me to be.

17. I release the power of discernment and wisdom in my relationships. I am able to recognize and navigate through manipulative dynamics, establishing healthy boundaries and fostering genuine connections.

18. I declare that I am an overcomer through Christ. I reject every manipulative stronghold that has been erected against me, and I stand firm in the victory that is mine in Jesus.

19. I release the power of the Holy Spirit to guide me in making wise decisions. I am not easily swayed or manipulated, but I am led by the Spirit into truth and freedom.

20. I declare that I am breaking free from manipulation, walking in the divine discernment that comes from God. I am empowered to live a life of authenticity, truth, and freedom in Jesus' mighty name. Amen.

# Chapter 5

# The Power of Prayer: Overcoming Jezebel's Influence

Prayer is a powerful weapon in our spiritual arsenal, enabling us to overcome the influence of the Jezebel spirit. In this chapter, we will explore the significance of prayer in our battle against Jezebel's tactics and strategies. We will discover how prayer empowers us to break free from manipulation, seek divine discernment, and walk in the freedom and victory that Christ has secured for us.

The Nature of Jezebel's Influence:

The Jezebel spirit seeks to exert control, manipulate, and hinder the purposes of God. Its influence can be felt in various spheres of life, including relationships, churches, workplaces, and communities. Jezebel operates through deception, seduction, and intimidation, seeking to subvert the authority of God and establish its dominion.

The Power of Prayer:

Prayer is our direct line of communication with God, enabling us to access His power, guidance, and intervention. It is through prayer that we engage in spiritual warfare, bringing the forces of heaven into alignment with our lives and circumstances. Here are key aspects of the power of prayer in overcoming Jezebel's influence:

1. Intimacy with God: Prayer deepens our intimacy with God, strengthening our relationship and aligning our hearts with His. It is in the place of prayer that we encounter His presence, receive His guidance, and are transformed by His love.

2. Seeking Divine Discernment: Prayer opens our spiritual eyes to discern the tactics and strategies of the Jezebel spirit. As we seek the Holy Spirit's guidance in prayer, He imparts discernment, helping us recognize manipulation, deception, and the counterfeit spirituality of Jezebel.

3. Breaking Strongholds: Through prayer, we can break the strongholds that Jezebel establishes in our lives and in the lives of others. As we intercede and wage spiritual warfare in prayer, we demolish every spiritual barrier and release the power of God to bring freedom and deliverance.

4. Overcoming Fear and Intimidation: Prayer empowers us to overcome the fear and intimidation that Jezebel employs. As we bring our fears and concerns before God, He fills us with His peace, courage, and boldness to resist the influence of Jezebel.

5. Establishing Boundaries: Prayer enables us to establish healthy boundaries in our relationships and interactions. By seeking God's wisdom

and guidance, we can set boundaries that protect us from manipulation and allow us to walk in the freedom and truth of Christ.

6. Strengthening Unity and Discerning False Unity: Prayer fosters unity among believers and exposes false unity that Jezebel promotes. Through prayer, we seek unity based on God's truth and love, guarding against the division and strife that Jezebel seeks to sow.

7. Releasing God's Truth: Prayer is a powerful avenue to release God's truth into every situation and circumstance. As we pray according to His Word, His truth exposes the lies and deception of Jezebel, bringing light and freedom.

8. Binding and Loosing: In prayer, we have the authority to bind the works of Jezebel and loose the power and purposes of God. Through prayer, we dismantle the influence of Jezebel, releasing the reign of God's kingdom in our lives and surroundings.

9. Intercession for Others: Prayer enables us to intercede on behalf of others who are affected by the influence of Jezebel. As we lift them up in prayer, we release the power of God's deliverance, healing, and restoration into their lives.

10. Seeking God's Strategies: In prayer, we seek God's strategies and guidance to effectively counter Jezebel's influence. God reveals specific

steps and actions to take in overcoming Jezebel, empowering us to walk in wisdom and authority.

Prayer Strategies to Overcome Jezebel's Influence:

1. Pray for Spiritual Discernment: Heavenly Father, I pray that you would sharpen my spiritual discernment to recognize the tactics and strategies of the Jezebel spirit. Open my eyes to see through deception, manipulation, and false spirituality. Fill me with your discernment, Holy Spirit, that I may walk in wisdom and truth.

2. Pray for Protection: Lord, I ask for your divine protection from the influence of Jezebel. Shield me with your armor, fortify me with your presence, and guard my heart and mind from manipulation and control. Surround me with your angels, Lord, as a wall of defense against the attacks of Jezebel.

3. Pray for Freedom and Deliverance: Heavenly Father, I declare freedom and deliverance from the influence of Jezebel in my life and in the lives of those around me. I break every chain and stronghold established by Jezebel's deception and manipulation. I release the power of your Holy Spirit to bring liberation and restoration.

4. Pray for Strength and Courage: Lord, empower me with your strength and courage to resist the fear and intimidation of Jezebel. Fill me with your

boldness and confidence that I may stand firm in your truth and walk in the freedom that Christ has won for me.

5. Pray for Healing and Restoration: Father, I pray for your healing and restoration in every area of my life that has been affected by Jezebel's influence. Heal the wounds of manipulation, restore broken relationships, and bring wholeness to my identity and purpose. Pour out your healing love and restoration, Lord, and make me whole.

6. Pray for Unity and Genuine Relationships: Lord, I pray for unity among believers and genuine relationships built on your love and truth. Expose any false unity that Jezebel seeks to promote and establish genuine connections that honor and glorify you. Help us to walk in love, forgiveness, and unity, strengthening one another in the battle against Jezebel.

7. Pray for Wisdom and Guidance: Heavenly Father, grant me your wisdom and guidance in navigating through the tactics of Jezebel. Show me the steps to take, the boundaries to establish, and the strategies to employ in overcoming Jezebel's influence. Lead me by your Spirit, Lord, and grant me the wisdom to discern your voice amidst the clamor of manipulation.

8. Pray for Jezebel's Exposure and Defeat: Lord, I pray for the exposure and defeat of Jezebel's influence in my life and in the lives of others. Let your light shine upon the works of darkness and bring every hidden agenda

and manipulation to light. I declare that Jezebel's influence is crushed by the power of your name, Jesus.

9. Pray for Transformation and Renewal: Father, transform my mind and heart by the renewing power of your Holy Spirit. Replace the lies and deception of Jezebel with your truth. Renew my thoughts, attitudes, and beliefs according to your Word, that I may walk in alignment with your will.

10. Pray for Bold Proclamation of Truth: Lord, fill my mouth with your words and empower me to boldly proclaim your truth. Let your truth dismantle the lies and deception of Jezebel. Use me as a vessel of your light and truth, that others may be set free from the influence of Jezebel.

---

Prayer is a powerful tool in our battle against Jezebel's influence. Through prayer, we cultivate intimacy with God, seek divine discernment, break strongholds, overcome fear, establish healthy boundaries, strengthen unity, release God's truth, and bind the works of Jezebel. As we engage in fervent and strategic prayer, we tap into the supernatural power of God, enabling us to walk in the freedom, discernment, and victory that Christ has secured for us. Let us commit ourselves to a lifestyle of prayer, unleashing its power to overcome Jezebel's influence and experience the fullness of God's purposes in our lives.

## Deliverance Prayer

1. Heavenly Father, I come before you in the name of Jesus, and I take authority over every influence of the Jezebel spirit in my life and in the lives of those around me. I declare that its power is broken, and its hold is shattered by the power of prayer.

2. I declare that I am a person of prayer, empowered by the Holy Spirit to overcome the tactics and strategies of Jezebel. I release the power of prayer to dismantle every stronghold and deception of the enemy.

3. I break every chain of manipulation and control that Jezebel has attempted to establish in my relationships, workplace, and community. I declare my freedom and autonomy in Christ, and I release the power of prayer to bring restoration and healing.

4. I release the fire of the Holy Spirit to expose every hidden agenda and manipulation of Jezebel. Let your light shine upon the works of darkness, revealing the truth and setting captives free.

5. I declare that my prayers are powerful and effective. I release the power of prayer to bind the works of Jezebel and loose the purposes and plans of God in my life and in the lives of those around me.

6. I pray for divine discernment to recognize the tactics and strategies of Jezebel. Open my spiritual eyes, Holy Spirit, to see through deception, manipulation, and false spirituality. Guide me into truth and empower me to walk in wisdom.

7. I pray for the protection of your angels, Lord, to surround me and guard me from the attacks and influence of Jezebel. I am covered by your heavenly army, and no weapon formed against me shall prosper.

8. I release the power of forgiveness to those who have manipulated and deceived me. I choose to forgive them, releasing them into your hands, Lord, and trusting in your justice.

9. I pray for strength and courage to resist the fear and intimidation of Jezebel. Fill me with your Holy Spirit, Lord, and empower me to stand firm in your truth and walk in boldness and confidence.

10. I break every soul tie and ungodly attachment formed through manipulation. I declare my independence and autonomy in Christ, severing any unhealthy connections that have been used to manipulate and control me.

11. I release the power of prayer to establish healthy boundaries in my relationships and interactions. I seek your wisdom and guidance,

Lord, in setting boundaries that protect me from manipulation and allow me to walk in freedom and truth.

12. I pray for unity among believers, rooted in your love and truth. Expose any false unity that Jezebel seeks to promote and establish genuine connections that honor and glorify you. Let love and unity prevail in the body of Christ.

13. I release the power of prayer to bring healing and restoration in every area of my life that has been affected by Jezebel's influence. Heal the wounds of manipulation, restore broken relationships, and bring wholeness to my identity and purpose.

14. I declare that I walk in the authority given to me by Jesus Christ. I release the power of prayer to dismantle the influence of Jezebel and release the reign of God's kingdom in my life and surroundings.

15. I pray for divine strategies and guidance in countering Jezebel's influence. Show me the steps to take, the boundaries to establish, and the strategies to employ in overcoming Jezebel. Lead me, Holy Spirit, and grant me the wisdom to discern your voice amidst the clamor of manipulation.

16. I pray for Jezebel's exposure and defeat. Let your light shine upon the works of darkness, bringing every hidden agenda and

manipulation to light. I declare that Jezebel's influence is crushed by the power of your name, Jesus.

17. I release the power of prayer to transform my mind and heart. Renew my thoughts, attitudes, and beliefs according to your Word. Replace the lies and deception of Jezebel with your truth, Lord.

18. I pray for bold proclamation of your truth. Fill my mouth with your words and empower me to boldly proclaim your truth in the face of deception and manipulation. Let your truth dismantle the works of Jezebel.

19. I pray for the release of your deliverance and healing upon those who have been affected by the influence of Jezebel. I intercede on their behalf, releasing the power of your Holy Spirit to bring freedom, healing, and restoration.

20. I declare that through the power of prayer, I overcome Jezebel's influence. I walk in the victory and freedom that Christ has secured for me. In Jesus' name, I pray. Amen.

## Chapter 6

# Decreeing Victory: Activating the Authority of Christ

As believers, we have been given the authority and power of Christ to overcome every spiritual battle we face. In this chapter, we will explore the significance of decreeing victory and activating the authority of Christ in our lives. Through the power of our words and the faith-filled declarations we make, we can align ourselves with God's purposes, release His power, and walk in the victory that has been secured for us through Jesus Christ.

Understanding Our Authority in Christ:

Before we can effectively decree victory, it is crucial to understand the authority we possess as followers of Christ. Through His death, resurrection, and ascension, Jesus defeated the powers of darkness, disarmed the enemy, and gave us authority over all the works of the enemy (Luke 10:19). Our authority is not based on our own strength or merit, but on the finished work of Christ on the cross.

Activating the Authority of Christ:

Activating the authority of Christ involves aligning our words and declarations with the truth of God's Word and the leading of the Holy Spirit. By doing so, we release the power of God, enforce His kingdom, and manifest His victory in every area of our lives. Here are key principles to activate the authority of Christ and decree victory:

1. Knowing God's Word: To effectively decree victory, we must know and meditate on God's Word. His Word is the foundation of our authority, and it provides the truth and promises on which we stand. By immersing ourselves in His Word, we align our thoughts, words, and declarations with His truth.

2. Believing and Speaking in Faith: Decreeing victory requires unwavering faith in the power of God and the authority we have in Christ. We must believe that our words carry weight and have the power to shape reality. By speaking in faith and declaring God's truth, we activate His power and authority.

3. Aligning with God's Will: Effective decrees are in alignment with God's will and purposes. We must seek His heart, understand His plans, and declare His truth accordingly. By aligning our decrees with God's will, we release His power and authority to bring about His desired outcomes.

4. Enforcing the Victory of the Cross: Through the victory of the cross, Jesus triumphed over sin, death, and every principality and power. By decreeing and enforcing the victory of the cross, we declare that the enemy

has been defeated and that we walk in the freedom and authority that Christ has won for us.

5. Resisting the Enemy: Decreeing victory involves actively resisting the enemy and his works. We stand firm in our authority, rebuking the enemy and his tactics. By declaring our victory in Christ, we enforce his defeat and release God's power to bring breakthrough and deliverance.

6. Prophesying God's Promises: Our decrees are not mere wishful thinking; they are prophetic proclamations of God's promises. By prophesying God's promises over our lives, circumstances, and relationships, we align ourselves with His purposes and release His power to bring fulfillment.

7. Praying in Agreement with Heaven: Our decrees are strengthened when we pray in agreement with heaven. By seeking the leading of the Holy Spirit, we pray according to God's will and partner with Him in bringing about His purposes on earth. Our prayers and decrees become powerful instruments of transformation.

8. Walking in Obedience: Obedience is vital in activating the authority of Christ. We must align our lives with God's Word, obey His commands, and live in righteousness and holiness. By walking in obedience, we position ourselves to decree victory and release His power.

9. Persisting in Faith: Decreeing victory requires persistence and steadfastness in faith. We continue to speak God's truth and declare His promises even when circumstances seem contrary. By persevering in faith, we overcome opposition and experience the manifestation of God's victory.

10. Maintaining an Attitude of Gratitude: Gratitude is a powerful posture that activates the authority of Christ. By maintaining an attitude of gratitude, we acknowledge God's faithfulness and goodness. Gratitude aligns our hearts with God's purposes and opens the door for His power and provision.

Decreeing Victory in Various Areas of Life:

1. Decreeing Victory in Spiritual Warfare:
   - Heavenly Father, I decree victory over every spiritual battle I face. I am equipped with the armor of God, and no weapon formed against me shall prosper.
   - I decree that I walk in authority and power, demolishing every stronghold and taking captive every thought that exalts itself against the knowledge of God.
   - I declare that I am more than a conqueror through Christ who strengthens me, and I have the victory in every spiritual battle.

2. Decreeing Victory in Relationships:

- I decree victory in my relationships, Lord. I release forgiveness, love, and reconciliation. I break every chain of discord and division, and I declare unity, peace, and harmony to prevail.
- I decree that I walk in wisdom and discernment, recognizing manipulative tactics and setting healthy boundaries. I release the power of restoration and healing in my relationships.

3. Decreeing Victory in Finances:
- Heavenly Father, I decree victory in my finances. I declare that You are my provider, and You supply all my needs according to Your riches in glory.
- I break the power of lack and poverty, and I release the abundance and provision of God into every area of my financial life. I decree wisdom in financial stewardship and the multiplication of resources.

4. Decreeing Victory in Health:
- I decree victory over sickness and disease in my body. By the stripes of Jesus, I am healed and whole. I release the healing power of God to flow through every cell, tissue, and organ of my body.
- I decree divine health and vitality, and I resist every attack of the enemy against my well-being. I walk in the fullness of health and strength that Christ has secured for me.

5. Decreeing Victory in Career and Ministry:

- I decree victory in my career and ministry. I declare that I walk in God's favor and promotion. I release the power of God to open doors of opportunity and to use my gifts and talents for His glory.
- I decree success and impact in my work and ministry endeavors. I resist every hindrance and limitation, and I walk in the divine breakthrough and fruitfulness that God has ordained for me.

6. Decreeing Victory in Family:
- Heavenly Father, I decree victory in my family. I release the power of Your love to heal and restore broken relationships. I break every generational curse and release the blessing of unity, love, and reconciliation.
- I decree that my family is a stronghold of faith and righteousness. I declare that we walk in Your wisdom, guidance, and protection. I release the power of restoration and transformation in my family.

---

Decreeing victory is a powerful tool in our spiritual arsenal. By activating the authority of Christ through our words and declarations, we align ourselves with God's truth, release His power, and walk in the victory that He has secured for us. Understanding our authority in Christ, aligning with God's will, resisting the enemy, and persisting in faith are key principles to decreeing victory. Whether in spiritual warfare, relationships, finances, health, career, or family, our decrees release God's power and bring transformation. Let us continually activate the authority of Christ through our decrees, confident that we walk in the victory that He has declared over our lives.

## Chapter 7

# The Fire of Holiness: Burning Away Jezebel's Stronghold

The Jezebel spirit thrives in an atmosphere of compromise, deception, and unholiness. In this chapter, we will explore the vital role of holiness in overcoming Jezebel's stronghold. We will delve into the fire of holiness, understanding its purifying and transformative power, and how it ignites a passionate pursuit of God, leading to the destruction of Jezebel's influence in our lives and communities.

The Nature of Jezebel's Stronghold:

Jezebel's stronghold is built upon manipulation, deception, and the promotion of ungodly values and practices. It thrives in environments that tolerate compromise and lack of accountability. Jezebel seeks to infiltrate churches, families, workplaces, and other spheres of influence, hindering the advancement of God's kingdom and distorting His truth.

Understanding Holiness:

Holiness is not merely a set of rules or religious rituals; it is a reflection of God's character and nature. To be holy means to be set apart, consecrated, and dedicated to God's purposes. It involves surrendering our lives to God, allowing His transforming power to work in us, and conforming our thoughts, words, and actions to His perfect will.

The Fire of Holiness:

The fire of holiness is a powerful force that burns away impurity, exposes hidden sins, and purifies our hearts. It is the fire that God uses to refine us, transforming us into vessels fit for His glory. Here are key aspects of the fire of holiness and its role in burning away Jezebel's stronghold:

1. Conviction and Repentance: The fire of holiness brings conviction, illuminating areas of compromise and sin in our lives. It exposes the tactics and influence of Jezebel, prompting us to repent and turn away from any ungodly practices or alliances.

2. Purification and Sanctification: The fire of holiness purifies our hearts, removing every impurity and refining us as vessels of honor. It sanctifies us, setting us apart for God's purposes and empowering us to resist the influence of Jezebel.

3. Surrender and Obedience: The fire of holiness demands our complete surrender to God. It requires obedience to His Word, a willingness to let go of anything that hinders our pursuit of holiness, and a desire to align our lives with His truth and righteousness.

4. Intimacy and Passion for God: The fire of holiness ignites a deep intimacy with God and a passionate pursuit of Him. It fuels our hunger for righteousness and a genuine desire to know and please Him above all else. This intimacy and passion extinguish the allure of Jezebel's false spirituality and counterfeit love.

5. Discernment and Spiritual Clarity: The fire of holiness sharpens our discernment, enabling us to recognize and reject the lies, manipulation, and deception of Jezebel. It brings spiritual clarity, allowing us to distinguish between true and false teachings, genuine love and counterfeit affection.

6. Accountability and Community: The fire of holiness promotes accountability and healthy community. It fosters an environment of transparency, where we can address and overcome the influence of Jezebel through mutual support, correction, and prayer.

7. Empowerment and Authority: The fire of holiness empowers us to walk in the authority given to us by Christ. It strengthens our spiritual foundations, equips us for spiritual warfare, and enables us to resist Jezebel's tactics with confidence and boldness.

8. Transformation and Impact: The fire of holiness transforms us from the inside out, aligning our thoughts, words, and actions with God's truth. It

empowers us to be salt and light in the world, impacting our families, communities, and spheres of influence for the glory of God.

Embracing the Fire of Holiness:

1. Surrendering to God:
   - Heavenly Father, I surrender my life to You completely. I invite the fire of Your holiness to consume me, purify me, and transform me into Your likeness. Burn away every impurity and stronghold that Jezebel has established in my life.

2. Embracing Conviction:
   - Holy Spirit, I welcome Your convicting fire. Illuminate areas of compromise and sin in my life. Show me any alliances, practices, or mindsets that have allowed Jezebel's influence to take hold. I repent and turn away from them, desiring to walk in holiness before You.

3. Seeking Intimacy:
   - Lord, ignite a passionate pursuit of You within my heart. Set my soul on fire with love for You. Increase my hunger for righteousness and my desire to know You intimately. Let my pursuit of holiness extinguish the allure of Jezebel's counterfeit spirituality.

4. Pursuing Obedience:

- Heavenly Father, help me to walk in obedience to Your Word. Give me the strength to let go of anything that hinders my pursuit of holiness. Grant me the grace to align my thoughts, words, and actions with Your truth and righteousness.

5. Praying for Purification:
- Lord, I pray for Your purifying fire to burn away every impurity in my heart. Purify my motives, desires, and intentions. Refine me as a vessel fit for Your glory. Empower me to resist the influence of Jezebel and to walk in purity and righteousness.

6. Cultivating Discernment:
- Holy Spirit, sharpen my spiritual discernment. Open my eyes to recognize the tactics, lies, and manipulation of Jezebel. Grant me wisdom to discern true from false teachings, genuine love from counterfeit affection. Lead me in the path of truth and righteousness.

7. Walking in Accountability:
- Lord, I thank You for the gift of community and accountability. Surround me with believers who walk in holiness and share my desire to overcome Jezebel's influence. Help us to support, encourage, and correct one another in love. May our accountability foster an environment of transparency and growth.

8. Embracing Empowerment and Authority:

- Heavenly Father, I receive the empowerment and authority You have given me through Christ. Clothe me with the armor of God, equipping me for spiritual warfare. Help me to walk in confidence and boldness, resisting Jezebel's influence and advancing Your kingdom.

9. Impacting the World:
- Lord, empower me to be a vessel of Your fire, salt, and light in the world. Use my life to impact my family, community, and spheres of influence for Your glory. Let the fire of holiness radiate from me, drawing others to Your truth and love.

---

The fire of holiness is a powerful force that burns away Jezebel's stronghold. It convicts us, purifies us, and empowers us to walk in alignment with God's truth and righteousness. As we surrender to God, embrace conviction, seek intimacy, pursue obedience, pray for purification, cultivate discernment, walk in accountability, and embrace empowerment and authority, we unleash the fire of holiness in our lives and communities. Let us be a generation that burns with the fire of holiness, overcoming Jezebel's influence and living as beacons of God's truth and love.

## Chapter 8

## Jezebel in Disguise: Identifying Modern-day Expressions

The Jezebel spirit is not limited to a particular time or era; it continues to manifest in various forms in our modern society. In this chapter, we will explore the modern-day expressions of the Jezebel spirit and learn how to identify its deceptive disguises. By understanding these manifestations, we can equip ourselves with discernment and wisdom to recognize and confront Jezebel's influence in our lives and communities.

The Adaptive Nature of Jezebel:

Jezebel is a cunning and adaptable spirit that adjusts its tactics to fit the cultural and social context of each era. It operates through deception, manipulation, control, and the distortion of truth. It seeks to establish its dominion in churches, families, workplaces, and other spheres of influence. By recognizing the modern-day expressions of Jezebel, we can effectively guard ourselves and stand against its influence.

Identifying Modern-day Expressions of Jezebel:

1. Manipulative Leadership:

- Jezebel often manifests in leaders who use manipulation, control, and intimidation to exert their influence. They may abuse their authority, silence opposing voices, and promote their own agenda rather than seeking the welfare of those under their leadership.

2. Seductive Spirituality:
- Jezebel employs a seductive spirituality that lures people away from true worship of God. It promotes counterfeit spiritual practices, false teachings, and a focus on self-gratification rather than surrender to God's will and His Word.

3. Sexual Immorality and Seduction:
- The spirit of Jezebel often entices individuals into sexual immorality and seduction. It promotes promiscuity, pornography, adultery, and other forms of sexual sin. Jezebel seeks to distort God's design for sexuality and destroy the sanctity of marriage.

4. Divisiveness and Strife:
- Jezebel fosters divisiveness, sowing seeds of discord and strife within relationships, families, churches, and communities. It promotes gossip, slander, and a spirit of competition that undermines unity and hinders the advancement of God's kingdom.

5. Narcissism and Self-Centeredness:
- Jezebel encourages a self-centered mindset that exalts personal desires, ambitions, and achievements above God and others. It

promotes a sense of entitlement, manipulation for personal gain, and a lack of empathy for the needs and feelings of others.

6. Deception and False Prophecy:

- Jezebel operates through deception and false prophecy. It distorts and misuses spiritual gifts, leading people astray with false teachings and counterfeit signs and wonders. Jezebel seeks to undermine the authority of God's Word and replace it with deceptive ideologies.

7. Jealousy and Envy:

- The spirit of Jezebel fuels jealousy and envy, causing individuals to covet what others possess. It promotes a spirit of competition and comparison, leading to bitterness, strife, and the destruction of relationships.

8. Control through Manipulative Relationships:

- Jezebel establishes manipulative relationships, seeking to control and dominate others. It employs emotional manipulation, gaslighting, and coercive tactics to keep individuals under its influence, hindering their personal growth and freedom.

9. Attack on God-Ordained Authority:

- Jezebel seeks to undermine and attack God-ordained authority structures. It promotes rebellion, disrespect, and disregard for spiritual leaders, parents, and those in positions of authority.

Jezebel seeks to replace divine authority with humanistic ideologies.

10. Witchcraft and Occult Practices:
- The spirit of Jezebel promotes witchcraft and occult practices, enticing individuals into sorcery, divination, and other forms of spiritual deception. It seeks to draw people away from the worship of the true God and into bondage to demonic forces.

Recognizing Jezebel's Influence:

To identify Jezebel's influence, we must be vigilant and discerning. Here are key indicators that Jezebel may be at work:

1. Manipulation and Control:
- Jezebel operates through manipulation, control, and the silencing of opposing voices. It seeks to impose its agenda and suppress authentic expressions of faith and truth.

2. Distortion of God's Word:
- Jezebel distorts and misuses God's Word to promote its own agenda and teachings. It cherry-picks Scriptures and twists their meaning to fit its deceptive narrative.

3. Seductive Appeals:

- Jezebel employs seductive appeals, enticing people with false promises, counterfeit spirituality, and worldly pleasures. It seeks to distract and draw people away from the true worship of God.

4. Division and Strife:
- Jezebel fosters division, strife, and a spirit of competition. It promotes gossip, slander, and the undermining of relationships and unity.

5. Intimidation and Fear:
- Jezebel uses intimidation, fear, and threats to maintain control and silence opposition. It seeks to instill a climate of fear and manipulation.

6. Resistance to Accountability:
- Jezebel resists accountability and correction. It rejects constructive criticism and surrounds itself with enablers who affirm its behavior.

7. Undermining of God-Ordained Authority:
- Jezebel undermines God-ordained authority structures and seeks to replace them with its own ideologies. It fosters rebellion and disrespect towards spiritual leaders, parents, and those in positions of authority.

8. False Prophecy and Deception:

- Jezebel promotes false prophecy, deception, and counterfeit signs and wonders. It seeks to lead people astray from the truth of God's Word and distort their understanding of God's character and His ways.

Guarding Against Jezebel's Influence:

1. Cultivating Discernment:
   - Cultivate a deep relationship with God and a knowledge of His Word. Seek the guidance of the Holy Spirit and develop discernment to recognize Jezebel's tactics and deceptions.

2. Testing the Spirits:
   - Test every teaching, prophecy, and spiritual experience against the truth of God's Word. Hold fast to the unchanging truth of Scripture and reject anything that contradicts it.

3. Pursuing Holiness:
   - Embrace a lifestyle of holiness, surrendering every area of your life to God. Pursue righteousness, purity, and integrity in thought, word, and action.

4. Building Healthy Relationships:
   - Surround yourself with godly, accountable relationships. Seek out mentors and leaders who exhibit humility, wisdom, and a commitment to God's truth.

5. Exercising Spiritual Authority:
   - Walk in the authority given to you by Christ. Resist Jezebel's influence through prayer, fasting, and the power of God's Word. Bind its works and release the power of God's kingdom.

6. Standing Firm in Truth:
   - Stand firm in the truth of God's Word, refusing to compromise or be swayed by Jezebel's deceptive appeals. Hold fast to the foundational principles of faith and righteousness.

7. Seeking Godly Wisdom:
   - Seek Godly wisdom in decision-making and discernment. Consult trusted spiritual leaders and seek their guidance in navigating Jezebel's influence.

---

Jezebel's influence is not confined to the past; it continues to manifest in various forms in our modern society. By understanding the modern-day expressions of Jezebel and being vigilant in discernment, we can guard ourselves and our communities against its deceptive influence. Through the power of God's Word, prayer, and the guidance of the Holy Spirit, we can confront Jezebel, exposing its lies and promoting the truth of God's kingdom. Let us be alert, discerning, and committed to walking in holiness, standing firm in truth, and resisting Jezebel's influence in our lives and communities.

## Deliverance Prayer

1. Heavenly Father, in the name of Jesus, I take authority over every manifestation of the Jezebel spirit in my life, my family, and my community. I decree that its influence is exposed and destroyed by the power of your Holy Spirit.

2. I declare that I am filled with the discernment and wisdom of the Holy Spirit to recognize the deceptive disguises of Jezebel in my surroundings. I reject every form of manipulation, control, and seductive spirituality that seeks to lead me astray.

3. I break every stronghold of division and strife that Jezebel has established. I release the power of unity, love, and reconciliation in my relationships, family, and community. Let the spirit of Jezebel be silenced and disarmed.

4. I declare that my mind is aligned with the truth of God's Word. I reject any distortion or misinterpretation of Scripture promoted by the spirit of Jezebel. I stand firm in the unchanging truth of God's Word and resist all false teachings and ideologies.

5. Heavenly Father, I release your fire of holiness to purify my heart, thoughts, and motives. Burn away any impurity, selfishness, and

narcissism that Jezebel seeks to promote. Fill me with your love and humility.

6. I break every chain of sexual immorality and seduction that Jezebel has used to ensnare me or others. I declare freedom and purity in my thoughts, actions, and relationships. I embrace God's design for sexuality and the sanctity of marriage.

7. I renounce every form of witchcraft and occult practices associated with Jezebel. I declare my allegiance to the one true God and reject any involvement with sorcery, divination, or other deceptive spiritual practices.

8. I release the power of forgiveness, releasing those who have been influenced by the spirit of Jezebel. I choose to forgive and pray for their deliverance and restoration. I break the cycle of jealousy and envy in my own heart and declare contentment and gratitude.

9. I declare that I walk in submission to God-ordained authority structures. I resist the spirit of rebellion and disrespect that Jezebel promotes. I honor and pray for my spiritual leaders, parents, and those in positions of authority.

10. Heavenly Father, I ask for an increase of discernment and spiritual clarity. Open my eyes to recognize the tactics, lies, and

manipulation of Jezebel. Help me to distinguish between genuine spiritual experiences and counterfeit signs and wonders.

11. I release the power of accountability and correction in my life. Surround me with godly mentors and friends who will speak truth and hold me accountable. I humbly receive correction and submit to the refining fire of holiness.

12. I decree that the power of Jezebel is broken over my life, my family, and my community. I release the fire of God to burn away every influence and stronghold. I proclaim that the authority of Christ prevails over Jezebel's deception and control.

13. I resist every spirit of fear, intimidation, and manipulation that Jezebel seeks to instill. I walk in boldness and courage, knowing that God has not given me a spirit of timidity but of power, love, and a sound mind.

14. I declare that I am not subject to the opinions and approval of others influenced by Jezebel. I find my identity and worth in Christ alone. I reject any attempts to control or manipulate me for personal gain.

15. Heavenly Father, I release your healing power to those who have been wounded by Jezebel's influence. Bring restoration and

freedom to their lives. Break the chains of bondage and release them into a renewed sense of purpose and identity in Christ.

16. I declare that Jezebel's influence is uprooted and expelled from my workplace, church, and community. I release the power of God's kingdom to establish an atmosphere of truth, integrity, and righteousness.

17. I decree that the plans and strategies of Jezebel are exposed and rendered ineffective. Every plot, scheme, and assignment is brought to naught by the power of God. I release confusion into the enemy's camp and declare divine intervention in every situation.

18. I bind every spirit of deception and false prophecy associated with Jezebel. I release the spirit of truth and discernment to prevail in my life and in the lives of those around me. Let the light of God's truth shine brightly, exposing every lie.

19. I release the power of God's love and forgiveness to heal wounds caused by Jezebel's influence. I break the power of bitterness, resentment, and unforgiveness. Let the healing balm of Your love bring restoration and reconciliation.

20. Heavenly Father, I thank you for the victory you have secured over Jezebel's influence through the finished work of Jesus Christ. I walk in the authority and power you have given me. I decree that

Jezebel is defeated, and your truth and righteousness prevail in my life and in the world around me. In Jesus' mighty name, I pray. Amen.

## Chapter 9

# Unleashing God's Word: Sword of Truth against Jezebel

In our battle against the Jezebel spirit, we have been given a powerful weapon—the Word of God. In this chapter, we will explore the significance of God's Word as a sword of truth in combating Jezebel's influence. We will delve into the transformative power of Scripture, understanding how to wield it effectively, and unleashing its authority to expose, confront, and defeat the Jezebel spirit in our lives and communities.

The Power of God's Word:

God's Word is not just a collection of ancient writings; it is alive, active, and powerful (Hebrews 4:12). It is the inspired revelation of God's truth, revealing His character, His ways, and His promises. The Word of God carries inherent authority and possesses the power to transform lives, break strongholds, and release freedom.

Understanding Jezebel's Resistance to God's Word:

Jezebel, by nature, resists and distorts God's Word. It seeks to undermine the authority and power of Scripture, replacing it with deception and false teachings. Jezebel knows that when the Word of God is unleashed with faith and authority, its influence is weakened, and its tactics are exposed.

Wielding the Sword of Truth:

To effectively combat Jezebel's influence, we must learn to wield the sword of truth—the Word of God. Here are key principles to unleash God's Word against Jezebel:

1. Study and Meditate on God's Word:
   - Immerse yourself in the study and meditation of God's Word. Allow its truth to penetrate your heart, renew your mind, and transform your perspective. The more intimately you know God's Word, the better equipped you are to confront Jezebel's deception.

2. Declare God's Promises:
   - Speak forth God's promises over your life, circumstances, and relationships. Declare His truth with boldness and authority. When confronted with the lies of Jezebel, counter them with the truth of God's Word.

3. Rebuke and Renounce False Teachings:
   - Identify and renounce any false teachings or ideologies influenced by Jezebel. Speak the truth of God's Word against them, rebuking their influence in your life and the lives of others. Reject anything that contradicts the truth of Scripture.

4. Pray and Declare Scripture:
   - Pray and declare specific Scriptures that address Jezebel's tactics and influence. Use the Word of God as a weapon in your prayers, releasing its power to dismantle Jezebel's strongholds and to establish God's kingdom.

5. Stand Firm in the Word:
   - Stand firm in the truth of God's Word, refusing to compromise or be swayed by Jezebel's deceptive appeals. Let the Word of God be your foundation, your anchor, and your guide. Do not waver in your commitment to God's truth.

6. Use Scripture to Expose Deception:
   - Use the Word of God to expose Jezebel's deception. Compare its teachings and practices to the truth of Scripture, pointing out any discrepancies and revealing the true motives behind Jezebel's influence.

7. Release God's Word with Love and Authority:
   - Speak the Word of God with love, compassion, and authority. Let the Holy Spirit guide your words as you confront Jezebel's influence. Remember that the goal is not to attack individuals but to expose the spirit behind the deception.

8. Cultivate a Lifestyle of Obedience to the Word:

- Live in obedience to the Word of God. Let it guide your decisions, actions, and relationships. Walk in alignment with its teachings, allowing the power of God's Word to flow through your life.

9. Seek the Holy Spirit's Guidance:
- Depend on the Holy Spirit to illuminate the Scriptures and guide your understanding. Allow the Spirit to reveal the deeper truths of God's Word, equipping you with wisdom and discernment to effectively combat Jezebel's influence.

10. Share the Word with Others:
- Share the truth of God's Word with others who are influenced by Jezebel. Be a vessel of God's truth and love, helping others recognize and reject the lies of Jezebel. Offer hope, encouragement, and guidance through the power of Scripture.

Examples of Scriptures to Unleash against Jezebel:

1. 2 Corinthians 10:4-5:
- "For the weapons of our warfare are not of the flesh but have divine power to destroy strongholds. We destroy arguments and every lofty opinion raised against the knowledge of God, and take every thought captive to obey Christ."

2. Ephesians 6:17:

- "And take the helmet of salvation, and the sword of the Spirit, which is the word of God."

3. James 4:7:
- "Submit yourselves therefore to God. Resist the devil, and he will flee from you."

4. 1 John 4:4:
- "Little children, you are from God and have overcome them, for he who is in you is greater than he who is in the world."

5. Psalm 119:105:
- "Your word is a lamp to my feet and a light to my path."

6. Psalm 139:23-24:
- "Search me, O God, and know my heart! Try me and know my thoughts! And see if there be any grievous way in me, and lead me in the way everlasting!"

7. Isaiah 54:17:
- "No weapon that is fashioned against you shall succeed, and you shall confute every tongue that rises against you in judgment. This is the heritage of the servants of the Lord and their vindication from me, declares the Lord."

8. Jeremiah 23:29:

- "Is not my word like fire, declares the Lord, and like a hammer that breaks the rock in pieces?"

9. Matthew 4:4:

- "But he answered, 'It is written, "Man shall not live by bread alone, but by every word that comes from the mouth of God."

10. Hebrews 4:12:

- "For the word of God is living and active, sharper than any two-edged sword, piercing to the division of soul and of spirit, of joints and of marrow, and discerning the thoughts and intentions of the heart."

---

The Word of God is a powerful weapon against the influence of Jezebel. By studying, meditating on, and declaring God's Word, we unleash its transformative power to expose, confront, and overcome Jezebel's deception. Let us wield the sword of truth with faith, love, and authority, knowing that God's Word is alive and active, capable of breaking every stronghold and establishing His kingdom. May the Word of God be our guide, our strength, and our source of victory in our battle against Jezebel's influence.

## Deliverance Prayer

1. Heavenly Father, I thank you for the power and authority of your Word. I declare that your Word is a sword of truth against Jezebel's influence in my life and in my community. I wield the Word of God with faith and authority.

2. I rebuke every lie and deception of Jezebel in my thought life. I declare that my mind is renewed by the truth of your Word. I cast down every argument and every thought that exalts itself against the knowledge of God.

3. I declare that your Word is a lamp to my feet and a light to my path. It guides me in discerning the tactics and strategies of Jezebel. I walk in the wisdom and clarity of your Word.

4. I renounce every false teaching and ideology influenced by Jezebel. I declare that I stand firm in the truth of your Word. I reject any distortion or misinterpretation of Scripture promoted by Jezebel.

5. I release the power of your Word to expose the lies and deception of Jezebel. Let your truth penetrate every area of my life and reveal any hidden motives and agendas of the enemy.

6. I declare that the Word of God is alive and active within me. It penetrates my soul and spirit, discerning the thoughts and

intentions of my heart. I yield to the transformative power of your Word.

7. I resist the influence of Jezebel with the sword of the Spirit, which is the Word of God. I declare that every stronghold of Jezebel is broken by the power of your Word. I release freedom and deliverance in its place.

8. I declare that the Word of God prevails over the spirit of Jezebel. I release the authority of your Word to dismantle Jezebel's strongholds, expose its deception, and bring forth truth and restoration.

9. I declare that I am rooted and grounded in your Word. I am established in the truth, and no lie can take hold of me. I walk in discernment and resist every attempt of Jezebel to deceive and manipulate.

10. I release the power of the Scriptures to bring healing and restoration to those who have been wounded by Jezebel's influence. Let your Word bring comfort, hope, and freedom to their lives.

11. I pray for divine revelation and understanding of your Word. Illuminate the Scriptures and open my eyes to the deeper truths

contained within. Let your Word come alive in my heart and transform me from the inside out.

12. I release the power of your Word to dismantle the spirit of control and manipulation associated with Jezebel. I break every chain of bondage and release others into the freedom and liberty found in your truth.

13. I declare that your Word is a weapon of warfare. I wield it against every demonic assignment and attack orchestrated by Jezebel. I release the power of your Word to defeat the enemy and establish your kingdom.

14. I declare that Jezebel's influence is weakened and destroyed by the authority of your Word. I release the fire of your Word to burn away every form of manipulation, deception, and seduction.

15. I release the power of your Word to bring unity and reconciliation in relationships and communities affected by Jezebel's divisive tactics. Let your Word heal wounds and restore brokenness.

16. I declare that the Word of God is my source of strength and encouragement. I stand on your promises, knowing that you are faithful to fulfill every word spoken in your Scriptures.

17. I pray for a hunger and thirst for your Word to increase within me. Let me desire your truth more than the deceptive allure of Jezebel. Fill me with a love for your Word and a passion to share it with others.

18. I release the power of Scripture to convict and transform hearts that have been influenced by Jezebel's lies. Let your Word pierce through hardened hearts and bring repentance and restoration.

19. I declare that the gates of hell cannot prevail against the Word of God. I stand on the authority of your Word, knowing that Jezebel's influence is no match for your truth and power.

20. Heavenly Father, I thank you for the victory I have through the Word of God. I declare that your Word prevails over every manifestation of Jezebel's spirit. I walk in the freedom, authority, and truth of your Word. In Jesus' name, Amen.

## Chapter 10

# Walking in Spiritual Purity:
## Shielding Yourself from Jezebel's Seduction

In our battle against the Jezebel spirit, it is crucial to maintain spiritual purity. Jezebel seeks to seduce and corrupt through various means, tempting us to compromise our values and principles. In this chapter, we will explore the importance of walking in spiritual purity and the strategies to shield ourselves from Jezebel's seductive influence. By guarding our hearts, minds, and actions, we can resist Jezebel's allure and stand firm in righteousness.

The Seductive Nature of Jezebel:

Jezebel is a spirit of seduction, enticing individuals into compromising their spiritual integrity. It capitalizes on our weaknesses, desires, and vulnerabilities, presenting counterfeit love, acceptance, and fulfillment. Jezebel employs sensual appeal, manipulation, and false spirituality to draw people away from God's truth and righteousness.

Understanding Spiritual Purity:

Spiritual purity is more than abstaining from immorality; it encompasses the alignment of our hearts, minds, and actions with God's standards and values. It involves a wholehearted devotion to God, an unwavering commitment to His truth, and a separation from anything that compromises our relationship with Him.

Strategies for Walking in Spiritual Purity:

1. Guarding the Heart:
   - Guard your heart diligently, for out of it flow the issues of life (Proverbs 4:23). Be mindful of what you allow into your heart and mind—what you watch, listen to, and engage with. Protect your heart from the influences that can lead to compromise and spiritual pollution.

2. Cultivating Intimacy with God:
   - Deepen your relationship with God through prayer, worship, and the study of His Word. Seek to know Him intimately, allowing His presence to fill your heart and satisfy your deepest longings. The more intimately you know God, the less enticing the seduction of Jezebel becomes.

3. Renewing the Mind:
   - Allow the Word of God to renew your mind and transform your thinking. Reject the lies and distorted messages of Jezebel with the truth of Scripture. Let your mind be saturated with God's

Word, enabling you to discern and reject Jezebel's seductive tactics.

4. Practicing Discernment:
- Develop discernment through the guidance of the Holy Spirit. Ask God for the discernment to recognize Jezebel's seductive strategies and to discern between true love and counterfeit affection. Let discernment be your shield against the allure of Jezebel.

5. Fleeing Temptation:
- When faced with temptation and seduction, follow the example of Joseph and flee (Genesis 39:12). Do not entertain or indulge in situations or relationships that compromise your spiritual purity. Choose to separate yourself from anything that leads you away from God's truth.

6. Surrounding Yourself with Accountability:
- Seek accountability through trusted mentors, friends, or spiritual leaders who will help you stay on the path of purity. Share your struggles and victories with them, allowing them to speak truth and provide support. Accountability acts as a safeguard against Jezebel's seductive influence.

7. Developing Emotional Wholeness:

- Jezebel often preys on emotional wounds and insecurities. Seek healing and restoration for any emotional wounds that may make you susceptible to Jezebel's seduction. Allow God's love and grace to bring healing and wholeness to your heart and emotions.

8. Rejecting Compromise:
- Make a firm decision to reject compromise and stand firm in righteousness. Let your actions align with God's truth, even when faced with pressure or temptation. Choose integrity over momentary pleasure and the eternal rewards of obedience over the temporary allure of Jezebel.

9. Seeking Accountability in Relationships:
- Be cautious in your relationships and seek accountability within them. Surround yourself with individuals who encourage and support your pursuit of purity. Choose relationships that honor God and promote spiritual growth, rejecting those that lead you towards compromise.

10. Building a Strong Foundation:
- Build a strong foundation of faith, rooted in the love and truth of God. Let your identity be firmly established in Christ, knowing that your worth and fulfillment come from Him alone. The stronger your foundation, the less vulnerable you are to Jezebel's seduction.

11. Praying for Spiritual Discernment:
    - Pray for spiritual discernment and wisdom to recognize Jezebel's seductive tactics. Ask God to reveal any areas of vulnerability and to strengthen you against the allure of Jezebel. Seek His guidance and protection as you walk the path of purity.

12. Guarding Your Words:
    - Be mindful of the words you speak and the influence they can have. Guard your tongue from gossip, slander, and manipulation—tactics often employed by Jezebel. Let your words build others up, speak truth, and bring life.

13. Filling Your Mind with Truth:
    - Fill your mind with the truth of God's Word, positive and uplifting thoughts, and wholesome content. Avoid entertainment or media that promotes sensuality, deception, or compromise. Choose to feed your mind with that which strengthens and edifies your spirit.

14. Practicing Self-Control:
    - Develop self-control in every area of your life, including your thoughts, desires, and actions. Let the Holy Spirit empower you to overcome temptation and resist Jezebel's seductive allurements. Walk in self-control, surrendering to God's leading and guidance.

15. Seeking the Holy Spirit's Empowerment:

- Rely on the power of the Holy Spirit to empower you to walk in spiritual purity. Yield to His guidance, allowing Him to lead and direct your steps. By the Spirit's strength, you can overcome Jezebel's seductive influence and live a life pleasing to God.

16. Embracing God's Love and Acceptance:
- Find your ultimate love, acceptance, and fulfillment in God's perfect love for you. Let His love be the source of your identity and worth. When you grasp the depth of His love, the counterfeit affection of Jezebel loses its appeal.

17. Building Spiritual Resilience:
- Cultivate spiritual resilience to withstand Jezebel's seduction. Stay rooted in God's truth, maintain a strong prayer life, and surround yourself with supportive believers. Strengthen your faith through spiritual disciplines and the study of God's Word.

18. Recognizing the Consequences of Compromise:
- Understand the consequences of compromise and the destructive effects of Jezebel's seduction. Reflect on the stories of individuals who fell into Jezebel's trap and the harm it brought to their lives and relationships. Let their experiences serve as a warning and motivation to remain steadfast.

19. Pursuing Holiness:

- Pursue holiness as a lifestyle, continuously growing in righteousness and conformity to God's will. Embrace the call to be set apart and resist conformity to the ways of the world. Let your pursuit of holiness be a shield against Jezebel's seductive tactics.

20. Seeking Restoration and Deliverance:
- If you have fallen into Jezebel's seduction, seek restoration and deliverance through repentance and surrender to God's grace. Confess your sins, renounce any involvement with Jezebel's influence, and allow God's mercy to bring healing and restoration to your life.

---

Walking in spiritual purity is essential in shielding ourselves from Jezebel's seduction. By guarding our hearts, minds, and actions, and relying on the power of the Holy Spirit, we can resist Jezebel's allurements and stand firm in righteousness. Let us pursue spiritual purity, recognizing that it is through purity that we find true intimacy with God and the strength to overcome the seductive tactics of Jezebel. May our lives reflect the beauty of holiness as we walk in purity and bring glory to God.

## Deliverance Prayer

1. Heavenly Father, I come before you in the name of Jesus, taking authority over every seductive spirit of Jezebel. I declare that I am shielded by your grace and empowered to walk in spiritual purity.

2. I renounce and break every soul tie and ungodly attachment formed through Jezebel's seduction. I release myself from its grip and declare freedom in Christ.

3. I decree that my heart is guarded by the power of the Holy Spirit. I reject any form of impurity, sensuality, and compromise. I choose to honor you with my thoughts, desires, and actions.

4. I release the power of the blood of Jesus to cleanse me from every stain of Jezebel's seduction. I am washed and made pure in your sight, O Lord. I declare that I am a vessel set apart for your purposes.

5. I declare that I am rooted in your love, O God. I find my acceptance, worth, and fulfillment in you alone. I resist the counterfeit affection and false promises of Jezebel's seduction.

6. I release the power of the Holy Spirit to strengthen me against the allure of Jezebel's seduction. Fill me afresh with your presence, empowering me to resist temptation and walk in purity.

7. I renounce every form of entertainment, media, or influence that promotes sensuality and compromise. I choose to fill my mind with that which is pure, noble, and praiseworthy according to your Word.

8. I declare that my body is a temple of the Holy Spirit. I choose to honor you with my body, abstaining from any sexual immorality or impure practices. I yield my body to you as an instrument of righteousness.

9. I release the power of your Word to transform my thinking and guard my mind against Jezebel's seductive lies. Let your truth reign in my thoughts, renewing my mind day by day.

10. I resist every temptation and lure of Jezebel's seduction. I stand firm in righteousness, empowered by your Spirit to say no to sin and yes to obedience. Strengthen me, Lord, to withstand the enemy's schemes.

11. I pray for a spirit of discernment to recognize Jezebel's seductive tactics. Open my eyes to the hidden snares and enticements that seek to lead me astray. Give me wisdom to make righteous choices.

12. I release forgiveness and extend grace to those who have been influenced by Jezebel's seduction. I pray for their deliverance and

restoration. Let Your love flow through me as a testimony of Your transforming power.

13. I declare that my relationships are marked by purity and honor. I surround myself with those who encourage and support my pursuit of spiritual purity. I reject relationships that compromise my commitment to righteousness.

14. I renounce every form of manipulation and control that Jezebel employs to sway my decisions and actions. I choose to be led by your Spirit, walking in obedience to Your Word.

15. I release the power of the Holy Spirit to bring healing and restoration to any emotional wounds that make me susceptible to Jezebel's seduction. Let your love and grace fill every broken place.

16. I resist the spirit of seduction and sensuality that pervades our culture. I stand as a beacon of purity, shining your light in the midst of darkness. Let my life reflect your holiness and draw others to you.

17. I declare that I am an overcomer by the blood of the Lamb and the word of my testimony. I reject the lies of Jezebel's seduction and walk in the victory that Christ has secured for me.

18. I release the power of intercessory prayer over those who are ensnared by Jezebel's seduction. I lift them up before your throne, asking for their deliverance and the breaking of the chains that bind them.

19. I surrender my desires, ambitions, and dreams to your lordship, O God. Let your will be done in my life. I choose to seek your kingdom and righteousness above all else, resisting the temptations of Jezebel's seduction.

20. I declare that I am an instrument of purity and righteousness in the hands of the Almighty. I walk in the power of the Holy Spirit, shielded from Jezebel's seduction, and shining as a light in a dark world. In Jesus' mighty name, Amen.

## Chapter 11

## Confronting Jezebel's Familiar Spirits:
## Exposing Hidden Covenants

In our battle against the Jezebel spirit, it is important to recognize that Jezebel often operates through familiar spirits and hidden covenants. These spirits seek to establish ungodly agreements and alliances with individuals, leading them into bondage and compromise. In this chapter, we will explore the significance of confronting Jezebel's familiar spirits and exposing the hidden covenants that enable its influence. By understanding the nature of these spirits and breaking free from their grip, we can walk in freedom and victory over Jezebel's tactics.

Understanding Familiar Spirits:

Familiar spirits are demonic entities that masquerade as familiar or friendly beings, seeking to deceive and influence individuals. They operate in secrecy, often preying on vulnerabilities, wounds, and unhealed areas of our lives. These spirits establish ungodly connections and agreements, leading individuals into bondage and spiritual compromise.

Recognizing Hidden Covenants:

Hidden covenants are agreements or alliances that individuals unknowingly or knowingly enter into with familiar spirits. These covenants give the enemy legal ground to operate in our lives, allowing Jezebel's influence to take root. They may be formed through involvement in occult practices, generational ties, ungodly soul ties, or other forms of spiritual compromise.

Exposing Hidden Covenants:

1. Identifying Areas of Compromise:
   - Take an inventory of your life and identify any areas where compromise or ungodly agreements may have taken place. Examine your past involvement in occult practices, ungodly relationships, or other activities that may have opened doors to hidden covenants.

2. Repentance and Renunciation:
   - Repent for any involvement in ungodly practices or agreements that have allowed Jezebel's influence to operate in your life. Renounce any hidden covenants and break the power they hold over you through the blood of Jesus.

3. Seeking Inner Healing:
   - Seek inner healing for any wounds or unresolved issues that have made you vulnerable to familiar spirits. Allow the Holy Spirit to

bring healing and wholeness to those areas, closing the doors to the enemy's influence.

4. Praying for Discernment:
- Pray for discernment to recognize the presence of familiar spirits and hidden covenants. Ask the Holy Spirit to reveal any hidden agreements or alliances that may be operating in your life.

5. Engaging in Spiritual Warfare:
- Engage in spiritual warfare by praying fervently and using the authority given to you as a believer. Bind the activity of familiar spirits and break the power of hidden covenants in the name of Jesus.

6. Breaking Generational Ties:
- Break generational ties and curses that may have been established through hidden covenants. Declare freedom and deliverance over your bloodline, cutting off any spiritual inheritance from Jezebel's influence.

7. Seeking Deliverance Ministry:
- If necessary, seek deliverance ministry to receive freedom from familiar spirits and to break the power of hidden covenants. Allow experienced ministers to guide you through the process of deliverance and inner healing.

8. Guarding Against Re-Entry:

- Guard against re-entry of familiar spirits by maintaining a lifestyle of holiness, surrendering fully to God, and submitting every area of your life to His lordship. Be vigilant and discerning, rejecting any attempts of Jezebel to reestablish hidden covenants.

9. Filling the Void with God's Truth:

- Fill the void left by the breaking of hidden covenants with God's truth. Immerse yourself in His Word, meditate on His promises, and allow His truth to shape your identity and beliefs. Let the power of God's truth replace the lies of Jezebel's familiar spirits.

10. Building a Strong Foundation in Christ:

- Build a strong foundation in Christ through prayer, worship, fellowship, and discipleship. Deepen your relationship with Him, allowing His love and truth to anchor you securely and protect you from Jezebel's influence.

11. Developing Spiritual Discernment:

- Develop spiritual discernment through intimate fellowship with the Holy Spirit and studying God's Word. Let the Holy Spirit guide your decisions and actions, helping you to recognize and confront familiar spirits and hidden covenants.

12. Walking in Obedience to God's Word:

- Walk in obedience to God's Word, aligning your life with His commands and principles. This obedience serves as a safeguard against Jezebel's influence and establishes a strong defense against familiar spirits.

13. Seeking Accountability and Support:
   - Seek accountability and support from mature believers who can provide guidance, prayer, and encouragement as you confront Jezebel's familiar spirits. Share your struggles and victories, and invite others to stand with you in prayer.

14. Applying the Blood of Jesus:
   - Apply the blood of Jesus over every area of your life, covering yourself and your spiritual inheritance. Declare the power and authority of the blood to break every hidden covenant and to cleanse you from all unrighteousness.

15. Proclaiming God's Promises:
   - Proclaim the promises of God's Word over your life and declare them as the ultimate truth that supersedes any influence of Jezebel's familiar spirits. Stand on the authority of God's promises, knowing that they are irrevocable.

16. Guarding Your Gates:
   - Guard the gates of your heart, mind, eyes, and ears against the infiltration of Jezebel's familiar spirits. Be selective in what you

allow into your life, rejecting any form of entertainment, media, or influence that compromises your spiritual walk.

17. Strengthening Your Spiritual Foundation:
- Strengthen your spiritual foundation through prayer, fasting, and studying the Word of God. Let your relationship with Him grow deeper, establishing a solid grounding in the truth that fortifies you against the influence of Jezebel's familiar spirits.

18. Pursuing Holiness and Righteousness:
- Pursue holiness and righteousness as a lifestyle. Let your actions and choices reflect your commitment to follow God's ways. Reject compromise and embrace a life that honors Him in all areas.

19. Walking in the Spirit's Power:
- Walk in the power of the Holy Spirit, relying on His guidance and strength to resist the allure of Jezebel's familiar spirits. Allow the Spirit to empower you to live a life of victory and freedom.

20. Trusting in God's Deliverance:
- Place your trust in God's deliverance and faithfulness. Know that He is greater than any familiar spirit or hidden covenant. Trust in His ability to break every chain and set you free from the influence of Jezebel's tactics.

Confronting Jezebel's familiar spirits and exposing hidden covenants is a vital step in breaking free from Jezebel's influence. By recognizing the presence of these spirits, repenting of any involvement, and seeking God's deliverance, we can experience freedom and walk in spiritual victory. Let us be vigilant, guarding against re-entry and filling our lives with God's truth and presence. As we confront and expose Jezebel's familiar spirits, we can live in the fullness of God's purpose and walk in the freedom He has provided through Christ.

## Deliverance Prayer

1. Heavenly Father, I come before you in the name of Jesus, taking authority over every familiar spirit associated with Jezebel's influence. I declare that their power is broken by the blood of Jesus.

2. I renounce and break every hidden covenant and ungodly agreement formed with familiar spirits. I declare that I am released from their grip and influence by the power of the cross.

3. I repent for any involvement in occult practices, ungodly soul ties, or generational curses that have allowed familiar spirits to operate in my life. I renounce and reject their presence, declaring my allegiance to Jesus Christ alone.

4. I release the power of the Holy Spirit to expose and dismantle every hidden covenant that gives Jezebel's familiar spirits legal ground in my life. I declare that their influence is nullified and rendered powerless.

5. I declare that I am a child of God, covered by the blood of Jesus. I am sealed by the Holy Spirit, and no familiar spirit has any authority or access to my life. I am free from their manipulation and control.

6. I take authority over every hidden agenda and assignment of Jezebel's familiar spirits. I bind their operations and render them ineffective in the name of Jesus. I declare that their plans are thwarted and exposed.

7. I release the fire of God to consume every hidden covenant and alliance formed with familiar spirits. Let Your holy fire purify and cleanse every area of my life, removing any trace of their influence.

8. I declare that the light of God's truth exposes every hidden work of darkness. I pray for discernment to recognize the presence of familiar spirits and the courage to confront and expose them.

9. I release the power of forgiveness over those who have been influenced by Jezebel's familiar spirits. I break the power of

manipulation and control in their lives. May they experience healing and deliverance in Jesus' name.

10. I declare that my mind is renewed by the Word of God. I reject every lie and deception whispered by familiar spirits. I fill my mind with the truth of God's Word, fortifying my thoughts against their influence.

11. I release the power of the Holy Spirit to bring inner healing to any wounds or vulnerabilities that have made me susceptible to familiar spirits. Let your healing balm restore and strengthen me, closing the doors to their influence.

12. I declare that I am a vessel of honor, sanctified and set apart for God's purposes. I reject any unholy alliance or agreement formed with familiar spirits. I am dedicated to righteousness and purity.

13. I release the power of the blood of Jesus to cleanse me from any contamination or defilement caused by familiar spirits. I am washed clean and made whole by His precious blood.

14. I break the power of inherited familiar spirits and generational ties in my bloodline. I declare that the curse is broken, and I walk in the freedom and victory purchased for me by Jesus Christ.

15. I declare that I am equipped with the armor of God to stand against the schemes of Jezebel's familiar spirits. I take up the sword of the Spirit, which is the Word of God, to confront and overcome their influence.

16. I resist and reject every seductive lure and manipulation of familiar spirits. I declare that my heart is guarded by the truth and love of God. I am steadfast and unwavering in my devotion to Him.

17. I release the power of God's angels to surround and protect me from familiar spirits. I declare that they are encamped around me, shielding me from their attacks and guarding me from their influence.

18. I release the power of deliverance over those ensnared by familiar spirits. I pray that their eyes are opened to the truth, and they experience the freedom and liberation that comes through Jesus Christ.

19. I declare that Jezebel's familiar spirits have no place or authority in my life. I am submitted to God, and they must flee at the sound of His name. I stand firm in my position as a child of the Most High God.

20. I declare that I walk in the victory and authority of Jesus Christ. I am more than a conqueror through Him who loves me. No familiar spirit can withstand the power and authority that resides in me. In Jesus' mighty name, Amen.

## Chapter 12

# Destroying the Altars of Jezebel: Reclaiming Your Territory

The influence of the Jezebel spirit is often manifested through the establishment of altars that promote idolatry, compromise, and spiritual bondage. These altars serve as strongholds where Jezebel's influence is perpetuated and her agenda advanced. In this chapter, we will explore the importance of identifying and destroying the altars of Jezebel in our lives and communities. By reclaiming our spiritual territory, we can break free from her grip and experience the fullness of God's purposes.

Understanding Jezebel's Altars:

Jezebel's altars are not physical structures but spiritual strongholds that perpetuate her agenda. These altars can manifest in various forms, including idolatrous practices, false teachings, immorality, control, manipulation, and compromise. They operate through systems, institutions, and mindsets that promote Jezebel's influence and hinder the advancement of God's kingdom.

Recognizing the Altars in Your Life:

1. Examination of Beliefs and Practices:

- Examine your beliefs, practices, and habits to identify any altars that align with Jezebel's agenda. Look for areas of compromise, idolatry, or conformity to worldly values. Be willing to confront and renounce these altars.

2. Evaluation of Relationships:

- Evaluate your relationships and associations to discern if any foster Jezebel's influence. Consider whether these relationships promote compromise, control, or manipulation. Be willing to distance yourself from unhealthy alliances.

3. Reflection on Patterns and Behaviors:

- Reflect on patterns and behaviors in your life that perpetuate Jezebel's agenda. Look for signs of manipulation, fear, control, or compromise. Be honest with yourself and seek God's guidance in identifying and breaking free from these patterns.

4. Examination of Thought Patterns:

- Examine your thought patterns to identify any lies or deceptions influenced by Jezebel's altars. Pay attention to thoughts of unworthiness, fear, or false teachings. Reject these thoughts and replace them with God's truth.

Strategies for Destroying Jezebel's Altars:

1. Prayer and Intercession:
   - Engage in fervent prayer and intercession, seeking God's guidance and intervention in dismantling Jezebel's altars. Pray for His power to be released, exposing and destroying every stronghold associated with Jezebel's influence.

2. Repentance and Cleansing:
   - Repent for any involvement with Jezebel's altars and the compromise they represent. Ask God for forgiveness and cleansing. Break free from the entanglement of sin and renew your commitment to walk in righteousness.

3. Spiritual Warfare:
   - Engage in spiritual warfare, using the weapons of our warfare to pull down Jezebel's altars. Bind the influence of the Jezebel spirit, tear down the strongholds, and declare the victory of Jesus over every principality and power.

4. Prophetic Declaration:
   - Make prophetic declarations against Jezebel's altars, declaring the triumph of God's kingdom and the downfall of Jezebel's influence. Speak forth God's truth and His purposes for your life and community.

5. Consecration and Dedication:

- Consecrate yourself and your surroundings to the Lord, dedicating every area of your life to His purposes. Offer yourself as a living sacrifice, holy and pleasing to Him, resisting the allure of Jezebel's altars.

6. Pursuit of Truth and Discernment:
   - Pursue truth and discernment by immersing yourself in God's Word. Allow the truth of Scripture to guide your thoughts, decisions, and actions. Seek the wisdom and revelation of the Holy Spirit to expose Jezebel's altars.

7. Separation from Compromise:
   - Separate yourself from any form of compromise that aligns with Jezebel's agenda. Be willing to let go of relationships, activities, or practices that hinder your walk with God and perpetuate Jezebel's influence.

8. Filling the Void with God's Presence:
   - Fill the void left by the destruction of Jezebel's altars with the presence of God. Seek intimate fellowship with Him through prayer, worship, and meditation on His Word. Allow His presence to occupy every aspect of your life.

9. Community Transformation:
   - Engage in community transformation by standing against Jezebel's altars in your local community. Collaborate with other

believers to expose and confront Jezebel's influence, replacing it with the truth and love of God.

10. Cultivating a Spirit of Boldness:
- Cultivate a spirit of boldness and courage in confronting Jezebel's altars. Be unafraid to speak truth, expose deception, and stand up against compromise. Allow the Holy Spirit to empower you to confront Jezebel's influence with confidence.

11. Spiritual Discipleship and Mentoring:
- Engage in spiritual discipleship and mentoring relationships, seeking guidance from mature believers who can help you navigate the process of destroying Jezebel's altars. Learn from their wisdom and experience.

12. Guarding Your Gates:
- Guard the gates of your heart, mind, and senses against the infiltration of Jezebel's influence. Be intentional in what you allow into your life, choosing to fill your mind with God's truth and surround yourself with godly influences.

13. Operating in the Gifts of the Holy Spirit:
- Operate in the gifts of the Holy Spirit, allowing His supernatural gifts to flow through you. Let the gifts of discernment, prophecy, and wisdom enable you to identify and confront Jezebel's altars with divine insight and authority.

14. Persistence and Perseverance:
    - Be persistent and persevere in the destruction of Jezebel's altars. Do not grow weary in well-doing but continue to stand in faith and engage in spiritual warfare until every altar is demolished and every influence is eradicated.

15. Seeking Accountability and Support:
    - Seek accountability and support from other believers as you confront Jezebel's altars. Surround yourself with a community of faith that can encourage, pray, and stand with you in the battle against Jezebel's influence.

16. Walking in the Fear of the Lord:
    - Walk in the fear of the Lord, honoring His commands and seeking to align your life with His will. Let the reverential fear of God guide your decisions and actions, keeping you steadfast in the face of Jezebel's altars.

17. Cultivating a Lifestyle of Worship:
    - Cultivate a lifestyle of worship, offering your whole life as a sacrifice of praise to God. Let worship be a weapon against Jezebel's altars, ushering in the presence and power of God to dismantle and destroy their influence.

18. Exercising Kingdom Authority:

- Exercise your authority as a believer in Christ, taking authority over Jezebel's altars and declaring the dominion of God's kingdom in every area of your life. Release the power of Jesus' name and the authority of His blood to dismantle and destroy every stronghold.

19. Preaching and Teaching the Truth:
- Preach and teach the truth of God's Word, exposing the lies of Jezebel's altars and proclaiming the freedom and deliverance found in Christ. Equip others to identify and confront Jezebel's influence in their lives.

20. Walking in Kingdom Purpose:
- Walk in the fullness of your Kingdom purpose, pursuing God's calling and mission for your life. Let the passion for advancing God's kingdom fuel your resolve to destroy Jezebel's altars and reclaim territory for the glory of God.

---

Destroying the altars of Jezebel is crucial in reclaiming our spiritual territory and advancing the purposes of God. By identifying and confronting these altars, we can break free from the influence of Jezebel, experience spiritual freedom, and see the manifestation of God's kingdom in our lives and communities. Let us be diligent in seeking God's guidance, engaging in spiritual warfare, and standing firm in the truth of His Word.

As we destroy Jezebel's altars, we will see a transformation that brings glory to God and releases His people into their destiny.

## Deliverance Prayer

1. Heavenly Father, I come before you in the name of Jesus, taking authority over every altar of Jezebel in my life and community. I declare that these altars are demolished, and their influence is destroyed by the power of the Holy Spirit.

2. I renounce and break every ungodly agreement and alliance formed with Jezebel's altars. I declare that I am free from their grip and influence. I reclaim my spiritual territory for the glory of God.

3. I release the fire of God to consume every altar of compromise, idolatry, and manipulation established by Jezebel. Let your holy fire purify and cleanse every area of my life and community.

4. I repent for any participation in or tolerance of Jezebel's altars. I ask for your forgiveness, Lord, and I turn away from every form of compromise and ungodly alliance. I commit myself to walk in righteousness and purity.

5. I declare that the power and influence of Jezebel's altars are broken by the blood of Jesus. I cover myself and my community with the protection of His blood, nullifying every assignment of the enemy.

6.  I release the power of intercessory prayer against the altars of Jezebel. I stand in the gap for my community, praying for the exposure and dismantling of every stronghold associated with Jezebel's influence.

7.  I bind and cast out every familiar spirit operating through the altars of Jezebel. I command them to leave in the name of Jesus. Let their influence be completely broken and their power rendered powerless.

8.  I declare that the light of God's truth exposes every hidden work of darkness associated with Jezebel's altars. I speak forth the truth and declare freedom and deliverance from their influence.

9.  I release the power of God's love and grace to bring healing and restoration to those who have been ensnared by Jezebel's altars. Let your mercy flow, Lord, breaking every chain and bringing freedom.

10. I declare that Jezebel's altars have no authority or power over my life and community. I stand in the victory and authority of Jesus Christ. I reclaim my territory for the purposes of God.

11. I release the power of unity among believers to confront and destroy Jezebel's altars. Let us stand together, declaring the truth

and exposing the deception. May our unity bring a powerful shift in the spiritual atmosphere.

12. I break every generational tie to Jezebel's altars in my bloodline. I declare that the curse is broken, and I walk in the freedom and victory that Christ has secured for me.

13. I declare that my mind is renewed by the truth of God's Word. I reject every lie and deception perpetuated by Jezebel's altars. I align my thoughts with the mind of Christ.

14. I release the power of forgiveness over those who have been influenced by Jezebel's altars. I break the power of manipulation and control in their lives. Let them experience healing and deliverance in Jesus' name.

15. I release the power of worship and praise to dismantle the altars of Jezebel. Let the sound of worship shatter every stronghold and bring forth the manifest presence of God.

16. I declare that I am filled with the Holy Spirit, who empowers me to confront and destroy Jezebel's altars. I walk in the anointing and authority to bring forth transformation and revival.

17. I release the power of God's angels to dismantle Jezebel's altars. Let them go forth as ministering spirits, warring against the

powers of darkness and establishing God's kingdom in my life and community.

18. I declare that Jezebel's altars have no place in my thoughts, emotions, or actions. I submit every area of my life to the lordship of Jesus Christ. I am aligned with His will and purposes.

19. I declare that my community is a stronghold of God's presence and truth. I pray for the exposure and dismantling of every altar of Jezebel, bringing transformation and revival to our midst.

20. I release the power of restoration and restitution over the areas affected by Jezebel's altars. Let your healing and rebuilding begin, Lord. Reclaiming every lost territory for your glory and honor. In Jesus' mighty name, Amen.

# Chapter 13

## Prophetic Warfare: Unveiling Jezebel's Plans

In the battle against the Jezebel spirit, it is essential to engage in prophetic warfare. Prophetic warfare involves partnering with the Holy Spirit to receive divine insight and revelation regarding Jezebel's plans and strategies. Through prophetic discernment, we can unveil the hidden schemes of Jezebel and effectively counteract her attacks. In this chapter, we will explore the power of prophetic warfare and how it enables us to expose and overcome Jezebel's plans.

Understanding the Nature of Jezebel's Plans:

Jezebel is a cunning and strategic spirit that seeks to infiltrate and undermine the purposes of God. Her plans often involve manipulation, control, intimidation, and seduction. Jezebel operates through various means such as false prophetic words, counterfeit spiritual experiences, and deceptive teachings. She seeks to silence the prophetic voice and hinder the advancement of God's kingdom.

The Role of Prophetic Warfare:

1. Prophetic Discernment:

- Prophetic warfare begins with discerning the spirits at work. Through the Holy Spirit's guidance, we can discern the presence and influence of Jezebel in our midst. This discernment enables us to unveil her plans and strategies.

2. Intercessory Prayer:
- Prophetic warfare involves fervent intercessory prayer. As we partner with the Holy Spirit, we pray according to His leading, declaring God's purposes and resisting Jezebel's plans. Intercession acts as a spiritual weapon, dismantling Jezebel's strategies and releasing God's power.

3. Prophetic Insight and Revelation:
- Prophetic warfare is empowered by prophetic insight and revelation. Through intimacy with God, we receive divine downloads of His plans and strategies. These prophetic insights unveil Jezebel's schemes and enable us to counteract them effectively.

4. Exposing Deception and Falsehood:
- Prophetic warfare exposes the deception and falsehood propagated by Jezebel. The prophetic voice unveils the hidden agenda, false teachings, and counterfeit spiritual experiences employed by Jezebel. This exposure leads to freedom and deliverance for God's people.

5. Aligning with God's Purposes:
- Prophetic warfare aligns us with God's purposes. Through prophetic revelation, we gain insight into God's plans, enabling us to stand in alignment with His will. This alignment gives us authority to dismantle Jezebel's plans and advance God's kingdom.

Strategies for Prophetic Warfare:

1. Cultivating Intimacy with God:
- Cultivate intimacy with God through prayer, worship, and studying His Word. As we draw near to Him, He reveals His heart and purposes, equipping us for prophetic warfare.

2. Sensitivity to the Holy Spirit:
- Develop sensitivity to the leading of the Holy Spirit. Tune your spirit to His voice, recognizing His promptings and impressions. The Holy Spirit will unveil Jezebel's plans and guide you in warfare strategies.

3. Prophetic Intercession:
- Engage in prophetic intercession, praying according to the revelations received from the Holy Spirit. Pray strategically, declaring God's purposes and resisting Jezebel's plans. Let the prophetic voice be released in intercession.

4. Decreeing God's Word:

- Decree God's Word in prophetic warfare. Speak forth His promises and declarations against Jezebel's plans. The Word of God is a powerful weapon that dismantles the strategies of the enemy.

5. Spiritual Discernment:

- Cultivate spiritual discernment through prayer and training. Ask the Holy Spirit to sharpen your discernment, enabling you to identify Jezebel's tactics and plans. Discernment acts as a radar to unveil hidden schemes.

6. Walking in Humility and Obedience:

- Walk in humility and obedience before God. Humility opens our hearts to receive His revelation and wisdom. Obedience positions us in alignment with His will, empowering our prophetic warfare.

7. Operating in the Gifts of the Holy Spirit:

- Operate in the gifts of the Holy Spirit, particularly the gift of prophecy. Allow the Holy Spirit to release prophetic utterances that expose Jezebel's plans and strategies. Let the prophetic gifts be activated for warfare.

8. Spiritual Covering and Accountability:

- Seek spiritual covering and accountability from mature believers who can provide guidance and confirmation in prophetic warfare.

Submit your prophetic insights to trusted leaders for evaluation and guidance.

9. Testing the Spirits:

  - Test the spirits to ensure they align with the character and Word of God. Verify prophetic revelations through Scripture and seek confirmation from trusted spiritual leaders. Avoid being swayed by false or deceptive prophetic words.

10. Cultivating a Lifestyle of Prayer and Fasting:

  - Cultivate a lifestyle of prayer and fasting. Dedicate specific times for seeking God's face, interceding, and receiving prophetic insight. Fasting strengthens your spiritual sensitivity and sharpens your prophetic hearing.

11. Prophetic Worship:

  - Engage in prophetic worship, allowing the Holy Spirit to release prophetic songs and melodies. Let the atmosphere shift as the prophetic sound pierces through Jezebel's plans, releasing God's breakthrough.

12. Exposing Falsehood and False Teachers:

  - Courageously expose falsehood and false teachers influenced by Jezebel's spirit. Use prophetic discernment to identify those who propagate deception and lead God's people astray. Warn and redirect the flock with the truth of God's Word.

13. Praying for Divine Strategies:
- Pray for divine strategies that dismantle Jezebel's plans and expose her tactics. Seek God's wisdom and guidance, trusting Him to reveal His battle plans for prophetic warfare.

14. Walking in Love and Forgiveness:
- Walk in love and forgiveness towards those influenced by Jezebel's spirit. Let the love of Christ flow through you, breaking down walls of bitterness and division. Love is a powerful weapon that disarms Jezebel's plans.

15. Prophetic Acts and Declarations:
- Engage in prophetic acts and declarations that align with God's purposes and dismantle Jezebel's plans. Step out in faith, obeying the leading of the Holy Spirit in strategic actions that release God's power.

16. Operating in Spiritual Authority:
- Operate in the spiritual authority given to you as a believer in Christ. Recognize and confront Jezebel's plans with the authority of Jesus' name. Let the power of the Holy Spirit flow through you to dismantle her strongholds.

17. Guarding the Prophetic Voice:

- Guard the integrity of the prophetic voice by living a life of holiness and accountability. Uphold the biblical standard for prophets and prophetic ministry. Protect the prophetic mantle from contamination by Jezebel's influence.

18. Prophetic Declaration of God's Promises:
    - Prophetic declaration of God's promises is a powerful tool in prophetic warfare. Speak forth God's promises and prophetic words that counteract Jezebel's plans. Declare God's truth with boldness and authority.

19. Operating in the Spirit of Elijah:
    - Operate in the spirit of Elijah, confronting the false prophets and exposing Jezebel's plans. Stand in boldness, proclaiming the truth of God's Word and challenging the idolatry and compromise fostered by Jezebel.

20. Praying for Restoration and Revival:
    - Pray for restoration and revival in the wake of Jezebel's influence. Cry out for the restoration of true worship, the prophetic voice, and the purity of God's people. Intercede for a revival that dismantles Jezebel's plans and brings forth God's Kingdom.

---

Prophetic warfare is a vital aspect of the battle against Jezebel's plans. Through prophetic discernment, intercession, and obedience to the Holy

Spirit, we can unveil Jezebel's schemes and counteract her attacks. Let us cultivate intimacy with God, walk in spiritual discernment, and align ourselves with His purposes. By operating in prophetic warfare, we dismantle Jezebel's plans, release freedom and deliverance, and advance God's kingdom in power and authority. May the prophetic voice be raised, unveiling Jezebel's plans and releasing the fullness of God's purposes in our lives and communities.

## Deliverance Prayer

1. Heavenly Father, I come before you in the name of Jesus, taking authority over every plan and scheme of Jezebel that has been unveiled through prophetic discernment. I declare that these plans are exposed and rendered powerless by the light of your truth.

2. I renounce and break every assignment and strategy of Jezebel that has been unveiled through prophetic insight. I declare that these plans are nullified and ineffective in the name of Jesus.

3. I release the power of intercessory prayer to dismantle and destroy every plan of Jezebel. I pray for divine intervention and the release of angelic forces to thwart her schemes and bring them to naught.

4. I decree that the prophetic voice is restored and empowered to speak forth your truth and expose Jezebel's plans. Let the

prophetic mantle be purified and released to bring alignment with your purposes.

5. I declare that every false prophetic word and counterfeit spiritual experience perpetuated by Jezebel is exposed and brought down. I decree that the genuine prophetic flow is restored and operates in purity and accuracy.

6. I release the fire of the Holy Spirit to consume every false teaching and doctrine promoted by Jezebel. Let your truth prevail and set captives free from deception.

7. I declare that the plans of Jezebel to manipulate and control individuals and communities are nullified. I release the power of freedom and deliverance to break the chains of bondage and release the captives.

8. I release the power of discernment to your people, enabling them to recognize and reject the seductive tactics of Jezebel. Open their eyes to the schemes of the enemy and empower them to stand firm in your truth.

9. I declare that every counterfeit spiritual experience fostered by Jezebel is exposed and rejected. I release a hunger and thirst for genuine encounters with you, Lord, where your presence and power are manifest.

10. I release the power of forgiveness and reconciliation to heal the wounds caused by Jezebel's plans. Restore relationships, bring unity, and break down walls of division that Jezebel has erected.

11. I release the power of prophetic declarations to counteract Jezebel's plans. Let your truth be proclaimed with authority and boldness, dismantling the lies and confusion propagated by Jezebel.

12. I pray for the release of strategic prophetic insights and revelation to your people, enabling them to stay steps ahead of Jezebel's plans. Illuminate the path before them and empower them to navigate through the spiritual battles with wisdom.

13. I decree that the voice of Jezebel is silenced, and her influence is broken in the name of Jesus. Let her plans crumble and fall as your truth prevails and your Kingdom advances.

14. I release the power of restoration and revival to counteract the effects of Jezebel's plans. Let hearts be transformed, lives be renewed, and communities be revived by the fire of your Spirit.

15. I declare that the plans of Jezebel to hinder the prophetic voice are nullified. I decree that the voice of the prophets will arise with

clarity, authority, and accuracy to release your word and bring alignment with your purposes.

16. I release the power of discernment to identify false prophets influenced by Jezebel's spirit. Let their influence be exposed and their deceptive works be dismantled. Protect your people from their falsehood.

17. I declare that every plan of Jezebel to hinder the advancement of your Kingdom is destroyed. I decree that the gates of hell cannot prevail against your Church, and your purposes will be fulfilled.

18. I release the power of spiritual weapons to counteract Jezebel's plans. Let the sword of the Spirit, the Word of God, cut through the lies and deception. Let the shield of faith quench every fiery dart aimed by Jezebel.

19. I declare that your prophetic warriors are rising up, equipped with your anointing and power to unveil Jezebel's plans and release your strategies. Let them walk in boldness and authority, bringing forth your victory.

20. I declare that I walk in the authority of Jesus Christ, and no plan or scheme of Jezebel can prevail against me. I stand firm, fully equipped with the armor of God, and I declare victory in every spiritual battle. In Jesus' mighty name, Amen.

## Chapter 14

# The Anointing Breaks the Yoke:
# Breaking Free from Jezebel's Influence

In our battle against the Jezebel spirit, we must recognize that it is not by our own strength or might that we can overcome, but by the power of the Holy Spirit. The anointing of God breaks the yoke of Jezebel's influence and sets us free. In this chapter, we will delve into the importance of the anointing in breaking free from Jezebel's control and manipulation. We will explore the nature of the anointing, how it operates, and how we can activate it in our lives to experience true freedom and victory.

Understanding the Anointing:

The anointing is the empowering presence of the Holy Spirit that enables us to fulfill God's purposes. It is the supernatural enablement to walk in the authority and power of God. The anointing breaks the yoke, shatters bondage, and releases the freedom and deliverance that Christ has secured for us.

1. The Source of the Anointing:
   - The anointing originates from God Himself. It is the Holy Spirit who anoints and empowers believers to carry out His work. The

anointing flows from the Father, through the Son, and into our lives as we yield to Him.

2. Activation of the Anointing:
- The anointing is activated through intimacy with God. As we cultivate a deep and abiding relationship with Him, we position ourselves to receive His anointing. It is in the secret place of prayer, worship, and communion with God that the anointing is released.

3. The Purpose of the Anointing:
- The anointing is not merely for personal benefit but for the advancement of God's kingdom. It equips us to preach the gospel, heal the sick, cast out demons, and set the captives free. The anointing enables us to walk in supernatural power and authority.

4. The Anointing and Spiritual Warfare:
- The anointing is crucial in spiritual warfare, especially in combating the influence of Jezebel. It empowers us to discern and confront the schemes of the enemy. The anointing breaks the yoke of Jezebel's control, dismantles her strongholds, and releases freedom and victory.

The Anointing and Breaking Free from Jezebel's Influence:

1. Recognizing the Yoke of Jezebel:

- To break free from Jezebel's influence, we must first recognize the yoke she places upon us. This yoke can manifest in various ways, such as manipulation, control, intimidation, and seduction. The anointing breaks these yokes and releases us into true freedom.

2. Yielding to the Holy Spirit:
- To activate the anointing and break free from Jezebel's influence, we must yield ourselves fully to the Holy Spirit. We surrender our will, desires, and plans to Him, allowing Him to have complete control over our lives. It is through this surrender that the anointing flows and empowers us to overcome.

3. Prayer and Fasting:
- Prayer and fasting play a significant role in breaking free from Jezebel's influence. These spiritual disciplines create an atmosphere for the anointing to increase and manifest. Through focused prayer and fasting, we position ourselves to receive the power and authority needed to break the yoke of Jezebel.

4. Repentance and Inner Healing:
- Repentance and inner healing are essential steps in breaking free from Jezebel's influence. We must confront and renounce any participation in her schemes and seek God's forgiveness. Inner healing allows us to address wounds, trauma, and strongholds that Jezebel may have exploited.

5. Prophetic Activation:

- The prophetic activation of the anointing is a powerful tool in breaking free from Jezebel's influence. As we embrace our identity as prophetic people, we become sensitive to the Holy Spirit's leading and discern Jezebel's strategies. The prophetic anointing enables us to speak forth God's truth and dismantle her lies.

6. Discernment and Spiritual Warfare:

- Discernment is crucial in breaking free from Jezebel's influence. The anointing sharpens our spiritual discernment, enabling us to identify her tactics and strategies. We engage in spiritual warfare, using the weapons of our warfare to dismantle her strongholds and release God's freedom.

7. Operating in the Gifts of the Holy Spirit:

- Operating in the gifts of the Holy Spirit empowers us to break free from Jezebel's influence. The gift of discernment exposes her lies and manipulations. The gift of prophecy brings forth God's truth, demolishing the deceptions of Jezebel. The gifts of healing and deliverance set the captives free from her bondage.

8. Walking in Holiness and Purity:

- Walking in holiness and purity is essential in breaking free from Jezebel's influence. The anointing thrives in an atmosphere of holiness. We must renounce and reject any compromise or sin that Jezebel may tempt us with, and pursue a life of righteousness.

9. Seeking Accountability and Community:

- Seeking accountability and community is crucial in breaking free from Jezebel's influence. We need the support and prayers of other believers as we wage war against her. Accountability helps us to remain steadfast and provides a safe place for confession, healing, and growth.

10. Embracing the Cross and the Power of the Blood:

- Embracing the cross and the power of the blood of Jesus is key to breaking free from Jezebel's influence. The anointing was made possible through Jesus' sacrifice on the cross, and His blood cleanses us from all sin. We appropriate the power of the cross and the blood as we renounce Jezebel's influence and walk in the victory Jesus has won.

---

The anointing breaks the yoke of Jezebel's influence and releases us into freedom and victory. Through intimacy with God, prayer, fasting, repentance, prophetic activation, spiritual warfare, and walking in holiness, we can break free from Jezebel's control and manipulation. Let us embrace the anointing and allow the Holy Spirit to empower us to overcome every scheme and strategy of Jezebel. As we walk in the anointing, we will experience the fullness of God's purposes and see His Kingdom established in power and authority.

# Deliverance Prayer

1. Heavenly Father, I come before you in the name of Jesus, recognizing the yoke of Jezebel's influence in my life. I declare that by the power of the Holy Spirit and the anointing of God, I am breaking free from her control and manipulation.

2. I renounce and reject every lie, deception, and seductive tactic of Jezebel. I declare that her yoke is broken, and I am released into the freedom and victory that Christ has secured for me.

3. I activate the anointing of God in my life to break every stronghold of Jezebel. I release the power of the Holy Spirit to dismantle her control and manipulation in every area of my life.

4. I pray for a fresh infilling of the Holy Spirit and a fresh anointing to empower me to overcome Jezebel's influence. Fill me with your presence and power, Lord, and let the anointing break every chain.

5. I declare that the anointing breaks the yoke of fear and intimidation caused by Jezebel. I am filled with the spirit of power, love, and a sound mind. I walk in boldness and confidence, knowing that greater is He who is in me than he who is in the world.

6. I release the anointing of healing and deliverance to set the captives free from Jezebel's bondage. I declare freedom and wholeness in the lives of those who have been under her control.

7. I decree that the anointing breaks the yoke of manipulation and control that Jezebel has placed on relationships, ministries, and communities. I declare divine order and alignment with the will of God.

8. I pray for a heightened sensitivity to the leading of the Holy Spirit, that I may discern Jezebel's tactics and strategies. Let the anointing sharpen my discernment and give me supernatural insight to navigate through her schemes.

9. I release the anointing of prophetic discernment to expose Jezebel's plans and strategies. I declare that every hidden agenda is brought to light, and her deceptions are unveiled for all to see.

10. I declare that the anointing breaks the yoke of confusion and deception caused by Jezebel's false teachings. I am rooted in the truth of God's Word, and I discern every lie and falsehood that Jezebel tries to propagate.

11. I release the anointing of spiritual warfare to engage in battle against Jezebel and her demonic forces. I take up the weapons of

our warfare, declaring that no weapon formed against me shall prosper.

12. I decree that the anointing breaks the yoke of compromise and idolatry associated with Jezebel's influence. I am fully devoted to God and will not be swayed by her enticements.

13. I pray for the anointing of divine wisdom and revelation to navigate through Jezebel's snares and traps. Give me supernatural insight and strategy to counteract her attacks and walk in victory.

14. I release the anointing of restoration and reconciliation to heal the wounds caused by Jezebel's influence. Let relationships be restored, hearts be healed, and unity be established among your people.

15. I declare that the anointing breaks the yoke of Jezebel's seduction and immorality. I am empowered to walk in purity and holiness, guarding my heart and mind against her allurements.

16. I pray for the anointing to operate in the gifts of the Holy Spirit, especially the gift of discernment, prophecy, and healing. Let your gifts flow through me, bringing deliverance and freedom from Jezebel's influence.

17. I release the anointing of boldness and courage to confront Jezebel and her agents. I will not shrink back or be intimidated, but I will stand firm in the authority and power of Jesus Christ.

18. I decree that the anointing breaks the yoke of Jezebel's Jezebel spirit and her Jezebel spirit. I declare that every stronghold of Jezebel is demolished, and her influence is destroyed by the anointing of God.

19. I pray for divine encounters with your presence, Lord, where the anointing is intensified, and the yoke of Jezebel is shattered. Let your glory fill my life, saturating every area with Your anointing.

20. I declare that I am anointed for such a time as this. I am equipped and empowered to break free from Jezebel's influence. By the anointing of the Holy Spirit, I walk in freedom, victory, and the fullness of God's purposes. In Jesus' mighty name, Amen.

## Chapter 15

## Defeating Jezebel's Assassins: Strategies for Protection

As we engage in spiritual warfare against the Jezebel spirit, it is essential to recognize that Jezebel often employs various assassins to attack and undermine God's people. These assassins may manifest in the form of spiritual attacks, emotional manipulation, character assassination, and other tactics aimed at destroying our identity and purpose in Christ. In this chapter, we will explore strategies for protecting ourselves from Jezebel's assassins and standing strong in the face of her relentless attacks.

Understanding Jezebel's Assassins:

1. The Spirit of Offense:
   - Jezebel's spirit often uses the spirit of offense to create division, sow discord, and weaken the unity of God's people. This spirit targets our emotions, seeking to provoke anger, bitterness, and resentment.

2. The Accuser:
   - The Accuser is another assassin used by Jezebel to bring false accusations and slander against God's people. This spirit seeks to

tarnish our reputation, hinder our effectiveness, and create a negative perception of us.

3. Manipulation and Control:
- Jezebel's assassins often manifest in the form of manipulation and control. These tactics are used to dominate and influence others, exploiting their weaknesses and vulnerabilities for personal gain and control.

4. Witchcraft and Sorcery:
- Jezebel's assassins may also operate through witchcraft and sorcery. These occult practices seek to exert control and influence over individuals and situations, using demonic powers to manipulate and harm others.

Strategies for Protection against Jezebel's Assassins:

1. Guarding Your Heart:
- Protect your heart from the spirit of offense by cultivating forgiveness, love, and compassion. Choose to walk in humility and extend grace to others, refusing to be easily offended or hold grudges.

2. Clinging to Truth:
- Anchor yourself in the truth of God's Word. Renew your mind daily with the promises and principles found in Scripture. Let the

truth be your shield against the accusations and lies of Jezebel's assassins.

3. Discernment and Spiritual Awareness:
   - Develop spiritual discernment to recognize the tactics and strategies employed by Jezebel's assassins. Stay alert to the signs of manipulation, control, and false accusations. Test all things according to the Word of God.

4. Prayer and Intercession:
   - Engage in fervent prayer and intercession for protection against Jezebel's assassins. Pray for discernment, wisdom, and divine intervention in every situation. Cover yourself and others in prayer, asking God for His supernatural protection.

5. Surrounding Yourself with Godly Community:
   - Build a strong support network of godly individuals who can provide accountability, encouragement, and prayer. Surround yourself with people who will speak truth into your life and help guard against Jezebel's assassins.

6. Humility and Submission to God:
   - Cultivate a lifestyle of humility and submission to God. Submit every area of your life to His lordship, acknowledging that He is the ultimate authority. Surrender your will and desires to Him, resisting the temptation to exert control over others.

7. Spirit-led Decision Making:

- Seek the guidance of the Holy Spirit in every decision you make. Rely on His wisdom and discernment to avoid falling into the traps set by Jezebel's assassins. Trust in God's guidance and His ability to protect and lead you.

8. Walking in Love and Forgiveness:

- Choose to walk in love and forgiveness, even in the face of opposition and attack. Release any resentment or bitterness toward those who may be used as Jezebel's assassins. Let the love of Christ shine through you, disarming their tactics.

9. Accountability and Transparency:

- Embrace accountability and transparency in your relationships. Allow trusted individuals to speak into your life and provide guidance. Be open and honest about struggles and vulnerabilities, seeking help when needed.

10. Strengthening Your Identity in Christ:

- Ground your identity in Christ and His love for you. Understand who you are in Him and the authority you possess as a child of God. Let your identity in Christ serve as a strong foundation that Jezebel's assassins cannot shake.

11. Rejecting the Lies and Accusations:

-   Refuse to entertain the lies and accusations of Jezebel's assassins. Stand firm in the truth of God's Word and declare that you are protected and covered by the blood of Jesus. Do not allow their words to define you.

12. Engaging in Spiritual Warfare:
    -   Engage in spiritual warfare against Jezebel's assassins. Use the weapons of prayer, the Word of God, and the power of the Holy Spirit to dismantle their strategies and expose their works of darkness.

13. Seeking Inner Healing and Deliverance:
    -   Seek inner healing and deliverance from the wounds and strongholds that Jezebel's assassins may have caused. Invite the Holy Spirit to bring healing to any areas of hurt or brokenness, and renounce any agreements made with Jezebel's spirits.

14. Building a Strong Foundation in God's Word:
    -   Establish a strong foundation in the Word of God. Study and meditate on Scripture, allowing it to become a firm foundation in your life. Let the truth of God's Word be your shield and protection against Jezebel's assassins.

15. Relying on the Holy Spirit's Leading:
    -   Lean on the guidance and leading of the Holy Spirit in every situation. Trust in His wisdom and let Him direct your steps and

decisions. The Holy Spirit will empower you to navigate through the schemes of Jezebel's assassins.

16. Developing Emotional Resilience:
   - Cultivate emotional resilience to withstand the attacks of Jezebel's assassins. Develop a mindset of resilience and trust in God's faithfulness, knowing that He will sustain you through every trial and challenge.

17. Practicing Spiritual Disciplines:
   - Engage in spiritual disciplines such as prayer, fasting, worship, and meditation. These disciplines deepen your relationship with God and strengthen your spiritual defenses against Jezebel's assassins.

18. Seeking Professional Help:
   - If the attacks of Jezebel's assassins have caused significant emotional or psychological distress, seek professional help from counselors or therapists who align with biblical principles. They can provide guidance and support as you navigate the healing process.

19. Cultivating a Lifestyle of Worship:
   - Develop a lifestyle of worship and praise. Let worship be a weapon in your warfare against Jezebel's assassins. Lift up the

name of Jesus and declare His victory over every scheme and attack.

20. Trusting in God's Protection and Provision:
- Ultimately, trust in God's protection and provision. He is your strong tower and refuge in times of trouble. Rest in His love and know that He is faithful to protect you from Jezebel's assassins.

## Deliverance Prayer

1. Heavenly Father, I come before you in the name of Jesus, recognizing the attacks of Jezebel's assassins against my life. I declare that by the power of the Holy Spirit and through the strategies of protection outlined in this chapter, I am equipped to overcome and defeat every assault.

2. I take authority over the spirit of offense used by Jezebel's assassins. I declare that I am rooted in love and forgiveness, and I refuse to allow offense to take hold of my heart. I release forgiveness and extend grace to those who may try to provoke me.

3. I renounce and reject every false accusation and slander spoken against me by Jezebel's assassins. I declare that no weapon formed against me shall prosper, and every tongue that rises against me in judgment is condemned. I am covered by the blood of Jesus.

4. I break the power of manipulation and control exerted by Jezebel's assassins. I declare that I am free from their influence, and I walk in the liberty and authority given to me by Christ. I reject any attempts to manipulate or dominate me.

5. I bind and dismantle every work of witchcraft and sorcery used by Jezebel's assassins. I release the power of God's Word and the blood of Jesus to break every curse and demonic influence. I am protected by the blood of the Lamb.

6. I pray for discernment and spiritual awareness to recognize the tactics and strategies employed by Jezebel's assassins. Open my eyes, Lord, to see beyond the surface and discern the schemes of the enemy. I walk in spiritual sensitivity and discernment.

7. I cover myself and my loved ones in the blood of Jesus, asking for your divine protection against Jezebel's assassins. I declare that no weapon formed against us shall prosper, and every scheme or plan of the enemy is exposed and thwarted.

8. I surround myself with godly community and accountability, Lord. I pray for discerning and trustworthy relationships that provide protection, encouragement, and accountability. Help me to build a strong support network to guard against Jezebel's assassins.

9. I submit myself fully to Your lordship, Lord. I humbly yield to your leading and guidance in every area of my life. I declare that you are my ultimate authority, and I resist the temptation to exert control over others.

10. I walk in love and forgiveness, Lord, refusing to be swayed by the actions or words of Jezebel's assassins. I choose to extend grace and compassion, knowing that love disarms their tactics. Help me to reflect your love in every situation.

11. I engage in spiritual warfare against Jezebel's assassins, Lord. I take up the armor of God and use the weapons of our warfare to tear down strongholds. I declare that I am more than a conqueror through Christ who strengthens me.

12. I pray for inner healing and deliverance from the wounds and strongholds caused by Jezebel's assassins. I invite your Holy Spirit to bring healing and freedom to every area of my life. I renounce any agreements made with Jezebel's spirits.

13. I declare that I am built upon the foundation of your Word, Lord. I meditate on your truth day and night, and it becomes a shield and protection against Jezebel's assassins. I am secure in your promises and principles.

14. I trust in your guidance, Holy Spirit, and lean on your wisdom and discernment. Direct my steps and decisions, leading me away from the traps set by Jezebel's assassins. I trust in your protection and leading.

15. I reject the lies and accusations of Jezebel's assassins, Lord. I declare that I am a child of God, redeemed by the blood of Jesus. I am defined by your truth, and I will not be swayed by their false narratives.

16. I resist the spirit of fear and intimidation used by Jezebel's assassins. I declare that I am courageous and bold, empowered by the Holy Spirit to stand strong against every attack. I walk in the authority given to me by Christ.

17. I declare that I am an overcomer, Lord. By the power of your Spirit and through the strategies for protection outlined in this chapter, I am victorious over Jezebel's assassins. I walk in freedom, victory, and the fullness of your purposes.

18. I pray for divine favor and divine appointments, Lord. Open doors that no one can shut and close doors that no one can open. Let your favor surround me as a shield, protecting me from Jezebel's assassins.

19. I release the anointing of discernment and wisdom to navigate through the attacks of Jezebel's assassins. Let your Spirit guide me, granting me supernatural insight to see beyond the natural and recognize the spiritual battle at hand.

20. I trust in your protection and provision, Lord. You are my refuge and fortress, and I find safety in your presence. I declare that you are my defense and my strong tower, shielding me from the assaults of Jezebel's assassins. In Jesus' mighty name, Amen.

## Chapter 16

# Jezebel in the Church: Restoring God's Order

The Jezebel spirit is not limited to individuals; it can also infiltrate and influence the church. This chapter addresses the presence of Jezebel in the church and the importance of restoring God's order. We will explore how Jezebel seeks to undermine spiritual authority, sow division, and distort true worship. By understanding the tactics of Jezebel and implementing strategies to restore God's order, we can create an atmosphere of revival, unity, and spiritual growth within the church.

Recognizing the Presence of Jezebel in the Church:

1. Subverting Spiritual Authority:
   - Jezebel in the church seeks to subvert and undermine spiritual authority. It promotes rebellion, fosters division, and challenges God-appointed leaders. It opposes the leadership structure established by God.

2. Promoting False Teachings:
   - Jezebel in the church promotes false teachings and doctrines that deviate from the truth of God's Word. It distorts the Gospel,

leading people astray and compromising the integrity of biblical teachings.

3. Distorting True Worship:
- Jezebel in the church distorts true worship by introducing practices and beliefs contrary to God's Word. It promotes idolatry, sensualism, and the pursuit of personal gain, turning worship into a self-centered and manipulative experience.

4. Sowing Division and Strife:
- Jezebel in the church sows seeds of division, causing discord and strife among believers. It fosters a spirit of competition, jealousy, and self-centeredness, leading to fragmentation within the body of Christ.

Restoring God's Order in the Church:

1. Embracing Biblical Leadership:
- To restore God's order in the church, we must embrace and honor biblical leadership. Recognize and submit to the authority of those whom God has appointed as shepherds and overseers. Pray for leaders to walk in integrity, wisdom, and humility.

2. Exposing False Teachings:
- We must be diligent in studying God's Word and discerning truth from falsehood. Expose false teachings and doctrines that are

contrary to the Scriptures. Teach sound doctrine and equip believers to discern and reject Jezebel's deceptive influences.

3. Pursuing Genuine Worship:
   - Restore genuine worship in the church by centering it on God and His Word. Cultivate an atmosphere of reverence, humility, and surrender. Guard against worldly influences and seek the guidance of the Holy Spirit in all aspects of worship.

4. Building Unity and Community:
   - Foster unity and community within the church by promoting love, forgiveness, and reconciliation. Encourage open communication, transparency, and accountability among believers. Seek opportunities for fellowship and serve one another in humility.

5. Cultivating a Culture of Discipleship:
   - Restore God's order in the church by prioritizing discipleship. Equip believers to grow in their knowledge of God's Word, develop spiritual maturity, and walk in obedience to His commands. Encourage mentoring relationships and small group gatherings for mutual edification.

6. Engaging in Spiritual Warfare:
   - Engage in spiritual warfare to break the influence of Jezebel in the church. Pray fervently for the exposure and dismantling of

Jezebel's strongholds. Use the spiritual weapons of prayer, fasting, and the Word of God to push back the forces of darkness.

7. Pursuing Holiness and Purity:
    - Uphold holiness and purity within the church by addressing sin and promoting righteous living. Provide teaching and resources on sexual purity, integrity, and moral standards. Create a culture of accountability and restoration for those who stumble.

8. Nurturing Spiritual Gifts:
    - Encourage the activation and operation of spiritual gifts within the church. Empower believers to walk in their God-given anointing and use their gifts to edify the body of Christ. Equip and release individuals into their specific callings and ministries.

9. Seeking the Presence of God:
    - Pursue a deep and intimate relationship with God, seeking His presence above all else. Emphasize the need for prayer, worship, and reliance on the Holy Spirit in every aspect of church life. Foster an atmosphere of reverence and awe in encountering God.

10. Empowering the Body for Ministry:
    - Empower every member of the church to fulfill their role in the body of Christ. Recognize and celebrate the unique gifts and talents of individuals, providing opportunities for them to serve and minister according to their calling.

11. Implementing Accountability Structures:
   - Establish accountability structures within the church to ensure the spiritual health and well-being of its members. Develop processes for addressing conflicts, discipline, and restoration. Provide pastoral care and support for those who are vulnerable to Jezebel's influences.

12. Teaching Spiritual Discernment:
   - Equip believers with the tools and knowledge to exercise spiritual discernment. Teach on the nature of Jezebel's spirit, its tactics, and how to recognize its manifestations. Provide practical guidance on discerning the voice of God and differentiating it from counterfeit influences.

13. Encouraging a Culture of Honor:
   - Foster a culture of honor and respect within the church. Teach and model humility, servanthood, and love. Encourage mutual respect and appreciation among believers, honoring one another's giftings and contributions.

14. Promoting Authentic Relationships:
   - Promote authentic relationships within the church based on love, trust, and accountability. Encourage vulnerability and transparency, creating a safe space for individuals to share their struggles and receive support and encouragement.

15. Providing Pastoral Care and Equipping:
    - Invest in pastoral care and equipping ministries within the church. Provide counseling, mentoring, and discipleship programs to support individuals in their spiritual growth and personal development. Address specific needs and challenges posed by Jezebel's influences.

16. Praying for Spiritual Revival:
    - Pray fervently for spiritual revival within the church. Cry out for the Holy Spirit's presence to sweep through the congregation, bringing repentance, renewal, and a fresh passion for God. Seek God's heart for the church and intercede for His purposes to be fulfilled.

17. Conducting Teachings on Jezebel's Spirit:
    - Conduct teachings and seminars on Jezebel's spirit, its characteristics, and how to combat its influence. Educate the congregation on the dangers of Jezebel's strategies and equip them with the knowledge to stand against its deceptions.

18. Seeking Wisdom and Counsel:
    - Seek wisdom and counsel from experienced spiritual leaders and pastors who have confronted Jezebel's influences. Learn from their insights, experiences, and victories. Embrace a teachable spirit and be willing to learn and grow in understanding.

19. Engaging in Continuous Evaluation and Adjustment:
- Regularly evaluate the health and spiritual climate of the church. Be willing to make adjustments, address areas of weakness, and implement necessary changes to align with God's order and His purposes. Seek feedback from the congregation and remain open to the leading of the Holy Spirit.

20. Trusting in God's Sovereignty and Provision:
- Ultimately, trust in God's sovereignty and provision for the church. Rely on His grace, wisdom, and power to restore and establish His order. Believe that He is faithful to bring healing, revival, and transformation as His people align with His will and purposes.

---

Restoring God's order in the church requires a diligent and intentional pursuit of His presence, His truth, and His ways. By recognizing the presence of Jezebel in the church, implementing strategies for protection, and seeking God's guidance, we can restore a vibrant, unified, and healthy church body. Let us be steadfast in our commitment to upholding God's order, empowering His people, and allowing His Spirit to lead us into spiritual revival and transformation.

## Deliverance Prayer

1. Heavenly Father, I come before you in the name of Jesus, recognizing the presence of Jezebel in the Church and its destructive influence on your people. I declare that your order will be restored, and your purposes will prevail.

2. I take authority over every spirit of rebellion and defiance that seeks to undermine spiritual authority in the Church. I command every Jezebel spirit to be silenced and rendered powerless in the name of Jesus.

3. I bind and break the power of false teachings and doctrines that have infiltrated the Church through Jezebel's influence. I declare that the truth of your Word will prevail, and the Church will be rooted in sound doctrine and biblical principles.

4. I rebuke and dismantle every form of idolatry and false worship that Jezebel has introduced in the Church. I declare that true worship will be restored, where your name is exalted, and your presence is honored.

5. I pray for unity and harmony among believers in the Church. I bind the spirit of division and strife that Jezebel has sown. I declare a spirit of love, reconciliation, and mutual edification to permeate the Church.

6. I release the spirit of discernment upon the Church to recognize and expose Jezebel's tactics and deceptions. Open our eyes, Lord, to discern the spirit of Jezebel at work and grant us the wisdom to counter its influence.

7. I engage in spiritual warfare to dismantle every stronghold of Jezebel in the Church. I bind and cast out every demonic power operating through Jezebel's spirit. I declare that the gates of hell will not prevail against your Church.

8. I pray for the restoration of biblical leadership in the Church. Raise up godly leaders who will shepherd your people with integrity, humility, and wisdom. Remove any leaders who have been influenced by Jezebel's spirit and replace them with those who align with your heart.

9. I release the spirit of revival and renewal upon the Church. Ignite a passion for your presence, Lord, and draw your people into a deep intimacy with you. Let your Spirit move mightily, bringing transformation and spiritual awakening.

10. I pray for a culture of honor and respect to be established in the Church. Help us to honor and submit to spiritual authority, recognizing the importance of order and accountability. Let your love and humility guide our interactions with one another.

11. I bind the spirit of manipulation and control that Jezebel has used to manipulate the Church. I declare freedom from its influence, and I release the Spirit of truth and discernment to guard against such tactics.

12. I declare that the Church is a house of prayer and intercession. I release a spirit of fervent prayer and spiritual warfare to combat Jezebel's influence. Let your people rise up as mighty prayer warriors, tearing down strongholds and ushering in your kingdom.

13. I pray for healing and restoration in the Church. Heal the wounds caused by Jezebel's influence and bring reconciliation where there has been division. Restore broken relationships and renew a spirit of unity and love.

14. I release the anointing of spiritual gifts in the Church. Empower your people to operate in the gifts of the Holy Spirit for the edification and equipping of the body. Let the Church be a place where every member functions in their God-given calling and anointing.

15. I pray for divine strategies and wisdom to restore your order in the Church. Give leaders discernment to identify areas where Jezebel's influence has taken hold and guide them in implementing effective measures for restoration.

16. I bind the spirit of complacency and lukewarmness that Jezebel has fostered in the Church. I release a spirit of passion and zeal for your kingdom, Lord. Ignite a holy fire within your people to pursue you wholeheartedly.

17. I declare that the Church will be a beacon of light in a dark world. Let your love, truth, and power shine forth through your people, dispelling every trace of Jezebel's influence. Use the Church to bring transformation and revival to the nations.

18. I pray for divine connections and alliances within the body of Christ. Bring together like-minded believers who are committed to restoring your order in the Church. Let us join forces to combat Jezebel's influence and advance your kingdom.

19. I pray for spiritual discernment to recognize Jezebel's agents within the Church. Expose those who are aligned with her deceptive schemes and grant your people the courage to confront and overcome their influence.

20. I declare that the Church will arise in victory over Jezebel's influence. We will walk in your order, unity, and power. We will be a mighty force for your kingdom, advancing with boldness and authority. In Jesus' name, Amen.

## Chapter 17

# The Jezebel-Ahab Connection:
# Unmasking Toxic Relationships

The Jezebel spirit and the Ahab spirit are two destructive forces that often operate in tandem, creating toxic and dysfunctional relationships. This chapter explores the Jezebel-Ahab connection and sheds light on the dynamics that fuel these destructive unions. By understanding the characteristics of Jezebel and Ahab and the dynamics of their connection, we can unmask toxic relationships and seek healing and restoration.

Unveiling the Jezebel Spirit:

1. Manipulation and Control:
   - The Jezebel spirit is characterized by manipulation and control. It uses cunning tactics to dominate and influence others, often exploiting their weaknesses for personal gain and control.

2. Spirit of Rebellion:
   - Jezebel rebels against authority, both human and divine. It challenges and seeks to undermine God-given leadership, creating an atmosphere of rebellion and division.

3. Seduction and Deception:
- Jezebel employs seduction and deception to manipulate and ensnare her victims. She presents herself as alluring and charismatic, but her motives are self-serving and destructive.

4. Jealousy and Envy:
- Jezebel is driven by jealousy and envy. She resents the success, favor, and anointing of others, seeking to undermine and destroy those whom she perceives as a threat.

Understanding the Ahab Spirit:

1. Passivity and Weakness:
- The Ahab spirit is characterized by passivity and weakness. It lacks spiritual strength and moral courage, allowing the Jezebel spirit to exert control and influence over it.

2. Fear and Insecurity:
- Ahab is driven by fear and insecurity. He is easily manipulated by the Jezebel spirit, seeking to avoid conflict and confrontation at any cost.

3. Co-dependency:
- Ahab becomes co-dependent on the Jezebel spirit, relying on her for validation, identity, and decision-making. He allows her to dominate and control him, perpetuating a cycle of dysfunction.

4. Neglect of Spiritual Authority:

- Ahab neglects his role as a spiritual leader, failing to confront and resist the influence of Jezebel. He abdicates his responsibility and allows the Jezebel spirit to flourish.

Unmasking Toxic Relationships:

1. Recognizing the Jezebel-Ahab Dynamic:

- By understanding the Jezebel-Ahab dynamic, we can identify toxic relationships characterized by manipulation, control, passivity, and co-dependency. Recognizing these dynamics is the first step toward healing and restoration.

2. Examining Personal Patterns:

- It is essential to examine our own patterns and tendencies in relationships. Are we exhibiting characteristics of Jezebel or Ahab? Do we allow others to manipulate and control us? Are we passive and co-dependent? Honest self-reflection is crucial for breaking free from toxic patterns.

3. Healing from Emotional Wounds:

- Toxic relationships often stem from unresolved emotional wounds. Seek healing and restoration for past hurts and traumas. Addressing these wounds is crucial for breaking free from the grip of the Jezebel-Ahab connection.

4. Setting Healthy Boundaries:
   - Establishing healthy boundaries is essential in unmasking toxic relationships. Learn to say no to manipulation and control. Set limits on what is acceptable behavior. Value your own well-being and protect yourself from toxic influences.

5. Seeking Godly Counsel:
   - Seek wise and godly counsel to gain perspective on toxic relationships. Engage with mentors, pastors, or counselors who can provide guidance and support. Their wisdom can help you navigate the complexities of toxic relationships.

6. Breaking Free from Co-dependency:
   - Break free from the co-dependency that characterizes the Ahab spirit. Seek independence and emotional strength in God. Learn to rely on His affirmation and guidance, rather than seeking validation from toxic relationships.

7. Confronting the Jezebel Spirit:
   - Confronting the Jezebel spirit requires courage and discernment. Seek the guidance of the Holy Spirit to confront manipulation and control. Stand firm in truth and resist the Jezebel spirit's attempts to undermine your identity and purpose.

8. Developing Spiritual Strength:

- Develop spiritual strength to resist the influence of the Jezebel spirit. Build a strong foundation in God's Word. Cultivate intimacy with the Holy Spirit through prayer and worship. Allow the Lord to strengthen you from within, empowering you to resist and overcome toxic influences.

9. Reclaiming Spiritual Authority:
- Reclaim your spiritual authority as a child of God. Recognize the power and authority given to you by Christ. Step into your role as a spiritual leader and break free from the passivity of the Ahab spirit. Take responsibility for your spiritual life and resist the influence of Jezebel.

10. Embracing Accountability:
- Embrace accountability in your relationships. Surround yourself with godly individuals who can provide support, wisdom, and correction. Be accountable to spiritual leaders who can help you navigate the complexities of toxic relationships.

11. Seeking Restoration and Reconciliation:
- Pursue restoration and reconciliation where possible and appropriate. Pray for the salvation and transformation of those influenced by the Jezebel spirit. Extend forgiveness, but maintain healthy boundaries to protect yourself from further harm.

12. Emphasizing Self-care and Emotional Well-being:

- Prioritize self-care and emotional well-being. Engage in activities that bring you joy and promote healing. Seek professional help if needed to address any psychological or emotional effects of toxic relationships.

13. Praying for Deliverance and Protection:
- Pray for deliverance and protection from the Jezebel-Ahab connection. Declare the authority of Jesus over your life and relationships. Break every ungodly soul tie and renounce any agreements made with the Jezebel spirit.

14. Embracing Healthy Relationships:
- Seek out and cultivate healthy, God-centered relationships. Surround yourself with people who honor and respect you, and who support your spiritual growth. Invest in relationships that build you up and encourage you to walk in godliness.

15. Emphasizing Spiritual Discernment:
- Develop spiritual discernment to recognize the signs of toxic relationships. Rely on the guidance of the Holy Spirit to discern the spirits at work. Test every relationship against the plumb line of God's Word.

16. Growing in Emotional and Spiritual Maturity:
- Pursue emotional and spiritual maturity in all areas of your life. Allow God to refine your character and strengthen your resilience.

Let His love and truth transform you into a mature and healthy individual.

17. Modeling Healthy Relationships:
   - Model healthy relationships in your interactions with others. Demonstrate love, respect, and accountability. Share your experiences and journey of healing with others, offering hope and guidance to those trapped in toxic relationships.

18. Praying for Transformation in the Church:
   - Pray for transformation in the Church as a whole. Pray for leaders to recognize and confront the Jezebel-Ahab dynamic. Pray for the restoration of God's order and the establishment of healthy, godly relationships within the body of Christ.

19. Trusting in God's Healing and Restoration:
   - Trust in God's ability to heal and restore. Surrender your pain, wounds, and brokenness to Him. Allow His love and grace to bring healing and wholeness, as you seek to unmask toxic relationships and walk in freedom.

20. Moving Forward with Hope and Purpose:
   - Move forward with hope and purpose, knowing that God has a plan for your life. Embrace the journey of healing and restoration, trusting that He will lead you to healthier relationships and a

deeper walk with Him. Walk confidently in the freedom and victory that Christ has secured for you.

---

Unmasking the Jezebel-Ahab connection in toxic relationships is a journey of healing, restoration, and spiritual growth. By understanding the dynamics at play and seeking God's guidance, we can break free from manipulation, control, and dysfunction. Let us pursue healthy relationships, grounded in God's love and truth, and allow Him to restore His order in our lives. May His grace empower us to unmask toxic relationships and walk in freedom and wholeness.

## Deliverance Prayer

1. Heavenly Father, I come before you in the name of Jesus, recognizing the destructive nature of the Jezebel-Ahab connection in toxic relationships. I declare that your power and authority are greater than any manipulation or control.

2. I renounce and break every toxic soul tie formed through the Jezebel-Ahab connection. I sever and dissolve every ungodly bond, declaring freedom and healing in the name of Jesus.

3. I bind and cast out every spirit of manipulation, control, and rebellion operating in toxic relationships. I release the power of

the Holy Spirit to expose and dismantle the Jezebel-Ahab connection.

4. I declare that the power of the Holy Spirit is greater than any fear or insecurity associated with the Ahab spirit. I break the chains of passivity and weakness, and I release a spirit of courage and strength in the name of Jesus.

5. I release the spirit of discernment to recognize the signs of the Jezebel-Ahab connection in relationships. Let your light shine upon every hidden motive, manipulation, and control tactic. Grant wisdom to navigate and unmask toxic relationships.

6. I pray for the healing and restoration of those who have been wounded by toxic relationships. Bring comfort, healing, and restoration to their hearts and minds. Help them find their identity and worth in you alone.

7. I release the power of forgiveness and grace to those who have been influenced by the Jezebel-Ahab connection. Grant them the strength to forgive and release those who have manipulated and controlled them. Fill their hearts with your love and peace.

8. I pray for a spirit of repentance to come upon those who have operated in the Jezebel-Ahab dynamic. Open their eyes to the

harm they have caused and lead them to genuine repentance. Bring transformation and redemption to their lives.

9. I break every curse and negative influence that has been spoken over individuals in toxic relationships. I declare that they are released from the power of those words, and I release the blessings and favor of God upon them.

10. I pray for the restoration of godly authority in relationships affected by the Jezebel-Ahab connection. Let your truth and wisdom prevail. Raise up leaders and mentors who will guide and nurture individuals toward healthy, Christ-centered relationships.

11. I release a spirit of healing and reconciliation in toxic relationships. Bring forth restoration, understanding, and forgiveness. Let hearts be softened and hardened hearts be transformed by your love and grace.

12. I bind and rebuke every spirit of jealousy and envy that fuels the Jezebel-Ahab connection. I release the spirit of contentment and gratitude, filling hearts with joy and celebration for the successes of others.

13. I declare that the Church will be a place of refuge and healing for those affected by toxic relationships. Raise up ministries and

support systems that provide guidance, counsel, and prayer for those seeking deliverance and restoration.

14. I pray for divine connections and healthy relationships to replace the toxic ones. Lead individuals to godly friendships and partnerships that encourage, support, and edify one another.

15. I release a spirit of emotional healing and wholeness to those who have been wounded by the Jezebel-Ahab connection. Mend their broken hearts and restore their trust. Fill them with your peace and joy.

16. I bind and dismantle every stronghold of the Jezebel-Ahab connection in marriages and families. I release the power of your love and unity to restore broken relationships and bring healing to homes.

17. I pray for restoration in churches and ministries affected by the Jezebel-Ahab connection. Let your truth and order be established. Raise up leaders who operate in humility, integrity, and godly authority.

18. I declare that individuals influenced by the Jezebel-Ahab connection will no longer be defined by their past experiences. I speak identity and purpose over them. They are beloved children of God, called to walk in freedom and destiny.

19. I release a spirit of discernment and wisdom to navigate future relationships. Protect your people from falling into the trap of toxic connections. Grant them the ability to recognize red flags and walk away from unhealthy associations.

20. I pray for a revival of healthy relationships within the body of Christ. Let your love, truth, and grace permeate every interaction. May the Jezebel-Ahab connection be fully unmasked and replaced with relationships that glorify you and bring forth your Kingdom purposes.

## Chapter 18

## Jezebel's Witchcraft: Breaking the Curse of Control

The Jezebel spirit is known for its manipulative and controlling nature, often using various forms of witchcraft to exert its influence. This chapter delves into the realm of Jezebel's witchcraft and explores the strategies and tactics it employs to control and manipulate others. We will uncover the power of witchcraft and delve into the ways we can break free from its curse and establish God's freedom and authority in our lives.

Understanding Jezebel's Witchcraft:

1. Manipulation through Deception:
   - Jezebel employs witchcraft to deceive and manipulate others. It uses lies, false promises, and deceitful tactics to gain control over individuals and situations.

2. Emotional Manipulation and Soul Ties:
   - Jezebel's witchcraft operates through emotional manipulation, creating soul ties that bind and control others emotionally. It preys on vulnerabilities and wounds to establish dominance and control.

3. Controlling through Fear and Intimidation:

- Jezebel's witchcraft instills fear and intimidation in its victims, creating a sense of powerlessness and subjugation. It uses threats, coercion, and intimidation to maintain control over individuals and keep them bound to its influence.

4. Witchcraft in Spiritual Counterfeits:
- Jezebel's witchcraft can manifest in spiritual counterfeits, such as false prophetic words, divination, and manipulation of spiritual gifts. It uses these counterfeit manifestations to deceive and manipulate believers, leading them away from God's truth and authority.

Breaking the Curse of Jezebel's Witchcraft:

1. Identifying the Influence of Jezebel's Witchcraft:
- The first step in breaking the curse of Jezebel's witchcraft is to identify its presence and influence in our lives. Examine patterns of manipulation, control, and deception that may be operating. Seek the discernment of the Holy Spirit to expose its tactics.

2. Renouncing and Breaking Soul Ties:
- Renounce and break the soul ties established through Jezebel's witchcraft. Declare your freedom and separation from its influence. Cut off emotional attachments and dependencies on manipulative individuals.

3. Repenting from Involvement with Witchcraft:

- Repent from any involvement or association with witchcraft, including dabbling in occult practices or seeking power outside of God's authority. Confess and renounce any participation in witchcraft, seeking God's forgiveness and cleansing.

4. Embracing the Truth of God's Word:

- Combat Jezebel's witchcraft by immersing yourself in the truth of God's Word. Meditate on Scripture and allow it to renew your mind and expose the lies and deception of witchcraft. Embrace the truth that sets you free.

5. Praying for Deliverance and Breaking Generational Curses:

- Engage in fervent prayer for deliverance from the curse of Jezebel's witchcraft. Break generational curses that may have opened the door to its influence. Pray for God's healing and restoration in areas affected by witchcraft.

6. Seeking Inner Healing and Emotional Wholeness:

- Pursue inner healing and emotional wholeness to break free from the emotional manipulation of Jezebel's witchcraft. Seek God's healing touch in areas of woundedness, rejection, and fear. Allow His love to restore and strengthen your emotions.

7. Developing Spiritual Discernment:

- Develop spiritual discernment to recognize the counterfeit manifestations of Jezebel's witchcraft. Cultivate intimacy with the Holy Spirit, who will guide you into all truth and expose the works of darkness.

8. Resisting Fear and Intimidation:
- Stand firm against the fear and intimidation tactics of Jezebel's witchcraft. Declare your identity in Christ and your authority as a child of God. Resist the lies and threats with the truth of God's Word and the power of the Holy Spirit.

9. Surrounding Yourself with Godly Community:
- Surround yourself with a strong, godly community that can provide support, accountability, and prayer. Seek relationships with mature believers who operate in God's truth and authority, guarding against the influence of Jezebel's witchcraft.

10. Submitting to God's Authority:
- Surrender yourself fully to God's authority and submit to His leading in your life. Yield to the Holy Spirit's guidance and direction, allowing Him to lead you in paths of righteousness and freedom.

11. Forgiving and Releasing:
- Extend forgiveness to those who have operated in Jezebel's witchcraft. Release them from any resentment or bitterness,

entrusting them to God's justice and mercy. Walk in love and forgiveness, breaking the cycle of control.

12. Cultivating a Lifestyle of Worship and Prayer:
    - Cultivate a lifestyle of worship and prayer as a powerful antidote to Jezebel's witchcraft. Develop a deep intimacy with God through worship, intercession, and communion with the Holy Spirit. Let your heart be filled with the presence of God, breaking the power of witchcraft.

13. Operating in the Gifts of the Holy Spirit:
    - Engage in the proper operation of the gifts of the Holy Spirit. Seek the gifts of discernment, wisdom, and prophecy to expose and counteract Jezebel's witchcraft. Use the gifts for the edification and protection of the Body of Christ.

14. Filling Your Mind with Truth and Renewing Your Thoughts:
    - Fill your mind with truth by meditating on God's Word and rejecting the lies of Jezebel's witchcraft. Guard your thoughts, taking captive every thought that exalts itself against the knowledge of God. Renew your mind in the truth of God's Word.

15. Establishing Boundaries and Saying No to Manipulation:
    - Set healthy boundaries in relationships and learn to say no to manipulation and control. Guard your heart and emotions,

refusing to allow Jezebel's witchcraft to manipulate your decisions and actions.

16. Seeking Professional Help if Needed:
-   Seek professional help from counselors or pastors experienced in dealing with the effects of Jezebel's witchcraft if necessary. They can provide guidance, support, and specialized interventions for healing and deliverance.

17. Walking in Humility and Godly Authority:
-   Walk in humility, recognizing your need for God's grace and strength. Operate in godly authority, leading with love, humility, and wisdom. Reflect the character of Christ, who came not to be served but to serve.

18. Remaining Vigilant and Prayerful:
-   Remain vigilant and prayerful, continuously seeking God's guidance and protection. Be alert to the schemes of Jezebel's witchcraft and stand firm in the truth of God's Word. Pray for spiritual discernment and wisdom in all areas of your life.

19. Declaring God's Truth and Breaking Every Witchcraft Curse:
-   Declare the truth of God's Word and break every witchcraft curse spoken over your life. Proclaim the victory of Jesus Christ over witchcraft and renounce its hold on your life. Declare your freedom in Christ and release His power to break every chain.

20. Trusting in God's Deliverance and Restoration:

- Trust in the faithfulness of God to deliver you from the curse of Jezebel's witchcraft. Rest in His promises of restoration, healing, and freedom. Trust that He is able to redeem every aspect of your life affected by witchcraft and bring forth beauty from ashes.

---

Breaking the curse of Jezebel's witchcraft is a process that requires diligence, prayer, and a deep reliance on God's power and truth. By understanding its tactics and strategies, we can actively work towards breaking free from its control. As we embrace the truth of God's Word, develop spiritual discernment, and surround ourselves with a godly community, we can walk in freedom, authority, and victory over Jezebel's witchcraft. Let us continue to pursue healing, deliverance, and a life fully surrendered to God's authority, breaking the chains of control and stepping into the abundant life He has prepared for us.

## Deliverance Prayer

1. Heavenly Father, in the name of Jesus, I come before you to break the curse of Jezebel's witchcraft over my life and the lives of those affected by its control. I declare that your power is greater than any form of manipulation or deception.

2. I renounce and break every soul tie established through Jezebel's witchcraft. I sever and dissolve every emotional bond that has kept me bound to its influence. I declare my freedom in Christ and release myself from its control.

3. I repent of any involvement or association with witchcraft, including dabbling in the occult or seeking power outside of your authority. I ask for your forgiveness and cleansing, washing away any defilement caused by my participation.

4. I declare that your Word is my ultimate source of truth. I immerse myself in your Word, allowing it to renew my mind and expose the lies and deception of Jezebel's witchcraft. I choose to walk in the light of your truth.

5. I pray for deliverance from the power of witchcraft. I break every generational curse associated with Jezebel's witchcraft, declaring that it has no authority or power over my life. I am covered by the blood of Jesus.

6. I seek your inner healing and emotional wholeness, Lord. Heal the wounds caused by Jezebel's witchcraft and restore my emotions to alignment with your truth and love. Fill me with your peace, joy, and emotional stability.

7.  I pray for an increase in spiritual discernment. Open my eyes, Lord, to recognize the counterfeit manifestations of Jezebel's witchcraft. Grant me wisdom and insight to discern the works of darkness and stand against them.

8.  I resist the fear and intimidation tactics of Jezebel's witchcraft. I declare that I am a child of God, filled with the power of the Holy Spirit. I cast out all fear and intimidation, knowing that you have not given me a spirit of fear but of power, love, and a sound mind.

9.  I surround myself with a godly community that provides support, accountability, and prayer. I choose relationships that reflect your truth and love, guarding against the influence of Jezebel's witchcraft. Surround me with godly influences that build me up in faith.

10. I submit myself fully to your authority, Lord. I surrender my will, desires, and decisions to your guidance and direction. Help me to walk in obedience and humility, submitting every aspect of my life to you.

11. I extend forgiveness to those who have operated in Jezebel's witchcraft. I release them from any resentment or bitterness, knowing that vengeance belongs to you, Lord. I choose to walk in love and forgiveness, breaking the cycle of control.

12. I cultivate a lifestyle of worship and prayer. I draw near to you, Lord, through worship, intercession, and communion with the Holy Spirit. Let my life be marked by a deep intimacy with you, breaking the power of witchcraft in my life.

13. I operate in the gifts of the Holy Spirit. I seek the gift of discernment to expose and counteract Jezebel's witchcraft. I use the gifts for the edification and protection of the Body of Christ, discerning between what is of you and what is of the enemy.

14. I fill my mind with your truth and renew my thoughts. I meditate on your Word day and night, rejecting the lies and deceptions of Jezebel's witchcraft. I take captive every thought that exalts itself against your truth, aligning my thoughts with your Word.

15. I establish healthy boundaries and say no to manipulation and control. I guard my heart and emotions, refusing to allow Jezebel's witchcraft to manipulate my decisions and actions. I am empowered by your Spirit to walk in freedom and self-control.

16. I seek professional help if needed, Lord. If the effects of Jezebel's witchcraft have caused deep wounds or trauma, I seek the assistance of counselors or pastors experienced in deliverance and inner healing. Use them as vessels of your healing and restoration in my life.

17. I walk in humility and godly authority. I recognize my need for your grace and strength, Lord. I operate in godly authority, leading with love, humility, and wisdom. I reflect the character of Christ, who came to serve rather than to be served.

18. I remain vigilant and prayerful, Lord. I continue to seek your guidance and protection. Help me to discern the schemes of Jezebel's witchcraft and stand firm in your truth. Grant me spiritual discernment and wisdom in all areas of my life.

19. I declare your truth and break every witchcraft curse spoken over my life. I proclaim the victory of Jesus Christ over witchcraft and renounce its hold on my life. I am covered by the blood of Jesus, and no weapon formed against me shall prosper.

20. I trust in your deliverance and restoration, Lord. I rest in your faithfulness and know that you are able to redeem every aspect of my life affected by witchcraft. I walk in freedom, knowing that you have overcome the power of Jezebel's witchcraft.

## Chapter 19

## Overcoming Fear:
## Stepping into Boldness against Jezebel

Fear is one of the primary weapons used by the Jezebel spirit to control and manipulate individuals. In this chapter, we will explore the power of fear and its impact on our lives in relation to Jezebel's influence. We will delve into the strategies and tactics used by Jezebel to instill fear and discuss practical steps to overcome fear and step into boldness, walking in the authority and freedom that Christ has given us.

Understanding the Power of Fear:

1. Fear as a Control Mechanism:
   - Jezebel uses fear as a control mechanism to keep individuals bound to her influence. Fear of rejection, failure, and judgment can paralyze us and hinder us from walking in our God-given purpose.

2. Fear as a Tool of Manipulation:
   - Jezebel manipulates individuals by exploiting their fears. She uses fear to coerce, intimidate, and keep them submissive to her

control. Fear becomes a powerful tool in her hands to maintain dominance.

3. Fear as a Barrier to Spiritual Growth:
- Fear hinders our spiritual growth and stifles our potential. It holds us back from stepping out in faith, obeying God's call, and walking in the fullness of our giftings and destiny. Jezebel uses fear to keep us stagnant.

4. Fear as a Destructive Force:
- Fear has the power to consume and destroy. It breeds anxiety, doubt, and insecurity. It robs us of peace, joy, and confidence in God. Jezebel seeks to amplify and exploit our fears, trapping us in a cycle of bondage.

Breaking Free from Fear:

1. Identifying and Acknowledging Our Fears:
- The first step in overcoming fear is to identify and acknowledge our fears. We must confront the specific fears that Jezebel has used against us, bringing them into the light and refusing to let them hold power over us.

2. Embracing God's Love:
- Perfect love casts out fear. We must embrace and immerse ourselves in the love of God. Understand that His love for us is

unconditional, unwavering, and greater than any fear. Rest in His love and allow it to drive out fear.

3. Renewing Our Minds with Truth:
   - Overcoming fear requires renewing our minds with the truth of God's Word. Meditate on Scriptures that speak of God's faithfulness, His promises, and His protection. Replace fearful thoughts with thoughts of truth and faith.

4. Developing a Strong Prayer Life:
   - Prayer is a powerful weapon against fear. Spend time in prayer, pouring out your fears and anxieties to God. Seek His presence and allow His peace to guard your heart and mind. Pray for a spirit of boldness and confidence in Him.

5. Building a Foundation of Faith:
   - Cultivate a strong foundation of faith in God. Remember His faithfulness in your past, and trust that He will continue to be faithful. Stand on the promises of God, knowing that He is with you and will never leave you.

6. Surrounding Yourself with Encouragers:
   - Surround yourself with people who build you up and encourage you in your walk with God. Seek out mentors, friends, and community members who inspire you to step out in boldness and overcome fear. Allow their support to strengthen your faith.

7. Taking Steps of Faith:

- Overcoming fear requires taking steps of faith. Start small but step out of your comfort zone. As you obey God and trust His leading, you will experience His faithfulness and grow in confidence. Each step will help break the power of fear.

8. Seeking the Holy Spirit's Empowerment:

- Depend on the Holy Spirit for empowerment. He is our helper and source of strength. Allow the Holy Spirit to fill you, equipping you with boldness and courage to confront Jezebel's tactics and walk in freedom.

9. Guarding Your Thought Life:

- Guard your thought life against negative and fearful thinking. Replace anxious thoughts with thoughts of peace, confidence, and victory. Meditate on Philippians 4:8, focusing on whatever is true, noble, right, pure, lovely, admirable, excellent, or praiseworthy.

10. Practicing Gratitude and Thanksgiving:

- Cultivate an attitude of gratitude and thanksgiving. Give thanks to God for His goodness, faithfulness, and protection. Gratitude shifts our focus from fear to God's provision and care, reminding us of His presence in our lives.

11. Declaring God's Promises:

- Speak out loud the promises of God concerning fear and overcoming Jezebel's influence. Declare Scriptures such as 2 Timothy 1:7, which reminds us that God has not given us a spirit of fear but of power, love, and a sound mind.

12. Walking in Forgiveness:
- Forgive those who have used fear to manipulate and control you. Release any resentment or bitterness, knowing that forgiveness is a key to freedom. Allow God's love and grace to heal your heart and release you from the power of past hurts.

13. Strengthening Your Identity in Christ:
- Ground your identity in Christ and His love. Recognize that you are a child of God, chosen and accepted. Jezebel's tactics cannot diminish who you are in Christ. Walk in the confidence that comes from knowing your identity in Him.

14. Filling Your Mind with Positive and Inspirational Resources:
- Fill your mind with positive and inspirational resources that align with God's truth. Read books, listen to podcasts, and engage with content that encourages faith, courage, and freedom from fear. Let these resources strengthen your resolve to overcome Jezebel's control.

15. Celebrating Your Victories:

- Celebrate every victory, no matter how small. Acknowledge the progress you are making in overcoming fear and stepping into boldness. Give glory to God for His faithfulness and share your testimony with others to encourage them in their journey.

16. Embracing Discipline and Self-Control:
   - Practice discipline and self-control in all areas of your life. Develop healthy habits that promote a sound mind, body, and spirit. Take care of yourself physically, emotionally, and spiritually, as fear can often be amplified in times of neglect or imbalance.

17. Remaining Anchored in God's Presence:
   - Stay anchored in God's presence through consistent prayer, worship, and meditation on His Word. The more intimately we know God, the more we will trust Him and find courage to face our fears. Abide in Him, for apart from Him we can do nothing.

18. Surrendering to God's Plan and Timing:
   - Surrender your fears, plans, and desires to God. Trust that His plan and timing are perfect. Surrendering to Him allows Him to work in and through you, leading you into a future filled with purpose and freedom from fear.

19. Encouraging Others in Their Journey:

- Encourage others who are struggling with fear and Jezebel's control. Share your experiences, victories, and insights. Offer support, prayer, and guidance to help them overcome fear and step into boldness.

20. Trusting in God's Protection and Provision:
   - Ultimately, trust in God's protection and provision over your life. He is your refuge and strength, a very present help in times of trouble. Rest in the assurance that He will guide you, protect you, and empower you to overcome Jezebel's tactics.

---

Overcoming fear and stepping into boldness is a process that requires intentional effort, faith, and reliance on God's power. By understanding the power of fear and the tactics of Jezebel, we can actively work towards breaking free from its control. As we embrace God's love, renew our minds with truth, and step out in faith, we will experience the freedom and authority that Christ has secured for us. Let us press forward in boldness, knowing that we are more than conquerors through Him who loves us.

## Deliverance Prayer

1. Heavenly Father, in the name of Jesus, I come before you to break the power of fear and Jezebel's influence in my life. I declare that your perfect love casts out all fear, and I choose to walk in boldness and freedom.

2. I renounce and reject every spirit of fear that has been operating in my life through the tactics of Jezebel. I break its hold over my mind, emotions, and actions. I refuse to be controlled by fear any longer.

3. I declare that I am a child of God, and I have been given a spirit of power, love, and a sound mind. I embrace my identity in Christ and walk in the authority He has given me to overcome fear.

4. I submit myself to the leading and empowerment of the Holy Spirit. I rely on His strength and guidance to navigate through every situation that tries to instill fear. I trust in His power to break the chains of fear in my life.

5. I reject the lies and deception of Jezebel that seek to magnify my fears and keep me in bondage. I declare that I am rooted in the truth of God's Word, and I choose to meditate on His promises of protection, provision, and peace.

6. I take captive every thought that exalts itself against the knowledge of God. I demolish every stronghold of fear in my mind and replace it with thoughts of faith, courage, and victory. I choose to focus on what is true, noble, right, pure, lovely, admirable, excellent, and praiseworthy.

7.  I rebuke and cast out the spirit of fear from my life. I break every generational curse of fear and declare that it has no power or authority over me. I am free to walk in boldness and confidence in the Lord.

8.  I declare that I will not be paralyzed by fear, but I will step out in faith and obedience to God's call. I trust that He is with me, and I will not be shaken or intimidated by the tactics of Jezebel.

9.  I pray for divine courage and boldness to rise up within me. Let your Holy Spirit empower me to speak the truth, confront injustice, and stand against the manipulative tactics of Jezebel. Grant me the strength to walk in righteousness and integrity.

10. I resist the spirit of fear in every area of my life - in my relationships, career, ministry, and personal endeavors. I refuse to allow fear to dictate my decisions or limit my potential. I choose to trust in God's guidance and provision.

11. I surround myself with godly influences and support. I seek out community and fellowship with believers who encourage faith, courage, and boldness. I am strengthened by their testimonies and inspired to overcome fear.

12. I pray for those who have been victimized by Jezebel's control and manipulation. I intercede for their deliverance and freedom from

fear. I declare that they will step into boldness and walk in the fullness of their calling.

13. I bind and rebuke every spirit of intimidation and fear that Jezebel uses to hinder the advancement of God's Kingdom. I declare that the plans of Jezebel will be exposed and thwarted by the power of God.

14. I release forgiveness to those who have operated under the influence of Jezebel's fear tactics. I choose to forgive and release them from the hold they may have had over my life. I walk in freedom, extending grace and mercy.

15. I declare that I am more than a conqueror through Christ who strengthens me. I have been given authority over all the power of the enemy, and no weapon formed against me shall prosper. I walk in the victory that has been secured for me.

16. I resist the spirit of fear and embrace a spirit of boldness and courage. I choose to step out of my comfort zone, trusting in God's guidance and provision. I am not limited by fear but empowered by faith.

17. I pray for divine opportunities to overcome fear and demonstrate boldness. Open doors for me to speak truth, share my testimony,

and encourage others in their journey of overcoming fear. Use me as a vessel of your love and strength.

18. I declare that I will not shrink back or be silenced by fear. I will proclaim the truth of God's Word boldly and confidently. I will walk in the authority you have given me, breaking the power of fear in the lives of others.

19. I release a spirit of courage and boldness over my family, friends, and loved ones. May they be empowered to overcome fear and walk in the freedom and victory that you have provided. Let fear have no place in their lives.

20. I thank you, Lord, for the victory I have in Christ. I praise you for your faithfulness and for being my ever-present help in times of trouble. I choose to trust in you, walk in boldness, and live a life free from the grip of fear.

## Chapter 20

# Jezebel's Influence on Gender Roles: Restoring Biblical Identity

The Jezebel spirit not only seeks to control and manipulate individuals but also distorts and perverts gender roles as established by God. In this chapter, we will explore the influence of Jezebel on gender roles and its impact on society. We will delve into the tactics used by Jezebel to blur the lines of biblical identity and discuss the importance of restoring God's design for male and female roles.

Understanding Jezebel's Influence on Gender Roles:

1. Redefining Gender Roles:
   - Jezebel seeks to redefine and blur the distinctions between male and female roles established by God. It promotes a distorted view of gender, leading to confusion, conflict, and a loss of identity.

2. Undermining God's Order:
   - Jezebel's influence on gender roles undermines God's order and design. It encourages rebellion against the authority structures established by God, causing division and chaos.

3. Encouraging Female Empowerment at the Expense of Godly Submission:
   - Jezebel promotes female empowerment but often at the expense of godly submission. It distorts the concept of submission, leading to a rejection of biblical principles and a breakdown of healthy relationships.

4. Manipulating Male Authority:
   - Jezebel manipulates and emasculates men, undermining their God-given authority. It seeks to diminish their leadership role and replace it with female dominance, creating a power struggle and confusion in relationships.

5. Distorting God's Image in Humanity:
   - Jezebel's influence on gender roles distorts the reflection of God's image in humanity. It undermines the complementary nature of male and female, denying the beauty and purpose of God's design.

Restoring Biblical Identity:

1. Embracing God's Design for Gender:
   - To restore biblical identity, we must embrace and celebrate God's design for gender. Recognize that male and female are distinct and complementary, reflecting different aspects of God's character and purpose.

2. Understanding Godly Authority and Submission:

- Restore a proper understanding of godly authority and submission. Recognize that both men and women are called to submit to God and to one another in love, following the biblical principles of mutual submission and respect.

3. Cultivating Healthy Relationships:

- Foster healthy relationships based on mutual love, honor, and respect. Embrace the unique roles and giftings of both men and women, supporting one another's strengths and working together as a team.

4. Rediscovering the Strength of Biblical Womanhood:

- Rediscover the strength and influence of biblical womanhood. Women are called to be strong, courageous, and nurturing, reflecting the character of God. Embrace the unique opportunities and responsibilities that come with being a woman.

5. Encouraging Male Leadership and Godly Masculinity:

- Affirm and encourage male leadership and godly masculinity. Men are called to lead with humility, love, and servant-heartedness. Support and empower men to fulfill their God-given roles as leaders, protectors, and providers.

6. Equipping and Empowering Women in Their Callings:

- Equip and empower women to fulfill their unique callings and giftings. Provide opportunities for training, mentoring, and ministry involvement. Encourage women to use their God-given gifts to impact their families, communities, and the world.

7. Teaching Biblical Truth on Gender and Sexuality:
- Teach and uphold biblical truth on gender and sexuality. Provide sound teaching that upholds the sanctity of marriage, the importance of sexual purity, and the complementary nature of male and female relationships.

8. Discerning and Rejecting Jezebel's Influence:
- Discern and reject Jezebel's influence on gender roles. Be aware of the tactics and strategies used to distort biblical identity. Stand firm on God's Word and resist the pressure to conform to worldly ideologies.

9. Emphasizing Unity and Cooperation:
- Emphasize unity and cooperation between men and women. Recognize that we are co-laborers in God's kingdom, each contributing unique strengths and perspectives. Value and appreciate the diversity within the body of Christ.

10. Seeking God's Wisdom and Guidance:
- Seek God's wisdom and guidance in navigating gender roles. Pray for discernment and understanding of His design and purpose. Ask

for His help in embracing and restoring biblical identity in your own life and relationships.

11. Addressing Wounds and Restoring Wholeness:
   - Address the wounds and brokenness caused by the distortion of gender roles. Provide healing and restoration to those who have been affected by Jezebel's influence. Offer grace, empathy, and support to individuals as they seek to rediscover their true identity in Christ.

12. Raising Godly Children:
   - Raise children in the truth of God's Word concerning gender roles. Teach them the importance of embracing their God-given identities and fulfilling their unique callings. Model healthy relationships and godly authority within the family.

13. Challenging Cultural Norms:
   - Challenge cultural norms that undermine biblical gender roles. Speak out against societal pressures and ideologies that contradict God's Word. Be a voice for truth and advocate for God's design in your spheres of influence.

14. Celebrating God's Goodness in His Creation:
   - Celebrate God's goodness in creating male and female. Recognize the beauty and purpose in His design. Give thanks for the unique

qualities and contributions of both genders, and honor them as reflections of His image.

15. Extending Grace and Understanding:
   - Extend grace and understanding to those who may struggle with their identity or have been influenced by Jezebel's distortion of gender roles. Offer compassion, support, and a safe space for individuals to explore and rediscover their true identity in Christ.

16. Promoting Unity in the Body of Christ:
   - Promote unity in the body of Christ by embracing and valuing the diversity of gender roles. Recognize that we are part of one body, with different functions but a shared purpose. Encourage mutual respect, love, and collaboration among believers.

17. Resisting the Pressure to Conform:
   - Resist the pressure to conform to worldly ideologies and cultural trends regarding gender roles. Stand firm on the truth of God's Word and the timeless principles He has established. Trust in His wisdom and guidance above the shifting opinions of society.

18. Praying for Cultural Transformation:
   - Pray for cultural transformation concerning gender roles. Intercede for a restoration of biblical values and a rejection of Jezebel's influence. Pray for hearts to be turned toward God's design and for His kingdom to come on earth as it is in heaven.

19. Supporting Organizations and Resources:
- Support organizations and resources that promote biblical gender roles and provide guidance in navigating these issues. Engage with teachings, books, podcasts, and conferences that uphold biblical truth and provide practical wisdom for restoring biblical identity.

20. Trusting in God's Faithfulness and Provision:
- Trust in God's faithfulness and provision as you seek to restore biblical identity in the context of gender roles. He is the author of identity and design, and He will guide and empower you to walk in alignment with His purposes.

---

Restoring biblical identity in the context of gender roles requires a commitment to God's Word, a reliance on His guidance, and a willingness to challenge societal norms influenced by Jezebel's distortion. By embracing God's design, empowering one another, and seeking unity in the body of Christ, we can reclaim the beauty, purpose, and harmony that God intended for male and female roles. Let us continue to pursue biblical identity, walking in obedience and reflecting the image of our loving Creator.

## Deliverance Prayer

1. Heavenly Father, in the name of Jesus, I come before you to break the influence of Jezebel on gender roles and to restore biblical identity in my life and in the lives of others. I declare that your design for male and female is perfect and that your Word is the ultimate authority in all matters of identity.

2. I renounce and reject the lies and distortions of Jezebel's influence on gender roles. I break every stronghold and mindset that has been formed by her deception. I choose to align my beliefs and actions with your truth.

3. I declare that I am fearfully and wonderfully made, created in your image, and assigned a unique purpose. I embrace the beauty and dignity of being male/female as you intended. I reject any attempts to blur or pervert the distinctions you have established.

4. I release forgiveness to those who have propagated false teachings and ideologies regarding gender roles. I choose to extend grace and love, even to those who have been influenced by Jezebel's deception. I pray for their eyes to be opened to the truth of your Word.

5. I break every generational curse that has perpetuated distorted gender roles within my family line. I declare that in Christ, I am a new creation, and old patterns and mindsets no longer have power over me. I walk in the freedom and authority given to me by Jesus.

6. I pray for a restoration of biblical identity in the body of Christ. May we embrace and celebrate the unique roles and giftings you have given to men and women. May we honor and support one another, recognizing the strength and purpose in your design.

7. I declare that male/female relationships will reflect your love, harmony, and mutual submission. I rebuke any spirit of dominance, manipulation, or control that has infiltrated relationships. I pray for healing and restoration in marriages, families, and communities.

8. I pray for godly masculinity to be restored in men. May they embrace their roles as leaders, protectors, and providers, leading with humility, integrity, and sacrificial love. I pray for their empowerment and support in fulfilling their God-given callings.

9. I pray for godly femininity to be restored in women. May they embrace their roles as nurturers, helpers, and influencers, walking in strength, grace, and wisdom. I pray for their empowerment and support in fulfilling their God-given callings.

10. I bind and rebuke the spirit of confusion and rebellion that seeks to distort gender roles and promote division. I declare that in Christ, there is unity and harmony in fulfilling our roles and callings according to your Word.

11. I pray for discernment and wisdom in navigating cultural pressures and ideologies regarding gender roles. Help me to stand firm on your truth, even in the face of opposition. Grant me the courage to walk in obedience to your Word.

12. I pray for the transformation of societal norms and cultural perceptions regarding gender roles. May the influence of Jezebel be exposed and rejected. I pray for a revival of biblical values and a return to your design for male and female roles.

13. I break every spirit of emasculation that has weakened men and hindered them from walking in their God-given authority. I declare that they are strong, courageous, and empowered by your Spirit. I pray for a restoration of their confidence and leadership.

14. I break every spirit of rebellion and feminism that has distorted femininity and undermined godly submission. I declare that women are empowered by your Spirit to walk in strength, wisdom, and grace. I pray for a restoration of their identity and purpose.

15. I pray for healing and restoration for those who have been wounded by the distortion of gender roles. I ask for your comfort, love, and renewal to touch their hearts and minds. Bring healing to their identities and help them embrace their true biblical identity.

16. I pray for the empowerment of the younger generation to embrace biblical gender roles and reject the lies of Jezebel's influence. Equip them with discernment, wisdom, and a strong foundation in your Word.

17. I declare that my identity is rooted in Christ, not in societal expectations or cultural norms. I choose to walk in the freedom and confidence that comes from knowing who I am in you. I will live out my biblical identity with boldness and humility.

18. I pray for leaders, pastors, and teachers to faithfully teach and uphold biblical truths regarding gender roles. Grant them wisdom, courage, and anointing as they navigate these sensitive topics. May they be guided by your Word and your Holy Spirit.

19. I pray for unity and reconciliation among believers regarding gender roles. Help us to honor and respect one another's unique contributions, appreciating the diversity within the body of Christ. Let your love bind us together in a powerful testimony to the world.

20. I thank you, Lord, for your faithfulness in restoring biblical identity. I trust in your plan and purpose for male and female roles. Strengthen me to walk in obedience, confidence, and humility as I embrace and live out your design for my life.

## Chapter 21

# Divine Alignment:
# Partnering with Elijah to Confront Jezebel

In the biblical narrative, the confrontations between the prophet Elijah and the wicked Queen Jezebel serve as a powerful illustration of the battle between God's truth and the influence of the Jezebel spirit. In this chapter, we will explore the concept of divine alignment and how partnering with the spirit of Elijah can equip us to confront and overcome Jezebel's influence in our lives and in the world around us.

Understanding the Battle:

1. The Jezebel Spirit:
   - The Jezebel spirit is a deceptive and manipulative force that seeks to control, dominate, and undermine the authority of God. It operates through fear, manipulation, and seduction, distorting truth and perverting God's design for relationships and authority.

2. Elijah's Call and Anointing:
   - Elijah was a prophet chosen and anointed by God to confront and expose the influence of Jezebel. He stood as a voice of truth,

boldly confronting the idolatry and wickedness promoted by Jezebel and her followers.

3. Divine Alignment:
   - Divine alignment is the process of partnering with God and His purposes. It involves surrendering our will to His, seeking His guidance, and walking in obedience to His Word. When we align ourselves with God, we position ourselves to confront and overcome the influence of Jezebel.

4. Recognizing Jezebel's Tactics:
   - To confront Jezebel effectively, we must recognize her tactics and strategies. She operates through manipulation, control, intimidation, seduction, and witchcraft. By understanding her methods, we can guard ourselves against her influence and partner with God in the battle.

Divine Alignment and Confronting Jezebel:

1. Surrendering to God's Will:
   - Divine alignment begins with surrendering our will to God's will. We must submit ourselves fully to Him, seeking His guidance and trusting in His wisdom. Surrender allows God to lead us and empowers us to confront Jezebel with His authority.

2. Seeking Intimacy with God:

- Intimacy with God is vital in confronting Jezebel. We must cultivate a deep and personal relationship with Him through prayer, worship, and studying His Word. Intimacy with God equips us with discernment, wisdom, and the strength to confront the lies of Jezebel.

3. Embracing the Spirit of Elijah:
- Partnering with the spirit of Elijah involves embracing his boldness, uncompromising faith, and obedience to God. Like Elijah, we are called to be prophetic voices in a world influenced by Jezebel. We must boldly confront the lies and stand firm on God's truth.

4. Prophetic Discernment:
- Prophetic discernment is crucial in confronting Jezebel. We must seek the discernment of the Holy Spirit to identify the Jezebel spirit's presence and tactics. Through the Holy Spirit's guidance, we can expose the lies and deception of Jezebel and release God's truth.

5. Exposing Jezebel's Deception:
- We confront Jezebel by exposing her deception with the light of God's truth. Through prayer, studying God's Word, and reliance on the Holy Spirit, we can discern and expose the lies, manipulation, and false teachings promoted by Jezebel.

6. Operating in God's Authority:

- Divine alignment empowers us to operate in God's authority. By understanding and exercising the authority given to us through Jesus Christ, we can confront Jezebel's influence. We have the authority to bind and cast out the Jezebel spirit in Jesus' name.

7. Walking in Spiritual Warfare:

- Confronting Jezebel requires engaging in spiritual warfare. We must put on the full armor of God, praying, interceding, and using the spiritual weapons at our disposal. Through prayer, fasting, and spiritual disciplines, we can effectively battle against Jezebel's influence.

8. Surrounding Yourself with a Supportive Community:

- Divine alignment involves surrounding ourselves with a supportive community of like-minded believers. We need the encouragement, accountability, and support of fellow believers who are also committed to confronting Jezebel's influence.

9. Healing from Jezebel's Influence:

- Divine alignment brings healing from the wounds inflicted by Jezebel's influence. Through the power of the Holy Spirit, we can experience restoration and freedom from the effects of manipulation, control, and deception. God's healing brings wholeness and renewed strength.

10. Extending God's Love and Mercy:
   - Divine alignment compels us to extend God's love and mercy to those influenced by Jezebel. Instead of harboring resentment or judgment, we are called to extend grace and compassion, praying for their deliverance and restoration.

---

Divine alignment with God and partnering with the spirit of Elijah equips us to confront and overcome Jezebel's influence. By surrendering to God's will, seeking intimacy with Him, embracing boldness and prophetic discernment, operating in His authority, and walking in spiritual warfare, we can expose the lies and deceptions of Jezebel and experience victory in Christ. Let us align ourselves with God's purposes, confront Jezebel with courage and love, and reclaim God's truth and authority in our lives and in the world around us.

## Deliverance Prayer

1. Heavenly Father, in the name of Jesus, I come before you to seek divine alignment and to partner with the spirit of Elijah in confronting the influence of Jezebel in my life and in the world. I surrender my will to yours and align myself with your purposes.

2. I declare that I am a vessel of your truth and light. I embrace the boldness and unwavering faith of Elijah as I confront the lies and

deceptions of Jezebel. I walk in obedience to your Word and stand firm in your authority.

3. I pray for intimacy with you, Lord. Draw me closer to your heart, that I may discern your voice and receive your wisdom. Guide me through your Holy Spirit, that I may accurately discern the tactics and strategies of Jezebel.

4. I renounce and break every stronghold of manipulation, control, intimidation, and seduction that Jezebel has established in my life. I declare that I am free from her influence, and I release the power of your truth to expose and dismantle her deception.

5. I bind and rebuke the Jezebel spirit in the name of Jesus. I declare that it has no authority or power over me. I release the fire of your Holy Spirit to consume every assignment and influence of Jezebel in my life and in the lives of others.

6. I embrace the spirit of Elijah, standing as a prophetic voice in the midst of a world influenced by Jezebel. I boldly declare your truth, confronting the lies and promoting righteousness, justice, and godly authority.

7. I operate in the authority you have given me through Jesus Christ. I bind every demonic force associated with Jezebel and release the

power of your Word to break every chain of bondage. I walk in the freedom and authority you have secured for me.

8. I put on the full armor of God, equipping myself for spiritual warfare. I take up the sword of the Spirit, which is your Word, and I use it to expose and defeat the lies of Jezebel. I stand firm in the truth, righteousness, faith, and salvation you have provided.

9. I pray for divine discernment to recognize the presence of Jezebel's influence in my relationships, communities, and spheres of influence. Help me to expose her tactics and to guide others to freedom and restoration in you.

10. I surround myself with a supportive community of believers who are also aligned with your purposes. We stand united in confronting Jezebel, encouraging and empowering one another to walk in boldness and obedience to your Word.

11. I receive your healing from the wounds inflicted by Jezebel's influence. I declare that I am restored and made whole in your love and mercy. I release forgiveness to those who have operated under Jezebel's influence, knowing that your grace is sufficient.

12. I pray for those who are currently under the influence of Jezebel. I intercede for their deliverance and restoration. I ask that you

open their eyes to see the truth, break the chains that bind them, and bring them into divine alignment with your purposes.

13. I resist every attempt of Jezebel to manipulate and control my emotions, thoughts, and actions. I submit myself fully to your authority and choose to walk in obedience to your Word. I declare that I am free to live according to your design and calling for my life.

14. I pray for a revival of righteousness and godly authority in my family, church, community, and nation. May your truth prevail over the influence of Jezebel, and may your kingdom come, and your will be done in every sphere of influence.

15. I release your love, mercy, and compassion to those who have been wounded by Jezebel's influence. May they experience your healing touch and find restoration in you. Use me as an instrument of your grace to bring hope and restoration to their lives.

16. I resist the spirit of fear that Jezebel seeks to instill. I declare that I walk in the power, love, and sound mind that you have given me. I cast out all fear and embrace the courage and boldness that come from partnering with you.

17. I pray for divine opportunities to confront Jezebel's influence and release your truth and freedom. Open doors for me to speak boldly,

to bring healing and deliverance, and to lead others into divine alignment with your purposes.

18. I pray for a generation of Elijahs to rise up, equipped and anointed by your Spirit, to confront and overcome Jezebel's influence. Raise up prophetic voices who will boldly proclaim your truth, exposing the lies and leading others to freedom.

19. I declare that the spirit of Jezebel will not prevail in my life, my relationships, or my sphere of influence. I release the fire of your Holy Spirit to burn away every trace of her influence. I choose to partner with you, walking in divine alignment and experiencing victory.

20. I thank you, Lord, for the victory I have in Christ. I praise you for the power of divine alignment and the authority you have given me to confront and overcome Jezebel. I walk in confidence, knowing that you are with me and that I am more than a conqueror through Christ Jesus.

## Chapter 22

# The Jehu Anointing: Rising as God's Avenger

In the biblical narrative, the story of Jehu provides a powerful example of a leader anointed by God to confront and bring judgment upon the influence of Jezebel. In this chapter, we will explore the concept of the Jehu anointing and how it empowers believers to rise as God's avengers against the works of darkness and the influence of the Jezebel spirit.

Understanding the Jehu Anointing:

1. Jehu's Call and Commission:
   - Jehu was chosen and anointed by God as a king to execute judgment upon the wickedness of Jezebel and the house of Ahab. He was given a specific mandate to dismantle Jezebel's influence and restore righteousness in the land.

2. Characteristics of the Jehu Anointing:
   - The Jehu anointing is characterized by zeal, boldness, and an uncompromising spirit. It empowers believers to confront and overthrow the works of darkness, bringing justice and restoration in alignment with God's will.

3. Confronting Jezebel's Influence:
-   The Jehu anointing equips believers to confront and expose the influence of Jezebel. It empowers them to boldly confront false teachings, manipulative control, and the perversion of God's design for relationships and authority.

4. Prophetic Discernment:
-   Those walking in the Jehu anointing possess a heightened level of prophetic discernment. They are able to identify the works of darkness, discern the strategies of the enemy, and expose the deception of Jezebel.

5. Divine Strategy and Timing:
-   The Jehu anointing operates in divine strategy and timing. Jehu received specific instructions from the Lord on how to execute judgment upon Jezebel and her followers. Likewise, those operating in the Jehu anointing rely on God's guidance and timing to confront and dismantle the influence of Jezebel.

Walking in the Jehu Anointing:

1. Embracing Zeal and Righteous Anger:
-   The Jehu anointing is characterized by zeal and righteous anger against the works of darkness. We must cultivate a holy passion to see God's truth prevail and His righteousness established. Channel

your anger towards injustice and ungodliness, aligning it with God's purposes.

2. Aligning with God's Word:
   - The Jehu anointing requires alignment with God's Word. Study and meditate on His Word, allowing it to shape your thoughts, actions, and decisions. Let His Word be the foundation upon which you confront and dismantle Jezebel's influence.

3. Walking in Boldness and Confidence:
   - The Jehu anointing empowers believers to walk in boldness and confidence. Do not shrink back or be intimidated by the influence of Jezebel. Stand firm in your identity as a child of God, knowing that He has equipped you with the power of His Spirit.

4. Confronting False Teachings and Doctrines:
   - Those walking in the Jehu anointing confront false teachings and doctrines promoted by Jezebel. Expose the lies and deceptions that have infiltrated the Church and society. Speak the truth in love, rooted in the authority of God's Word.

5. Exercising Authority in Spiritual Warfare:
   - The Jehu anointing empowers believers to exercise authority in spiritual warfare. Bind the influence of Jezebel and release the power of God's Word to break every stronghold. Proclaim freedom, deliverance, and restoration in the name of Jesus.

6. Recognizing and Resisting Manipulation and Control:
- Those operating in the Jehu anointing discern and resist the manipulative control tactics employed by Jezebel. Do not allow yourself to be swayed or influenced by her strategies. Stand firm in the truth and authority of God's Word.

7. Pursuing Holiness and Righteousness:
- The Jehu anointing requires a commitment to holiness and righteousness. Live a life of integrity, obedience, and moral purity. Strive to walk in alignment with God's standards, refusing to compromise with the ways of Jezebel.

8. Executing God's Justice and Restoration:
- The Jehu anointing empowers believers to execute God's justice and restoration. Seek opportunities to bring justice to the oppressed, to expose corruption, and to restore what has been stolen or distorted by Jezebel's influence.

9. Submitting to Divine Strategy and Timing:
- Those walking in the Jehu anointing submit to divine strategy and timing. Seek the guidance of the Holy Spirit and rely on God's wisdom and direction. Execute your actions in alignment with His purposes and in His appointed time.

10. Praying for the Restoration of God's Order:

- Pray for the restoration of God's order in the Church and society. Intercede for leaders, influencers, and individuals who have been deceived or influenced by Jezebel. Pray for their eyes to be opened, their hearts to be softened, and their lives to be transformed.

---

The Jehu anointing empowers believers to rise as God's avengers against the influence of Jezebel. By embracing zeal, walking in boldness and confidence, confronting false teachings, exercising spiritual authority, resisting manipulation, pursuing holiness, executing justice and restoration, and submitting to divine strategy and timing, we can confront and overcome the works of darkness. Let us walk in the power of the Jehu anointing, aligned with God's purposes, and bring about transformation and restoration in our lives and in the world around us.

## Deliverance Prayer

1. Heavenly Father, in the name of Jesus, I thank you for the Jehu anointing that empowers me to rise as your avenger against the influence of Jezebel. I embrace the zeal and righteous anger that come from walking in this anointing.

2. I declare that I am aligned with your Word, and I reject every false teaching and deceptive doctrine promoted by Jezebel. I release the power of your truth to expose and dismantle her influence.

3.  I walk in boldness and confidence, knowing that you have equipped me with the Jehu anointing. I confront the works of darkness and the influence of Jezebel with courage, refusing to be intimidated or silenced.

4.  I exercise my authority in spiritual warfare, binding the influence of Jezebel and releasing the power of your Word to break every stronghold. I proclaim freedom, deliverance, and restoration in the name of Jesus.

5.  I discern and resist the manipulative control tactics employed by Jezebel. I refuse to be swayed or influenced by her strategies. I stand firm in the truth and authority of your Word.

6.  I pursue holiness and righteousness, living a life of integrity, obedience, and moral purity. I renounce compromise and refuse to conform to the ways of Jezebel. I walk in alignment with your standards.

7.  I execute your justice and restoration, bringing justice to the oppressed, exposing corruption, and restoring what has been stolen or distorted by Jezebel's influence. I release the power of your restoration in every area of my life and in the lives of others.

8. I submit to your divine strategy and timing. I seek your guidance and direction, relying on your wisdom and leading. I execute my actions in alignment with your purposes and in your appointed time.

9. I pray for the restoration of your order in the Church and society. I intercede for leaders, influencers, and individuals who have been deceived or influenced by Jezebel. I pray for their eyes to be opened, their hearts to be softened, and their lives to be transformed.

10. I release your fire to consume every assignment, stronghold, and influence of Jezebel in my life and in the lives of others. I declare that her power is broken, and I walk in victory through the Jehu anointing.

11. I break every generational curse associated with the influence of Jezebel. I declare that the cycles of manipulation, control, and deception are broken in the name of Jesus. I walk in the freedom and liberty you have provided.

12. I release forgiveness to those who have operated under the influence of Jezebel. I choose to extend grace and love, knowing that your mercy is sufficient. Help me to extend your compassion and forgiveness to those who need it.

13. I pray for a fresh outpouring of the Jehu anointing in my life and in the Church. Raise up a generation of believers who will boldly confront and overcome the works of darkness. Let your power and glory be manifested through us.

14. I resist every spirit of fear and intimidation that Jezebel seeks to instill. I declare that I walk in the power, love, and sound mind that you have given me. I cast out all fear and embrace the courage and boldness that come from partnering with you.

15. I release the spirit of discernment to accurately identify the works of darkness and the influence of Jezebel. Grant me wisdom and insight to expose her strategies and dismantle her influence. Let your light shine in the midst of darkness.

16. I pray for divine encounters and divine connections that will further empower me in the Jehu anointing. Connect me with like-minded believers who are also rising as your avengers. Together, we will make a greater impact for your kingdom.

17. I declare that the gates of hell will not prevail against the Church. I stand as a gatekeeper, partnering with you to confront and overthrow the influence of Jezebel. I release your authority and power to shift the spiritual atmosphere and bring about transformation.

18. I release the fire of revival, consuming every stronghold and barrier that Jezebel has erected. Let the fire of your Holy Spirit burn away every trace of her influence, purifying and renewing the Church and society.

19. I pray for divine wisdom and discernment in executing the Jehu anointing. Guide my steps, Lord, and let your strategies be revealed to me. Open doors and provide opportunities for me to confront and dismantle Jezebel's influence.

20. I thank you, Lord, for the Jehu anointing that empowers me to rise as your avenger. I walk in this anointing with humility, knowing that it is your power at work in me. I declare that I will bring glory to your name as I confront and overcome Jezebel's influence. In Jesus' mighty name, I pray and declare these warfare and deliverance prayer declarations. Amen.

Chapter 23

# Silencing Jezebel's False Prophets:
# Exposing Counterfeit Voices

In the battle against Jezebel and her influence, it is essential to address the false prophets and counterfeit voices that align themselves with her agenda. In this chapter, we will explore the tactics employed by Jezebel's false prophets, how to discern their deceptive messages, and the strategies to silence their influence. By exposing and silencing Jezebel's false prophets, we can protect the integrity of God's Word and lead others into truth.

Understanding Jezebel's False Prophets:

1. Jezebel's Manipulation of Prophecy:
   - Jezebel's false prophets distort and manipulate true prophetic gifts for their own agenda. They use their influence to promote false teachings, compromise with worldly values, and lead people astray from God's truth.

2. Characteristics of Jezebel's False Prophets:
   - Jezebel's false prophets often exhibit charismatic personalities, persuasive speech, and a facade of spirituality. They may appear

to have the signs of prophetic gifting, but their messages are tainted with deception and manipulation.

3. Deceptive Messages and Teachings:
- Jezebel's false prophets propagate messages that undermine biblical truths, promote compromise, and justify sinful behavior. They twist Scripture, dilute the message of repentance, and falsely claim to speak for God while promoting their own self-interest.

4. Exploiting Spiritual Hunger:
- Jezebel's false prophets prey on the spiritual hunger and vulnerability of individuals. They offer false promises, false prophecies, and counterfeit experiences to deceive and manipulate those seeking a genuine encounter with God.

5. Engaging in Spiritual Witchcraft:
- Jezebel's false prophets employ spiritual witchcraft to gain control and influence over people's lives. They use manipulation, control, and intimidation tactics to exert their authority and silence those who oppose them.

Silencing Jezebel's False Prophets:

1. Cultivating Discernment through God's Word:
- To silence Jezebel's false prophets, we must cultivate discernment by immersing ourselves in God's Word. The Bible serves as our

232

foundation for truth, and it equips us to recognize and refute deceptive teachings.

2. Developing Intimacy with the Holy Spirit:
   - Intimacy with the Holy Spirit is crucial in discerning and silencing Jezebel's false prophets. The Holy Spirit reveals truth, exposes deception, and empowers us to speak with authority. Seek His guidance and discernment in all matters.

3. Testing Every Spirit:
   - We must test every spirit and examine the fruit of the messages proclaimed by Jezebel's false prophets. Compare their teachings with the principles and teachings of Scripture. Look for alignment with God's character and His revealed truth.

4. Exposing False Teachings and False Prophecies:
   - It is essential to expose false teachings and false prophecies of Jezebel's false prophets. Speak the truth in love, boldly confront the lies and deception, and point people back to the Word of God as the ultimate authority.

5. Praying for Spiritual Clarity and Protection:
   - Pray for spiritual clarity and protection for yourself and others. Ask God to reveal any hidden agendas, false teachings, or manipulative tactics employed by Jezebel's false prophets. Seek His guidance and discernment in all interactions.

6. Providing Authentic Spiritual Nourishment:
   - Counteract the influence of Jezebel's false prophets by providing authentic spiritual nourishment. Teach and preach the uncompromised truth of God's Word, leading people into a deeper relationship with Jesus and grounding them in biblical truth.

7. Encouraging Accountability and Discipleship:
   - Promote accountability and discipleship within the body of Christ to safeguard against the influence of Jezebel's false prophets. Foster an environment where believers can grow in spiritual maturity, ask tough questions, and hold one another accountable to the truth.

8. Cultivating a Berean Spirit:
   - Develop a Berean spirit within yourself and encourage it in others. Like the Bereans in Acts 17:11, search the Scriptures diligently to verify the accuracy and authenticity of teachings. Let God's Word be the final authority in all matters of faith and doctrine.

9. Exercising Spiritual Authority:
   - As believers, we have been given spiritual authority through Jesus Christ. Declare the authority of God's Word over the influence of Jezebel's false prophets. Bind their influence and release the power of God's truth to break every chain of deception.

10. Praying for Repentance and Restoration:

- Pray for repentance and restoration for those who have been deceived by Jezebel's false prophets. Intercede for their eyes to be opened, their hearts to be softened, and their lives to be transformed by the truth of God's Word.

---

Silencing Jezebel's false prophets requires discernment, a firm foundation in God's Word, and a reliance on the leading of the Holy Spirit. By cultivating discernment, testing every spirit, exposing false teachings, providing authentic spiritual nourishment, encouraging accountability and discipleship, exercising spiritual authority, and praying for repentance and restoration, we can effectively silence Jezebel's false prophets and lead others into truth and freedom. Let us remain vigilant, standing firm on the rock of God's Word, and exposing the counterfeit voices that seek to lead astray.

## Deliverance Prayer

1. Heavenly Father, in the name of Jesus, I thank you for your Word that exposes the deception of Jezebel's false prophets. I declare that their influence will be silenced, and your truth will prevail.

2. I bind and rebuke every false prophet aligned with Jezebel's agenda. I declare that their deceptive messages and teachings will be exposed and dismantled by the power of your Word.

3. I release discernment and wisdom to recognize the counterfeit voices of Jezebel's false prophets. Open my eyes to their manipulative tactics and deceptive strategies. Let your truth shine brightly, illuminating every lie and exposing every false prophet.

4. I pray for a hunger and thirst for your Word to increase in the hearts of your people. May they be rooted and grounded in the truth, so that they are not swayed by the false teachings of Jezebel's false prophets.

5. I declare that the power of the Holy Spirit is greater than the power of Jezebel's false prophets. I release the Spirit of truth to guide and lead your people into all truth, protecting them from deception.

6. I break the influence and control of Jezebel's false prophets over the minds and hearts of individuals. I release the power of freedom and deliverance, setting captives free from the lies and manipulation.

7. I pray for an outpouring of spiritual discernment and a spirit of testing among your people. Help them to examine every message and teaching against the plumb line of your Word. Let your truth prevail.

8. I release the fire of your Holy Spirit to consume every false prophecy and false teaching of Jezebel's false prophets. Let your fire purify and refine, bringing forth a pure and unadulterated Word.

9. I declare that the ears of your people will be attuned to your voice alone. They will not be swayed by the smooth words and enticing messages of Jezebel's false prophets. Your truth will resound in their hearts.

10. I pray for the repentance and restoration of those who have been led astray by Jezebel's false prophets. Open their eyes to the truth, soften their hearts, and bring them back into alignment with your Word.

11. I release the spirit of courage and boldness upon your people to confront and expose the false prophets of Jezebel. Let them rise up with conviction and speak your truth fearlessly, knowing that you are with them.

12. I pray for the dismantling of Jezebel's networks and platforms used by her false prophets to spread deception. Let their influence be weakened and their voices silenced, as your truth prevails.

13. I declare that Jezebel's false prophets will be held accountable for their deception and manipulation. Let their influence crumble, and let their followers be set free from their grip.

14. I release a spirit of unity among your people as they stand together against Jezebel's false prophets. Let them encourage one another, build each other up in the faith, and sharpen one another's discernment.

15. I declare that the true prophets and messengers of God will rise up with boldness and authority, overshadowing the voices of Jezebel's false prophets. Let their messages ring true and bring forth transformation.

16. I pray for a fresh anointing of your Spirit upon your true prophets and messengers. Empower them to speak with accuracy, clarity, and authority. Let their words cut through the deception and bring life to the hearers.

17. I release your divine strategies and divine connections to expose and silence Jezebel's false prophets. Connect your true prophets and messengers, giving them a platform to proclaim your truth and expose the counterfeit.

18. I pray for divine appointments and divine interventions to bring Jezebel's false prophets to repentance. Let them encounter your

love and truth in a way that transforms their hearts and leads them to true repentance.

19. I declare that the Church will rise up in discernment and wisdom, no longer tolerating the influence of Jezebel's false prophets. Let a wave of discernment and exposure sweep across the body of Christ.

20. I thank you, Lord, for the victory we have in you over Jezebel's false prophets. Strengthen us to stand firm in your truth, to expose deception, and to lead others into the freedom and liberty found in your Word. In Jesus' name, I pray and declare these warfare and deliverance prayer declarations. Amen.

## Chapter 24

# Demolishing Jezebel's Baal Worship:
# Restoring Pure Worship

In the battle against Jezebel and her influence, one of the key areas to address is the worship of Baal that she promoted. Baal worship was characterized by idolatry, compromise, and the distortion of true worship. In this chapter, we will explore the tactics of Jezebel in promoting Baal worship, the consequences of idolatry, and the strategies to demolish Jezebel's Baal worship and restore pure worship to God alone.

Understanding Jezebel's Baal Worship:

1. Jezebel's Promotion of Baal Worship:
   - Jezebel actively promoted the worship of Baal, an idolatrous practice that involved sacrificing to false gods and engaging in immoral acts. She sought to replace the worship of the one true God with a distorted form of worship.

2. Characteristics of Baal Worship:
   - Baal worship was characterized by idolatry, compromise, and syncretism. It involved the worship of false gods, the offering of

sacrifices, and the participation in immoral rituals. It enticed the people of God to turn away from Him and pursue other gods.

3. Consequences of Baal Worship:
- The worship of Baal brought about severe consequences for the people of God. It led to spiritual adultery, moral decay, and the judgment of God. The people suffered drought, famine, and defeat in battle as a result of their disobedience and idolatry.

4. Distortion of True Worship:
- Baal worship distorted the true nature of worship. It replaced the worship of the Creator with the worship of created things. It compromised the holiness and purity of worship and led people away from the presence of God.

Demolishing Jezebel's Baal Worship:

1. Recognizing and Repenting of Idolatry:
- To demolish Jezebel's Baal worship, we must first recognize and repent of any idolatry in our lives. We must examine our hearts and remove anything that competes with God's rightful place of worship in our lives.

2. Returning to the True God:
- Demolishing Baal worship requires a return to the true God. We must wholeheartedly seek after Him, love Him with all our hearts,

241

and worship Him alone. Let us embrace the truth that there is no other God besides Him.

3. Destroying Idolatrous Altars:

-   Just as the prophet Elijah destroyed the altars of Baal, we must destroy every idolatrous altar in our lives. Tear down the altars of false gods, worldly desires, and sinful practices. Dedicate our hearts solely to the worship of the one true God.

4. Pursuing Holiness in Worship:

-   To restore pure worship, we must pursue holiness in every aspect of our lives. Let our worship be marked by integrity, purity, and reverence. Reject compromise and seek to honor God in both our private and corporate worship.

5. Embracing Spirit-led Worship:

-   Allow the Holy Spirit to lead our worship. Let us be sensitive to His presence and follow His leading in our worship gatherings. Seek His guidance as we choose songs, engage in prayer, and respond to His prompting.

6. Engaging in Scriptural Worship:

-   Anchor our worship in the truth of God's Word. Let the Scriptures guide our songs, prayers, and expressions of worship. Let the Word of God dwell richly in us as we worship Him in spirit and in truth.

7. Cultivating a Lifestyle of Worship:
- Worship is not confined to a Sunday service but encompasses our entire lives. Cultivate a lifestyle of worship by surrendering every area of our lives to God, living in obedience to His Word, and offering our bodies as living sacrifices.

8. Breaking Free from Cultural Influences:
- Demolishing Jezebel's Baal worship requires breaking free from the cultural influences that promote idolatry and compromise. Be willing to stand apart from the world and embrace the distinctiveness of true worship.

9. Proclaiming God's Supremacy:
- Declare the supremacy of God over every false god and idol. Proclaim His greatness, His power, and His unmatched glory. Let our worship be a declaration of His worthiness and a testimony to His sovereignty.

10. Prayer and Intercession for Spiritual Awakening:
- Pray fervently for a spiritual awakening that will demolish Jezebel's Baal worship. Intercede for the Church and the nations to turn away from false gods and return to the true God. Pray for a revival of pure worship that will bring transformation.

Demolishing Jezebel's Baal worship and restoring pure worship requires recognizing and repenting of idolatry, returning to the true God, destroying idolatrous altars, pursuing holiness, embracing Spirit-led and scriptural worship, cultivating a lifestyle of worship, breaking free from cultural influences, proclaiming God's supremacy, and engaging in prayer and intercession. As we align our hearts with God's heart and worship Him in spirit and in truth, we will experience the power and presence of God in our lives and witness the restoration of pure worship in our churches and communities. Let us demolish every counterfeit form of worship and exalt the name of the one true God.

## Deliverance Prayer

1. Heavenly Father, in the name of Jesus, I declare that Jezebel's Baal worship is demolished, and that pure worship is restored in our lives, churches, and communities.

2. I renounce and break every form of idolatry and compromise in my life. I repent for turning my heart away from you and pursuing false gods. I choose to worship you alone, the one true God.

3. I bind and cast out every spirit of idolatry and deception that has influenced my worship. I declare that I am free from the grip of Baal worship, and I embrace pure worship that honors and exalts you, Lord.

4. I tear down every altar of Baal in my life and in the spiritual realm. I declare that no false god will have any place of influence or authority in my worship. I dedicate myself wholly to the worship of the true God.

5. I pursue holiness and righteousness in my worship. I surrender every area of my life to you and invite your Holy Spirit to cleanse and purify me. Let my worship be marked by integrity and purity.

6. Holy Spirit, lead and guide me in my worship. I yield to your presence and follow your prompting. Empower me to worship in spirit and in truth, engaging in a genuine and heartfelt connection with you.

7. I anchor my worship in your Word, Lord. Let your truth dwell richly in me as I sing, pray, and respond to your presence. Let every aspect of my worship be in alignment with your revealed truth.

8. I cultivate a lifestyle of worship, offering my whole life as a living sacrifice to you. I worship you not only with my words and songs but also with my actions, attitudes, and choices. May my life be a continual act of worship unto you.

9. I break free from cultural influences that promote idolatry and compromise in worship. I choose to stand apart from the world

and embrace the distinctiveness of true worship. I am not conformed to this world but transformed by the renewing of my mind.

10. I proclaim your supremacy, Lord, over every false god and idol. You alone are worthy of all praise, honor, and glory. Let my worship be a declaration of your greatness and a testimony to your sovereignty.

11. I pray for a spiritual awakening that will shake the foundations of false worship and ignite a revival of pure worship. Pour out your Spirit upon the Church and the nations, turning hearts back to you and demolishing Jezebel's influence.

12. I intercede for the Church, that we may be delivered from the allure of false worship and embrace a passionate pursuit of your presence. Let our worship be a fragrance that draws others to you and brings transformation to our communities.

13. I pray for worship leaders and musicians to be anointed with a fresh fire of passion for your presence. Fill their hearts and minds with your songs, let their voices be instruments of praise, and let their worship lead others into a deeper encounter with you.

14. I bind and silence every counterfeit voice that seeks to distort true worship. I command every spirit of deception and manipulation to

be silenced and cast out in the name of Jesus. Let the true voices of worship rise up and be heard.

15. I declare that Jezebel's influence over worship is broken. Let the spirit of Baal be exposed and defeated. I release the power of your Holy Spirit to demolish every stronghold and restore pure worship in our churches and communities.

16. I pray for unity in worship, that we may join together in one accord to exalt your name. Remove any division or competition among worshippers and unify us in the pursuit of your presence.

17. I pray for a release of creativity and anointing in worship. Let new songs and melodies flow forth that exalt your name and declare your glory. Let your presence fill our worship gatherings and saturate every heart.

18. I ask for divine encounters in worship, where hearts are transformed, lives are restored, and breakthroughs are experienced. Let the atmosphere of worship become a gateway to your manifest presence and power.

19. I release the sound of worship as a weapon of warfare against Jezebel's influence. Let the praises of your people be like a mighty roar that shakes the foundations of darkness and proclaims your victory.

20. I thank you, Lord, for the restoration of pure worship. I declare that your name will be lifted high, and your glory will fill our worship. May our worship be pleasing to you and bring joy to your heart. In Jesus' name, I pray and declare these warfare and deliverance prayer declarations. Amen.

# Chapter 25

# Warrior Bride:
# Embracing Your Identity to Defeat Jezebel

In the battle against Jezebel and her deceptive influence, it is crucial to understand and embrace our identity as the Warrior Bride of Christ. Jezebel seeks to undermine our confidence, distort our identity, and rob us of our spiritual authority. In this chapter, we will explore what it means to be the Warrior Bride, how Jezebel attacks our identity, and the strategies to embrace our true identity and defeat Jezebel's schemes.

Understanding the Warrior Bride:

1. The Identity of the Warrior Bride:
   - As believers in Christ, we are called to be the Warrior Bride. We are not powerless victims but empowered conquerors, armed with the armor of God, and filled with the Holy Spirit. We are called to walk in victory and reflect the glory of our Bridegroom, Jesus Christ.

2. Embracing Our Spiritual Authority:
   - As the Warrior Bride, we have been given spiritual authority to defeat the works of darkness. We have the power to bind and

loose, to pray with authority, and to bring heaven's reality to earth. It is essential to understand and walk in the authority given to us by Christ.

3. The Intimacy of the Warrior Bride:
  - The Warrior Bride is not just a warrior; she is intimately connected to her Bridegroom, Jesus Christ. Our strength comes from our deep relationship with Him. Intimacy with Jesus is the foundation of our identity and the source of our power.

4. The Armament of the Warrior Bride:
  - The Warrior Bride is equipped with the armor of God, which includes the belt of truth, the breastplate of righteousness, the shoes of peace, the shield of faith, the helmet of salvation, and the sword of the Spirit. Understanding and utilizing this spiritual armament is crucial in defeating Jezebel's schemes.

Defeating Jezebel as the Warrior Bride:

1. Embracing Our Identity in Christ:
  - To defeat Jezebel, we must first embrace our true identity as the Warrior Bride. Recognize that we are chosen, loved, and empowered by God. Reject the lies of Jezebel that seek to undermine our confidence and distort our identity.

2. Walking in Intimacy with Jesus:

- Cultivate a deep and intimate relationship with Jesus. Spend time in prayer, worship, and meditation on His Word. Let His presence fill your life, empowering you to walk as the Warrior Bride.

3. Knowing and Using Our Spiritual Authority:
- Study and understand the authority given to us as believers. Know the power of the name of Jesus, the authority of His Word, and the role of the Holy Spirit in empowering us. Use this authority to bind Jezebel's influence and release the power of God's kingdom.

4. Recognizing Jezebel's Attacks on Our Identity:
- Jezebel seeks to attack our identity by fostering doubt, fear, and confusion. Be alert to her tactics and recognize when she is targeting your identity as the Warrior Bride. Reject her lies and stand firm in the truth of who you are in Christ.

5. Standing Firm in the Armor of God:
- Put on the full armor of God daily and stand firm against Jezebel's attacks. Let the truth of God's Word guard your mind, the righteousness of Christ protect your heart, and the peace of God guide your steps. Take up the shield of faith to extinguish every fiery dart of the enemy.

6. Discerning Jezebel's Manipulation and Deception:

- Jezebel is a master manipulator and deceiver. Develop spiritual discernment to recognize her tactics and strategies. Test every spirit and every message against the plumb line of God's Word.

7. Praying with Authority and Power:
- As the Warrior Bride, we have been given the privilege of praying with authority and power. Pray fervently and confidently, knowing that your prayers have an impact. Declare God's truth and His promises over your life, your family, your church, and your community.

8. Engaging in Spiritual Warfare:
- Engage in spiritual warfare, not in our own strength, but in the power of the Holy Spirit. Bind Jezebel's influence, demolish her strongholds, and release the power and presence of God in every situation.

9. Surrounding Ourselves with Spiritual Support:
- Seek out a community of fellow believers who understand their identity as the Warrior Bride. Surround yourself with those who can provide support, encouragement, and accountability in your spiritual journey.

10. Walking in Love and Forgiveness:
- The Warrior Bride fights with the weapon of love. Extend forgiveness to those who have been influenced by Jezebel and

pray for their deliverance. Let the love of Christ shine through you, overcoming evil with good.

---

As the Warrior Bride, we are called to embrace our identity, walk in intimacy with Jesus, know and use our spiritual authority, recognize Jezebel's attacks on our identity, stand firm in the armor of God, discern her manipulation and deception, pray with authority and power, engage in spiritual warfare, surround ourselves with spiritual support, and walk in love and forgiveness. By doing so, we will defeat Jezebel's schemes and manifest the victorious life that Christ has called us to. Let us rise up in the power of the Holy Spirit and embrace our identity as the Warrior Bride, walking in victory and bringing glory to our Bridegroom, Jesus Christ.

## Deliverance Prayer

1. Heavenly Father, I come before you in the name of Jesus, as a Warrior Bride, ready to embrace my true identity and defeat Jezebel's influence in my life and the lives of others.

2. I declare that I am chosen by you, Lord, to be a Warrior Bride, empowered by your Spirit to walk in victory and authority over every scheme of Jezebel.

3. I break every lie and deception of Jezebel that seeks to undermine my confidence and distort my identity. I declare that I am fearfully

and wonderfully made, created in your image, and called to be a mighty warrior in your Kingdom.

4. I renounce and bind every spirit of doubt, fear, and confusion that Jezebel tries to bring upon me. I release the power of your truth and Your Word to demolish every stronghold of the enemy.

5. I embrace intimacy with Jesus, my Bridegroom. I cultivate a deep and intimate relationship with Him, knowing that my strength and power come from being connected to Him.

6. I walk in the fullness of my spiritual authority as a Warrior Bride. I bind and cast out every spirit of Jezebel that tries to hinder my walk with you and the advancement of your Kingdom.

7. I put on the full armor of God, standing firm against the attacks of Jezebel. I gird myself with the belt of truth, put on the breastplate of righteousness, and take up the shield of faith to extinguish every fiery dart of the enemy.

8. I discern the tactics and strategies of Jezebel. I am alert to her manipulation and deception. I test every spirit and every message against the plumb line of your Word.

9. I pray with authority and power, declaring your truth and your promises over every situation. I release your kingdom authority to bind Jezebel's influence and release your divine purposes.

10. I engage in spiritual warfare, not in my own strength, but in the power of the Holy Spirit. I demolish every stronghold of Jezebel and release the power and presence of God in every area of my life.

11. I surround myself with spiritual support, aligning myself with fellow believers who understand their identity as Warrior Brides. Together, we stand united in faith, supporting and encouraging one another in the battle against Jezebel.

12. I walk in love and forgiveness, extending your grace to those who have been influenced by Jezebel. I pray for their deliverance and restoration, knowing that Your love has the power to overcome all evil.

13. I declare that Jezebel's influence is broken in my life and the lives of others. I release the power of your Holy Spirit to dismantle her works and bring forth freedom and victory.

14. I break every ungodly soul tie or covenant with Jezebel's spirits. I renounce and sever every connection with the spirit of control, manipulation, and rebellion.

15. I release the fire of the Holy Spirit to purify and refine my heart and mind. Let every impurity, compromise, and distortion be burned away, allowing your truth to shine brightly.

16. I declare that I am an overcomer through the blood of Jesus and the word of my testimony. I overcome every attack of Jezebel by the power of your Spirit and the authority you have given me.

17. I stand on the promises of your Word, Lord. Your Word is my sword, and I wield it with authority to cut through the lies and deceptions of Jezebel.

18. I pray for the deliverance of those who have been influenced by Jezebel. I intercede for their eyes to be opened, their hearts to be softened, and their lives to be transformed by your truth.

19. I release a fresh anointing of discernment and wisdom to navigate through Jezebel's schemes. Grant me supernatural insight to recognize her tactics and strategies and respond with divine wisdom.

20. I thank you, Lord, for the victory we have as Warrior Brides. I declare that we will rise up in the power of your Spirit, walking in our true identity, and defeating Jezebel's influence. In Jesus' name,

I pray and declare these warfare and deliverance prayer declarations. Amen.

## Chapter 26

# Jezebel in Politics: Engaging in Kingdom Transformation

Jezebel's influence extends beyond individual lives and infiltrates various spheres of society, including the realm of politics. In this chapter, we will delve into the impact of Jezebel's spirit in politics, explore the strategies used to manipulate and control, and uncover how we, as believers, can engage in Kingdom transformation within political arenas.

Understanding Jezebel's Influence in Politics:

1. Identifying Jezebel's Spirit in Politics:
   - Jezebel's spirit manifests in politics through the same characteristics seen in her biblical account: manipulation, control, intimidation, and the promotion of ungodly agendas. Her influence seeks to undermine godly principles and distort the purpose of government.

2. Tactics Used by Jezebel in Politics:
   - Jezebel utilizes various tactics in politics to achieve her goals. These may include deception, seduction, character assassination, intimidation, and the use of power and influence to silence opposition and promote her own agenda.

3. Jezebel's Control of Systems and Institutions:
- Jezebel seeks to gain control over political systems and institutions to further her own agenda. This includes influencing legislation, shaping public opinion, and manipulating the democratic process to advance ungodly ideologies.

4. Consequences of Jezebel's Influence in Politics:
- Jezebel's influence in politics can lead to the erosion of moral values, the suppression of religious freedoms, the promotion of injustice, and the disregard for the sanctity of life and biblical principles. It can have far-reaching consequences that impact society as a whole.

Engaging in Kingdom Transformation in Politics:

1. Prayer and Intercession:
- Engage in fervent prayer and intercession for political leaders, government officials, and those in positions of influence. Pray for God's wisdom, discernment, and righteous governance to prevail in political decision-making.

2. Embracing our Responsibility as Citizens:
- Recognize our responsibility as citizens to participate in the political process. Exercise our right to vote and actively engage in

advocating for godly values and principles within the political arena.

3. Pursuing Biblical Principles:
- As believers, we must seek to promote and uphold biblical principles in politics. Let the Word of God be our standard for evaluating policies, candidates, and political agendas. Stand for righteousness, justice, compassion, and the protection of human life.

4. Exposing Deception and Manipulation:
- Be vigilant in exposing deception and manipulation within politics. Seek the truth, examine information critically, and be discerning about the sources of information. Shine the light of God's truth on falsehoods and strive for transparency and integrity in political processes.

5. Encouraging and Supporting Godly Leaders:
- Identify and support leaders who demonstrate a commitment to godly values, righteousness, and justice. Encourage and uplift those who are called to serve in the political arena, providing them with prayer, encouragement, and wise counsel.

6. Engaging in Constructive Dialogue:
- Engage in respectful and constructive dialogue with those holding differing political views. Seek to understand perspectives, share

insights rooted in biblical truth, and promote unity in the pursuit of common goals that align with Kingdom principles.

7. Being Salt and Light:
- Be a positive influence within the political sphere, being salt and light in a world marked by corruption and darkness. Let our actions, words, and attitudes reflect Christ's love, grace, and truth.

8. Seeking God's Kingdom Agenda:
- Prioritize seeking God's kingdom agenda above any political affiliation or personal agenda. Align our hearts and actions with God's purposes, trusting in His sovereignty and His ability to bring about transformation.

9. Engaging in Grassroots Movements:
- Join or initiate grassroots movements that champion godly values and advocate for justice and righteousness within the political sphere. Collaborate with like-minded individuals and organizations to bring about change from the ground up.

10. Demonstrating Kingdom Values in Practical Ways:
- Live out Kingdom values in our daily lives, demonstrating love, compassion, and justice in practical ways. Engage in acts of service, support initiatives that promote the well-being of society, and extend a hand of kindness to those in need.

11. Seeking God's Wisdom and Guidance:

-   Continually seek God's wisdom and guidance in navigating the complexities of politics. Rely on the Holy Spirit to provide discernment, guidance, and the courage to take a stand for truth and righteousness.

12. Guarding Against Compromise:

-   Guard against compromise in the political arena. Resist the pressure to conform to ungodly agendas or compromise biblical principles for the sake of popularity or political gain. Stand firm in the truth, even in the face of opposition.

13. Embracing Unity and Collaboration:

-   Seek unity and collaboration with fellow believers and like-minded individuals in the pursuit of Kingdom transformation in politics. Recognize the power of collective efforts in bringing about lasting change.

14. Advocating for the Vulnerable:

-   Stand as a voice for the vulnerable and marginalized within political systems. Advocate for the rights and dignity of all individuals, championing policies that promote justice, equality, and the well-being of society's most vulnerable members.

15. Trusting in God's Sovereignty:

- Ultimately, place our trust in God's sovereignty over the political landscape. Remember that He is the ultimate ruler and that He can work through imperfect systems and flawed individuals to accomplish His purposes.

16. Proclaiming God's Truth:
- Proclaim God's truth boldly within the political sphere. Speak out against injustice, promote righteousness, and proclaim the transforming power of the Gospel. Let our words and actions be a reflection of God's love and grace.

17. Overcoming Evil with Good:
- Overcome the influence of Jezebel in politics by responding with good. Respond to hatred with love, respond to corruption with integrity, and respond to division with unity. Let our actions bring about positive change and transformation.

18. Resisting Fear and Discouragement:
- Resist the spirit of fear and discouragement that Jezebel seeks to instill in politics. Instead, anchor our hope and trust in God, knowing that He is greater than any political system or earthly power.

19. Praying for Revival and Spiritual Awakening:
- Pray earnestly for revival and spiritual awakening within the political sphere. Pray for God's Spirit to convict hearts, transform

lives, and raise up godly leaders who will influence politics with Kingdom values.

20. Trusting in the Long-Term Impact:
    - Trust in the long-term impact of Kingdom transformation in politics. Recognize that change may not happen overnight, but remain steadfast in prayer, action, and advocacy, knowing that God is faithful to bring about His purposes.

---

Jezebel's influence in politics is a significant challenge, but as believers, we are called to engage in Kingdom transformation within this sphere. By understanding Jezebel's tactics, engaging in prayer and intercession, embracing our responsibility as citizens, pursuing biblical principles, and being salt and light, we can effectively confront Jezebel's spirit and advance God's Kingdom agenda in politics. Let us stand firm, rooted in our identity as sons and daughters of the Most High God, and bring about lasting change that aligns with His will and purposes.

## Deliverance Prayer

1. Heavenly Father, I come before you in the name of Jesus, as a believer seeking to engage in Kingdom transformation within the sphere of politics. I take authority over the spirit of Jezebel that seeks to manipulate and control political systems and institutions.

2. I declare that the influence of Jezebel in politics is broken in the mighty name of Jesus. I release the power of your Holy Spirit to expose her tactics and bring about transformation in this realm.

3. I bind and cast out every spirit of deception, manipulation, and ungodly agenda that Jezebel uses to infiltrate politics. I release the power of truth, righteousness, and justice to prevail in every political decision-making process.

4. I pray for political leaders, government officials, and those in positions of influence. I ask for your wisdom, discernment, and righteous governance to guide their decisions and actions. Let your Kingdom principles permeate the political sphere.

5. I intercede for the removal of corrupt politicians and the exposure of their hidden agendas. Let every plan of Jezebel be thwarted and every ungodly influence be uprooted from the political arena.

6. I declare that your truth shines brightly in politics. Let the light of your Word expose falsehoods, lies, and manipulations. Grant discernment to voters, enabling them to see through deception and choose leaders who align with your values.

7. I release a spirit of unity and collaboration among believers engaging in politics. May we stand together, regardless of political

affiliations, in pursuit of Kingdom transformation. Let us set aside personal agendas and work towards the greater good.

8. I pray for divine appointments and strategic alliances within the political sphere. Connect believers with influence, wisdom, and godly values, enabling them to bring about significant change and Kingdom impact.

9. I decree that the voice of righteousness is amplified in political discourse. Raise up bold and courageous believers who fearlessly proclaim your truth, standing firm against the tide of ungodliness and compromise.

10. I release a fresh anointing of discernment to expose the strategies of Jezebel in politics. Grant believers the ability to discern between godly leaders and those under the influence of Jezebel. Help us identify those who promote righteousness, justice, and the well-being of society.

11. I declare that fear has no place in the hearts of believers engaging in politics. I release a spirit of boldness and courage to speak out against injustice, corruption, and ungodly agendas. Let us be unafraid to take a stand for righteousness.

12. I break every curse, spell, or assignment of Jezebel against godly leaders and individuals who seek to bring Kingdom values into

politics. I release the power of your blood to cleanse and protect them from the attacks of the enemy.

13. I pray for divine strategies and creative solutions to transform the political landscape. Give believers innovative ideas and effective methods to bring about lasting change in systems and structures.

14. I decree that the Church rises as a prophetic voice in politics, declaring your truth without compromise. Let the Church be a catalyst for change, influencing policies, and promoting godly principles within the political sphere.

15. I release a spirit of repentance and humility upon politicians and government officials. May they turn away from ungodliness and embrace your ways. Soften their hearts to your truth and convict them of the need for righteous governance.

16. I pray for a revival of godly values within political parties and institutions. Let your Spirit move mightily, transforming hearts and minds, and aligning political agendas with your Kingdom purposes.

17. I declare that corruption and bribery have no place in politics. I release a spirit of integrity and transparency to prevail, exposing and dismantling every form of dishonesty and unethical behavior.

18. I pray for protection and divine favor over believers engaging in politics. Shield them from false accusations, character assassinations, and attacks of Jezebel. Grant them supernatural wisdom and discernment to navigate political challenges.

19. I release a spirit of reconciliation and unity in the political arena. Heal divisions and foster a spirit of collaboration for the greater good. Let your love and grace flow through political processes, leading to unity and productive dialogue.

20. I thank you, Lord, for the transformational power of your Kingdom in politics. I trust in your sovereignty and authority to bring about lasting change. May your Kingdom come and your will be done in the political sphere, for your glory alone. Amen.

## Chapter 27

# The Spirit of Elijah: Igniting Revival against Jezebel

In the battle against Jezebel and her deceptive influence, God has raised up the Spirit of Elijah as a powerful force of revival and transformation. The Spirit of Elijah represents the prophetic mantle that confronts the spirit of Jezebel and brings forth revival, righteousness, and the restoration of God's purposes. In this chapter, we will explore the characteristics of the Spirit of Elijah, its role in igniting revival, and how we can partner with this anointing to overcome Jezebel's influence.

Understanding the Spirit of Elijah:

1. The Prophetic Anointing:
   - The Spirit of Elijah represents the prophetic anointing that confronts deception, exposes ungodliness, and calls for repentance. Elijah was a bold and fearless prophet who stood against the idolatry and wickedness perpetuated by Jezebel and Ahab.

2. Jezebel versus Elijah:
   - Jezebel symbolizes a spirit of manipulation, control, and ungodly influence, while Elijah represents the spirit of righteousness, truth,

and revival. The conflict between Jezebel and Elijah is a spiritual battle that manifests in various areas of society, including politics, culture, and the church.

3. The Mantle of Elijah:
   - The mantle of Elijah is not limited to one individual but can be carried by those who are anointed and empowered by the Holy Spirit. The Spirit of Elijah empowers believers to confront Jezebel's influence and release revival and restoration.

4. Characteristics of the Spirit of Elijah:
   - The Spirit of Elijah is characterized by boldness, courage, unwavering faith, and uncompromising devotion to God. It carries the fire of God's presence, the authority of His Word, and the power to bring about transformation and revival.

Igniting Revival against Jezebel:

1. Embracing the Spirit of Elijah:
   - We are called to embrace the Spirit of Elijah, allowing the Holy Spirit to ignite a fire within us. Surrender to His leading, be filled with His power, and step into the prophetic calling to confront Jezebel's influence and release revival.

2. Confronting Deception and Exposing Darkness:

- The Spirit of Elijah empowers us to confront deception and expose the works of darkness. Stand boldly against the lies and manipulation of Jezebel, shining the light of God's truth to bring about conviction and repentance.

3. Praying for Boldness and Divine Strategy:
- Pray for the release of boldness and divine strategy to confront Jezebel's influence. Ask the Holy Spirit to guide your steps and give you the words to speak as you engage in spiritual warfare against this spirit.

4. Prophesying Restoration and God's Purposes:
- Partner with the Spirit of Elijah to prophesy restoration, revival, and the fulfillment of God's purposes. Declare His promises, His plans, and His desire for righteousness and truth to prevail over Jezebel's deception.

5. Uniting in Prayer and Intercession:
- Join together with other believers to pray and intercede for revival and the defeat of Jezebel's influence. Pray for the Spirit of Elijah to be released across regions, nations, and the Church, igniting a fire of revival that cannot be extinguished.

6. Identifying and Discerning Jezebel's Tactics:
- Develop spiritual discernment to identify and discern Jezebel's tactics. Be alert to her strategies of manipulation, control, and

seduction. Test every spirit and every message against the plumb line of God's Word.

7. Repentance and Turning Back to God:
   - The Spirit of Elijah calls for repentance and turning back to God. Examine your own heart and life, and repent of any compromise or ungodliness. Lead by example, modeling a life of repentance and seeking after God's heart.

8. Breaking Jezebel's Strongholds:
   - Through the power of the Spirit of Elijah, break Jezebel's strongholds and dismantle her influence. Pray fervently, using the authority and power of the name of Jesus to bind and cast out the spirit of Jezebel from every area of society.

9. Restoring True Worship:
   - The Spirit of Elijah restores true worship that honors God alone. Stand against the idolatry and false worship promoted by Jezebel, declaring the supremacy of Jesus Christ and leading others into genuine worship and devotion.

10. Strengthening the Prophetic Voice:
    - Encourage and strengthen the prophetic voice within the Church. Equip believers to prophesy with accuracy, boldness, and love, releasing words that expose Jezebel's influence and bring forth God's truth and direction.

11. Reviving the Church:

- The Spirit of Elijah is instrumental in reviving the Church. Pray for a fresh outpouring of the Holy Spirit, revival, and restoration within the Body of Christ. May the Church arise in power, unity, and fervent pursuit of God's Kingdom purposes.

12. Empowering Godly Leadership:

- Pray for Godly leaders to rise up under the anointing of the Spirit of Elijah. Pray for pastors, ministers, and spiritual leaders to be filled with wisdom, courage, and discernment as they confront Jezebel's influence and lead with integrity and righteousness.

13. Engaging in Spiritual Warfare:

- Engage in spiritual warfare, not in our own strength, but in the power of the Holy Spirit. Put on the full armor of God and stand firm against the attacks of Jezebel. Use the spiritual weapons of prayer, fasting, and the Word of God to overcome her tactics.

14. Breaking Jezebel's Witchcraft and Manipulation:

- The Spirit of Elijah empowers us to break Jezebel's witchcraft and manipulation. Pray against every spell, curse, and assignment of Jezebel, declaring the power of the blood of Jesus to break every chain and set captives free.

15. Discerning and Embracing God's Timetable:

- Partner with the Spirit of Elijah to discern and embrace God's timetable. Seek His guidance and direction in the timing of confrontations, prophetic declarations, and strategic actions against Jezebel's influence.

16. Trusting in God's Victory:
- Place your trust in God's ultimate victory over Jezebel. Remember that He is greater than any spiritual force or principality. Trust in His faithfulness, knowing that the Spirit of Elijah within you empowers you to overcome.

17. Cultivating Intimacy with God:
- Cultivate intimacy with God as you embrace the Spirit of Elijah. Spend time in His presence, seek His face, and allow His fire to burn within you. It is from this place of intimacy that the power of the Spirit of Elijah flows.

18. Persevering in the Face of Opposition:
- The Spirit of Elijah calls for perseverance in the face of opposition. Do not be discouraged by Jezebel's resistance or the challenges that arise. Stand firm, knowing that the Spirit of Elijah empowers you to overcome every obstacle.

19. Raising a Prophetic Generation:
- Raise up a prophetic generation that carries the Spirit of Elijah. Disciple and equip young believers to walk in the prophetic

anointing, confront Jezebel's influence, and ignite revival wherever they go.

20. Proclaiming the Triumph of God's Kingdom:
- Proclaim the triumph of God's Kingdom over the works of Jezebel. Declare that revival is breaking forth, righteousness is prevailing, and God's purposes are being fulfilled. Proclaim the victory of the Spirit of Elijah over the spirit of Jezebel.

---

The Spirit of Elijah is a powerful force of revival, restoration, and righteousness that confronts the influence of Jezebel. By embracing the Spirit of Elijah, we become vessels for God's purposes, igniting revival, and standing boldly against the works of darkness. Let us partner with the Spirit of Elijah to bring about transformation, releasing God's Kingdom on earth and overcoming Jezebel's deception. As we walk in the prophetic anointing, let us declare the triumph of God's Kingdom and witness the power of the Spirit of Elijah igniting revival in our lives, communities, and nations.

## Deliverance Prayer

1. Heavenly Father, in the name of Jesus, I declare the release of the Spirit of Elijah to ignite revival and bring forth transformation in every area influenced by Jezebel. I take authority over the spirit of

Jezebel and command it to bow before the power of the Spirit of Elijah.

2. I declare that the fire of God's presence is falling upon every dry and desolate place affected by Jezebel's influence. Let the Spirit of Elijah bring forth a revival that burns away the works of darkness and restores righteousness and holiness.

3. I decree that the voice of the Spirit of Elijah will be heard loud and clear, exposing the deceptions of Jezebel and calling for repentance. Let the prophetic anointing flow through me as I confront the works of darkness and release God's truth.

4. I break every stronghold and bondage established by Jezebel's influence. I declare that the power of the Spirit of Elijah dismantles her structures and sets captives free from manipulation, control, and deception.

5. I release a fresh anointing of boldness and courage to confront Jezebel's spirit in every sphere of influence. Let the Spirit of Elijah rise within me, empowering me to stand fearlessly against ungodliness and release revival.

6. I bind and cast out every spirit of witchcraft and manipulation associated with Jezebel's influence. I declare that her spells and

curses are broken by the power of the Holy Spirit and the authority of Jesus' name.

7. I decree that the Spirit of Elijah awakens the Church to its prophetic calling. Let the Church rise up in power, declaring God's truth without compromise and releasing prophetic declarations that dismantle Jezebel's influence.

8. I pray for a fresh outpouring of the Holy Spirit, releasing a revival fire that spreads like wildfire, consuming Jezebel's strongholds and turning hearts back to God.

9. I pray for godly leaders anointed by the Spirit of Elijah to rise up in every sphere of society, including politics, education, media, and the Church. Let their voices carry authority and influence as they confront Jezebel's deception.

10. I release the power of God's Word to penetrate hearts and minds, exposing the lies and deceptions propagated by Jezebel. Let the truth of Scripture bring conviction, repentance, and transformation in the lives of those under her influence.

11. I pray for divine encounters with the Holy Spirit, where individuals encounter the fire of God's presence and are radically transformed. Let the Spirit of Elijah bring conviction, healing, and restoration to those bound by Jezebel's influence.

12. I declare that the Spirit of Elijah empowers me to walk in uncompromising righteousness and holiness. Let my life be a testimony of God's transforming power, drawing others out of Jezebel's deception and into the light of God's truth.

13. I release the power of unity among believers, as we stand together under the anointing of the Spirit of Elijah. Let us join forces, supporting one another, and confronting Jezebel's influence with a united front.

14. I pray for supernatural discernment to recognize and expose Jezebel's tactics. Grant me the ability to see beyond the surface and discern the spirits at work, enabling me to take strategic action and release God's victory.

15. I declare that the Spirit of Elijah restores true worship in every area influenced by Jezebel. Let the pure and authentic worship of God rise up, displacing every form of idolatry and false worship.

16. I release a spirit of repentance and turning back to God upon those influenced by Jezebel. May their hearts be softened, and may they recognize the need to renounce ungodliness and seek after God's righteousness.

17. I pray for divine encounters with the fear of the Lord, where hearts are awakened to the reality of God's holiness and sovereignty. Let the fear of the Lord displace the fear induced by Jezebel's manipulation and control.

18. I pray for divine strategies and divine appointments to confront Jezebel's influence head-on. Grant me wisdom, insight, and divine connections to expose her works and release God's power and authority.

19. I declare that Jezebel's influence is being replaced by the Spirit of Elijah's influence in every sphere of society. Let righteousness, justice, and truth prevail as revival spreads and transforms hearts and nations.

20. I thank you, Lord, for the power and anointing of the Spirit of Elijah. I thank you for the victory we have in Christ Jesus. May the Spirit of Elijah continue to ignite revival, dismantle Jezebel's influence, and usher in a mighty move of your Spirit. In Jesus' mighty name, amen.

## Chapter 28

# The Blood of Jesus: Ultimate Weapon against Jezebel

In the battle against the deceptive spirit of Jezebel, we have the ultimate weapon—the precious blood of Jesus Christ. The blood of Jesus holds unmatched power to defeat every work of darkness and break the influence of Jezebel in our lives, families, churches, and society. In this chapter, we will explore the significance of the blood of Jesus, its authority over Jezebel, and how we can apply its power in spiritual warfare.

Understanding the Power of the Blood of Jesus:

1. The Atoning Power:
   - The blood of Jesus is the foundation of our salvation and redemption. It was shed on the cross to atone for our sins and reconcile us to God. The blood cleanses us from all unrighteousness and empowers us to walk in victory.

2. Overcoming Satan's Accusations:
   - The blood of Jesus speaks a better word than the accusations of the enemy. It declares our forgiveness, righteousness, and freedom from condemnation. The blood silences the voice of Jezebel that seeks to accuse and manipulate.

3. Protection and Deliverance:

- The blood of Jesus serves as a powerful shield and deliverance from the influence of Jezebel. It covers us with divine protection, making us inaccessible to the enemy's schemes. The blood breaks every chain and sets the captives free.

4. Sanctification and Cleansing:

- The blood of Jesus sanctifies us and cleanses us from all defilement. It purifies our hearts, minds, and consciences, enabling us to live in holiness and righteousness. Through the blood, we are set apart for God's purposes.

5. Authority over Demonic Forces:

- The blood of Jesus carries ultimate authority over demonic forces, including the spirit of Jezebel. It disarms and defeats the enemy, rendering him powerless against the believer who applies the blood in faith.

6. Access to God's Presence:

- The blood of Jesus grants us access to God's presence and enables us to boldly approach His throne. It removes the barrier of sin and opens the way for intimate communion with our Heavenly Father.

Applying the Power of the Blood of Jesus against Jezebel:

1. Personal Cleansing and Renewal:
   - Apply the blood of Jesus to your own life, confessing your sins and receiving His forgiveness. Let the blood cleanse you from all unrighteousness and renew your heart, mind, and spirit.

2. Breaking Generational Curses:
   - Apply the blood of Jesus to break generational curses associated with Jezebel's influence. Declare the power of the blood to sever every ungodly tie and release the blessings and promises of God upon your family line.

3. Renouncing and Rejecting Jezebel's Influence:
   - Take a stand against Jezebel's influence by renouncing and rejecting her tactics. Declare the authority of the blood of Jesus to break every attachment and stronghold she has established in your life.

4. Breaking Soul Ties and Ungodly Connections:
   - Apply the blood of Jesus to break soul ties and ungodly connections formed under Jezebel's influence. Declare the power of the blood to sever every unholy attachment and restore your soul to wholeness.

5. Protection and Deliverance from Jezebel's Attacks:
   - Apply the blood of Jesus as a protective shield against Jezebel's attacks. Declare the covering of the blood over yourself, your

loved ones, and your sphere of influence, trusting in God's divine protection.

6. Praying in the Power of the Blood:
   - Engage in warfare prayer, applying the power of the blood of Jesus. Pray with confidence, knowing that the blood has already secured the victory. Declare the blood of Jesus over every situation and every area affected by Jezebel's influence.

7. Binding and Casting Out Jezebel's Spirits:
   - Exercise your authority in the name of Jesus and by the power of His blood to bind and cast out the spirits associated with Jezebel. Declare their defeat and expulsion from your life and the lives of others.

8. Breaking Jezebel's Control and Manipulation:
   - Apply the blood of Jesus to break Jezebel's control and manipulation over your thoughts, emotions, and actions. Declare your freedom in Christ and reject every lie and deception she tries to impose.

9. Restoring God's Order and Authority:
   - Apply the blood of Jesus to restore God's order and authority in every area influenced by Jezebel. Declare the supremacy of Jesus Christ and His lordship over every aspect of your life, church, and society.

10. Proclaiming the Triumph of the Blood of Jesus:

- Proclaim the triumph of the blood of Jesus over Jezebel's influence. Declare that the power of the blood is greater than any works of darkness and that Jezebel is defeated by the blood of the Lamb.

11. Communion and Remembrance:

- Regularly partake in communion as a way to remember and apply the power of the blood of Jesus. Let the act of communion remind you of the sacrifice of Christ and His victory over Jezebel and all spiritual forces of darkness.

12. Experiencing the Fullness of the Blood's Power:

- Embrace the fullness of the power of the blood of Jesus in your life. Meditate on its significance, study Scriptures that speak of its power, and cultivate a deep reverence for the blood that was shed for your redemption.

---

The blood of Jesus is the ultimate weapon against Jezebel and her deceptive influence. By understanding the power and significance of the blood, we can confidently apply it in spiritual warfare, breaking every stronghold and releasing God's victory. Let us continually rely on the blood of Jesus, knowing that through it, we overcome the works of darkness and walk in the fullness of God's redemption and freedom. May the blood of Jesus be our constant source of strength, protection, and deliverance as we stand against Jezebel and advance God's Kingdom on earth.

## Deliverance Prayer

1. Heavenly Father, I come before you in the mighty name of Jesus, covered by the precious blood that was shed for my redemption. I declare the power and authority of the blood of Jesus over every work of Jezebel in my life and in the lives of others.

2. I plead the blood of Jesus over my mind, emotions, and will, cleansing me from every thought, feeling, or desire influenced by Jezebel. Let the power of the blood purify my thoughts and align them with your truth.

3. I declare that the blood of Jesus breaks every chain of control and manipulation that Jezebel has attempted to establish. I renounce every agreement, soul tie, or ungodly connection formed under her influence. I am free by the power of the blood.

4. I apply the blood of Jesus to break generational curses associated with Jezebel's influence in my family line. I declare the power of the blood to sever every ungodly tie and release the blessings and promises of God upon my family.

5. I cover myself and my loved ones with the blood of Jesus, declaring divine protection from every attack of Jezebel. Let the blood form a shield around us, rendering us inaccessible to her schemes and strategies.

6. I take authority in the name of Jesus and by the power of His blood to bind and cast out every spirit associated with Jezebel. I command them to leave my life, my family, and my sphere of influence, never to return.

7. I apply the blood of Jesus to break every curse, spell, or assignment sent by Jezebel to hinder my spiritual growth, relationships, or destiny. I declare that the power of the blood overrules and nullifies every work of darkness.

8. I release the power of the blood of Jesus to cleanse and purify the atmosphere in my home, church, workplace, and community. Let the blood drive out every spirit of deception, manipulation, and control, replacing it with your presence and truth.

9. I declare that the blood of Jesus silences the voice of Jezebel, her accusations, and her lies. I receive the forgiveness and righteousness secured by the blood, walking in the freedom and authority that comes from being covered by the blood.

10. I pray for divine discernment and wisdom to recognize Jezebel's tactics and strategies. Let the blood of Jesus illuminate the hidden works of darkness and expose her deceptions, enabling me to take strategic action in spiritual warfare.

11. I release the power of the blood of Jesus to break every stronghold and addiction formed under Jezebel's influence. I declare that the power of the blood sets me free from every bondage, enabling me to walk in victory and wholeness.

12. I declare that the blood of Jesus sanctifies and separates me from the works of darkness. I am set apart for your purposes, empowered to walk in holiness, righteousness, and purity by the power of the blood.

13. I proclaim the triumph of the blood of Jesus over Jezebel's influence. I declare that through the blood, I overcome every work of darkness and release your Kingdom on earth. Let the power of the blood be evident in my life.

14. I apply the blood of Jesus to my thought life, breaking every negative and destructive thought pattern influenced by Jezebel. I declare that my mind is renewed by the power of the blood, aligning with your truth and purpose.

15. I plead the blood of Jesus over my physical body, declaring divine health, healing, and wholeness. Let the power of the blood cleanse and restore every aspect of my being, releasing your divine life and vitality within me.

16. I apply the blood of Jesus to every area of my finances, breaking the spirit of poverty, lack, and greed associated with Jezebel. I declare your abundance and provision flow into my life by the power of the blood.

17. I pray for divine encounters with the presence of Jesus through the power of His blood. Let me experience the fullness of His love, forgiveness, and redemption as I meditate on the power and significance of His blood.

18. I declare that the blood of Jesus disarms and defeats every weapon formed against me by Jezebel. I am more than a conqueror through Him who loved me and shed His blood for my victory.

19. I release the power of the blood of Jesus to restore true worship in my life and in the Church. Let the blood cleanse our worship from every form of idolatry and false worship, enabling us to worship you in spirit and in truth.

20. I thank you, Lord, for the power and authority of the blood of Jesus. I declare that through the blood, I am an overcomer, and

Jezebel's influence is broken. I walk in victory, covered by the blood and empowered by your Spirit. In Jesus' name, amen.

## Chapter 29

# Breaking Jezebel's Generational Curses: Releasing God's Blessings

Generational curses are patterns of negative behaviors, attitudes, and circumstances that can be traced back through family lines. Jezebel, with her manipulative and controlling spirit, has often been a source of generational curses that affect individuals, families, and even entire communities. In this chapter, we will explore the nature of generational curses, their connection to Jezebel's influence, and how we can break free from these curses and release God's blessings in our lives.

Understanding Generational Curses:

1. Definition and Origins:
   - Generational curses are patterns of negative consequences that are passed down from one generation to another. They can result from ungodly practices, sinful behaviors, or open doors to the enemy in previous generations.

2. Identification of Generational Curses:
   - Generational curses can manifest in various ways, such as addiction, poverty, broken relationships, health issues, or patterns

of destructive behavior. Identifying these patterns is the first step toward breaking free from them.

3. Connection to Jezebel's Influence:
   - Jezebel's influence can perpetuate generational curses by promoting ungodly behaviors, attitudes, and spiritual strongholds. Her manipulative and controlling spirit seeks to establish a generational legacy of rebellion and destruction.

4. Breaking Free from Generational Curses:
   - The power of Jesus Christ and His finished work on the cross is sufficient to break every generational curse. Through faith, repentance, and the application of biblical principles, we can be set free and release God's blessings in our lives.

Breaking Jezebel's Generational Curses:

1. Repentance and Confession:
   - Begin by acknowledging any generational sins or ungodly behaviors that have been perpetuated in your family line. Confess these sins before God, asking for His forgiveness and cleansing.

2. Renunciation of Jezebel's Influence:
   - Renounce and reject Jezebel's influence in your family line. Declare that you and your family are breaking free from her

manipulations and control. Take authority over her works by the power of Jesus' name.

3. Prayer of Forgiveness:
- Forgive any ancestors who may have been involved in perpetuating generational curses. Release them from the burden of guilt and extend forgiveness, declaring that you are no longer bound by their choices.

4. Covering with the Blood of Jesus:
- Apply the blood of Jesus over yourself and your family, declaring the power of His blood to break every generational curse. Proclaim that the blood of Jesus covers and protects you, setting you free from the consequences of past sins.

5. Reclaiming God's Promises:
- Identify the specific promises of God's Word that counteract the generational curses in your family line. Declare these promises over your life and the lives of your descendants, appropriating God's blessings and restoration.

6. Prayer for Healing and Restoration:
- Pray for healing and restoration in every area affected by the generational curses. Ask the Holy Spirit to bring divine healing and wholeness to your family line, breaking the cycle of destruction and releasing God's restoration.

7. Breaking Ungodly Soul Ties:
-   Cut off ungodly soul ties that have contributed to the perpetuation of generational curses. Declare the power of the Holy Spirit to sever these ties, releasing you from their influence and establishing healthy connections based on godliness and love.

8. Living in Obedience to God's Word:
-   Walk in obedience to God's Word and His commands, breaking the cycle of disobedience that may have contributed to the generational curses. Live a life of holiness, righteousness, and submission to God's will.

9. Seeking Deliverance and Inner Healing:
-   Seek deliverance and inner healing through prayer, counseling, and the support of fellow believers. Invite the Holy Spirit to bring healing to wounded areas of your life and to break the chains of bondage imposed by generational curses.

10. Proclaiming God's Blessings:
-   Proclaim God's blessings over yourself, your family, and your future generations. Declare that the cycle of generational curses is broken, and the cycle of God's blessings is activated in your life and your family line.

11. Walking in the Authority of Jesus:

- Walk in the authority given to you by Jesus Christ. Declare that you are a child of God, redeemed by the blood of Jesus, and empowered to overcome the effects of generational curses through the power of the Holy Spirit.

12. Continual Prayer and Warfare:
- Engage in continual prayer and spiritual warfare, staying vigilant against any attempts by Jezebel to reestablish her influence. Maintain a strong connection with God and seek His guidance in every area of your life.

---

Breaking generational curses associated with Jezebel's influence is a process of repentance, forgiveness, prayer, and the application of God's Word. Through the power of Jesus' sacrifice on the cross and the authority He has given us, we can break free from the cycle of destruction and release God's blessings in our lives and future generations. Let us step out in faith, trusting in the power of the Holy Spirit to bring healing, restoration, and transformation. As we do so, we will experience the freedom and abundant life that God desires for us and for our families.

## Deliverance Prayer

1. Heavenly Father, I come before you in the name of Jesus, covered by the blood of the Lamb. I declare that I am breaking free from every generational curse associated with Jezebel's influence. I

release your blessings and favor over my life and the lives of my descendants.

2. I repent on behalf of myself and my ancestors for any involvement with Jezebel's spirit and the perpetuation of generational curses. I renounce and reject her influence in my family line, declaring that her power is broken by the blood of Jesus.

3. I break every ungodly soul tie and connection formed under Jezebel's influence. I command these ties to be severed by the power of the Holy Spirit, releasing me and my family from the bondage of generational curses.

4. I plead the blood of Jesus over my family line, covering every past, present, and future generation. I declare that the power of the blood breaks every curse and releases your blessings and restoration upon my family.

5. I forgive and release any ancestors who may have contributed to the perpetuation of generational curses. I declare that their choices no longer have a hold on me, and I choose to walk in forgiveness and freedom.

6. I declare that I am a new creation in Christ Jesus, and the old patterns and cycles of generational curses no longer define me or my family. I am an overcomer through the blood of Jesus.

7. I take authority over every generational curse, declaring that it has no power or authority over me or my family. I release the power of God's Word to counteract and nullify every negative influence passed down through the generations.

8. I proclaim your blessings and promises over my life and the lives of my descendants. I declare that we are blessed, favored, and set apart for your purposes. We walk in the abundance and victory that you have provided.

9. I pray for divine healing and restoration in every area affected by generational curses. I release your healing power to bring wholeness to our hearts, minds, bodies, relationships, and finances.

10. I break every spirit of poverty, addiction, sickness, strife, and any other manifestation of generational curses. I command these spirits to leave my life and my family in the name of Jesus.

11. I release the power of the Holy Spirit to bring deliverance and freedom from the effects of generational curses. Let your Spirit flow through us, bringing transformation and breakthrough in every area of our lives.

12. I declare that the cycle of generational curses is broken, and a new cycle of blessings and favor is activated in my family line. I declare that we are a generational blessing, impacting future generations with your love and truth.

13. I declare that I am an agent of change and restoration in my family. I stand in the gap, interceding and praying for the release of generational blessings and the dismantling of generational curses.

14. I release the power of forgiveness and reconciliation in my family, breaking the cycle of division and strife. I declare that love, unity, and harmony reign supreme in our relationships.

15. I pray for wisdom and discernment to make godly choices and break free from any patterns or behaviors associated with generational curses. I choose to walk in obedience to your Word and your ways.

16. I declare that your blessings and favor overtake me and my family. I am a recipient of your grace, and I walk in the fullness of your provision and protection.

17. I release the power of the Holy Spirit to restore broken dreams, lost opportunities, and wasted years caused by generational curses. I declare a season of restoration and acceleration in my life and the lives of my descendants.

18. I pray for divine alignment with your purposes and plans. Let your will be done in my life and my family, as it is in heaven. I surrender every area of my life to your lordship.

19. I declare that I am an overcomer by the blood of the Lamb and the word of my testimony. I am victorious over every generational curse, walking in the fullness of your blessings and favor.

20. I give you all the glory, honor, and praise, knowing that you are faithful to break every generational curse and release your abundant blessings in my life and the lives of my descendants. In Jesus' name, amen.

## Chapter 30

# Jezebel's Throne: Dethroning the Queen of Control

Jezebel, the queen of control and manipulation, has been a destructive force throughout history, seeking to establish her throne of influence in families, churches, and society. In this chapter, we will delve into the nature of Jezebel's throne, the tactics she employs to gain and maintain control, and how we can effectively dethrone her by relying on the power of God.

Understanding Jezebel's Throne:

1. The Nature of Jezebel's Throne:
   - Jezebel's throne represents her position of authority and influence, from which she operates to exert control, sow division, and promote ungodliness. Her throne is built on deception, manipulation, and rebellion against God's order.

2. Tactics of Control:
   - Jezebel uses various tactics to establish and maintain control, such as manipulation, intimidation, seduction, and false spirituality. She seeks to dominate and subjugate others, leaving destruction in her wake.

3. The Effects of Jezebel's Throne:
- Jezebel's throne brings chaos, division, and spiritual oppression. It stifles spiritual growth, hinders the work of the Holy Spirit, and promotes ungodly practices and beliefs. It leads people astray from the truth and enslaves them in bondage.

4. Identifying Jezebel's Throne:
- Jezebel's throne can be identified by the presence of control, manipulation, and a spirit of rebellion against God's authority. It manifests in personal relationships, churches, workplaces, and even in societal structures.

Dethroning Jezebel:

1. Recognizing Jezebel's Tactics:
- Develop discernment and spiritual insight to recognize Jezebel's tactics of control and manipulation. Be alert to her subtle influences and strategies.

2. Exposing Jezebel's Deceptions:
- Shine the light of God's truth on Jezebel's deceptions and false teachings. Study and understand God's Word to discern and expose her lies.

3. Walking in the Fear of the Lord:

- Cultivate a deep reverence for God and a desire to honor His authority above all else. The fear of the Lord will protect you from falling into Jezebel's traps.

4. Seeking God's Order and Authority:
- Submit to God's divine order and authority in your life, church, and community. Allow Him to establish His throne of righteousness and justice.

5. Embracing Humility and Servanthood:
- Counter Jezebel's spirit of control by embracing humility and servanthood. Let the example of Jesus guide your actions and interactions with others.

6. Breaking Free from Jezebel's Influence:
- Renounce and reject Jezebel's influence in your life and the lives of those around you. Break free from any agreements or attachments formed under her influence.

7. Engaging in Spiritual Warfare:
- Engage in spiritual warfare, using the weapons of prayer, fasting, and the power of God's Word to dethrone Jezebel. Declare the victory of Jesus Christ over her throne of control.

8. Building a Strong Foundation in God's Word:

- Build a strong foundation in God's Word, studying and meditating on it daily. Let His truth be your anchor, guiding you away from Jezebel's deceptions and into freedom.

9. Surrounding Yourself with Discerning Believers:
- Connect with other discerning believers who can provide support, accountability, and prayer in the battle against Jezebel's influence. Seek wise counsel and advice from trusted spiritual mentors.

10. Praying for Jezebel's Salvation:
- Pray for the salvation of those influenced by Jezebel's spirit, including Jezebel herself. Ask God to intervene, bring conviction, and extend His mercy and grace to her.

11. Cultivating a Spirit of Love and Unity:
- Counter Jezebel's divisive spirit by cultivating a spirit of love, unity, and forgiveness. Seek to build healthy relationships based on God's love and reconciliation.

---

Dethroning Jezebel requires a steadfast commitment to the truth of God's Word, an unwavering trust in His authority, and a dependence on the power of the Holy Spirit. By recognizing Jezebel's tactics, exposing her deceptions, and walking in God's divine order, we can dismantle her throne of control and establish the reign of God's righteousness and love. Let us stand firm, united in our purpose to dethrone Jezebel and advance God's Kingdom on earth.

## Deliverance Prayer

1. Heavenly Father, I come before you in the name of Jesus, taking authority over Jezebel's throne of control and manipulation. I declare that her reign is overthrown, and your righteous rule is established in my life and in every area influenced by her.

2. I renounce and reject every lie and deception propagated by Jezebel. I declare that I am a child of truth, and I refuse to be ensnared by her web of manipulation and deceit.

3. I break every agreement and soul tie formed with Jezebel's spirit. I declare that I am free from her influence and control. I sever every ungodly connection and declare that I am aligned only with the Spirit of God.

4. I release the power of the Holy Spirit to expose and dismantle Jezebel's strategies of control and manipulation. I pray for discernment and wisdom to recognize her tactics and resist her attempts to gain influence in my life and in my sphere of influence.

5. I take authority in the name of Jesus over every spirit associated with Jezebel's throne. I bind and cast out the spirit of control,

manipulation, seduction, and rebellion. I declare that these spirits have no power or authority over me.

6. I declare that the fear of the Lord is my guide and protection. I choose to honor God's authority above all else and to walk in obedience to His Word. I reject the spirit of rebellion and embrace humility and servanthood.

7. I pray for a deep revelation of God's love, which casts out all fear. I declare that I am secure in His love, and I will not be swayed or controlled by the manipulative tactics of Jezebel.

8. I release forgiveness and extend grace to those who have been influenced by Jezebel's spirit. I pray for their deliverance and transformation, that they may experience the freedom and love found only in Christ.

9. I pray for a revival of discernment and godly wisdom in the Church. I ask for a spirit of unity and love to prevail, breaking down the walls of division and strife caused by Jezebel's influence.

10. I declare that Jezebel's throne is replaced by the throne of Jesus Christ. I invite the Holy Spirit to take His rightful place of authority in every aspect of my life, in my family, in my church, and in the world.

11. I declare that Jezebel's influence is nullified by the power of the blood of Jesus. I plead the blood over my mind, my emotions, my will, and every area affected by her control. I am covered and protected by the blood of the Lamb.

12. I release the power of the Holy Spirit to bring healing and restoration to those wounded by Jezebel's influence. I pray for the broken-hearted to be mended, for the captive to be set free, and for the wounded to experience the love and restoration of God.

13. I pray for divine encounters with the presence of God, where Jezebel's lies are exposed, and God's truth prevails. I invite the Holy Spirit to reveal any areas of my life that need to be transformed and renewed.

14. I break every generational curse associated with Jezebel's influence. I declare that the cycle of control and manipulation is broken, and the blessings of God's Kingdom flow freely in my life and in the lives of future generations.

15. I pray for the dismantling of Jezebel's influence in society, in politics, and in cultural norms. I declare that righteousness and justice prevail, and the spirit of Jezebel is exposed and rendered powerless.

16. I declare that I am an agent of change, standing against Jezebel's influence and advancing God's Kingdom agenda. I will not be silent or passive, but I will take a bold stand for truth and righteousness.

17. I pray for divine strategies and insights to combat Jezebel's influence. I ask for the wisdom to engage in spiritual warfare effectively and to see breakthrough and victory in every area affected by her control.

18. I declare that Jezebel's throne is dismantled, and the people of God are released into their true identity and purpose. I pray for a revival of passion for Jesus and a fervent pursuit of His presence.

19. I release the fire of God to consume Jezebel's throne. Let every stronghold and power associated with her control be consumed by the fire of God's holiness and righteousness.

20. I declare that I am an overcomer through Jesus Christ, and I will walk in the freedom and authority He has given me. I am empowered by the Holy Spirit to dethrone Jezebel and establish the reign of God's love, truth, and righteousness. In Jesus' mighty name, amen.

## Chapter 31

# The Mantle of Authority:
# Stepping into Spiritual Leadership

Spiritual leadership is a calling and a responsibility that requires a deep understanding of God's authority, a heart for servanthood, and a passion to lead others into a closer relationship with Him. In this chapter, we will explore the significance of the mantle of authority, the qualities of a spiritual leader, and practical steps to step into the role of spiritual leadership.

Understanding the Mantle of Authority:

1. The Meaning of the Mantle:
   - The mantle symbolizes the calling and authority given by God to individuals to lead and serve others in spiritual matters. It is a divine empowerment that carries with it the responsibility to represent God's kingdom on earth.

2. The Source of Authority:
   - The ultimate source of spiritual authority is God Himself. He delegates authority to individuals who are aligned with His will, equipped by His Spirit, and committed to His purposes.

3. Walking in Humility:
- Spiritual leaders must cultivate a heart of humility, recognizing that their authority is a privilege and not a position of superiority. They must serve as examples of Christ's humility, leading with love and compassion.

4. Responsibility and Accountability:
- Those who carry the mantle of authority are accountable to God and to the people they lead. They must steward their authority with integrity, seeking God's guidance and being accountable to wise counsel.

Qualities of a Spiritual Leader:

1. Intimacy with God:
- A spiritual leader must prioritize cultivating a deep and intimate relationship with God. They must seek His guidance, listen to His voice, and draw strength and wisdom from Him through prayer, worship, and the study of His Word.

2. Servant's Heart:
- A spiritual leader must embody the heart of a servant, following the example of Jesus Christ. They should serve others with humility, compassion, and a genuine desire to see others grow in their faith.

3. Discernment and Wisdom:

-   Spiritual leaders need discernment and wisdom to navigate the complexities of spiritual matters and make decisions that align with God's will. They must seek the guidance of the Holy Spirit and rely on His wisdom in all situations.

4. Integrity and Character:

-   A spiritual leader must demonstrate integrity and godly character in all aspects of life. They should be people of honesty, transparency, and moral uprightness, reflecting the image of Christ to those they lead.

5. Vision and Direction:

-   A spiritual leader must have a clear vision and direction inspired by God. They should communicate this vision to others, providing guidance and encouragement as they lead them towards the fulfillment of God's purposes.

6. Effective Communication:

-   Spiritual leaders must possess effective communication skills to articulate God's truth, inspire others, and foster healthy relationships. They should be able to listen attentively, speak with clarity, and adapt their communication style to different audiences.

7. Empowering Others:
- A spiritual leader should empower others, equipping them with the necessary tools, resources, and encouragement to fulfill their God-given purposes. They should invest in the development and growth of those they lead.

8. Embracing Diversity:
- Spiritual leaders should embrace and celebrate the diversity within the body of Christ. They should foster an inclusive environment where every individual feels valued, respected, and empowered to contribute their unique gifts and talents.

Stepping into Spiritual Leadership:

1. Seek God's Will:
- Seek God's guidance and confirmation concerning your calling to spiritual leadership. Spend time in prayer and seek wise counsel to discern if this is the path God is calling you to walk.

2. Develop a Strong Foundation:
- Build a strong foundation in your faith through consistent prayer, studying God's Word, and participating in discipleship and leadership development programs. Seek opportunities to grow in your understanding of spiritual leadership.

3. Cultivate Humility and Servanthood:

- Embrace the heart of a servant and cultivate humility as you prepare to step into spiritual leadership. Seek opportunities to serve others, both within and outside of the church community.

4. Invest in Personal Growth:
- Continuously invest in personal growth by attending leadership conferences, reading books on leadership and spiritual growth, and seeking mentorship from experienced spiritual leaders. Develop the necessary skills and knowledge to effectively lead others.

5. Surround Yourself with Supportive Community:
- Surround yourself with a supportive community of fellow believers who can provide encouragement, guidance, and accountability. Seek out mentors and spiritual leaders who can pour into your life and help you grow in your leadership journey.

6. Embrace Opportunities for Leadership:
- Be proactive in seeking out opportunities to lead within your church or community. Volunteer for leadership positions, serve on ministry teams, and look for ways to use your gifts and talents to impact others.

7. Develop Healthy Relationships:
- Build healthy relationships with those you lead and those you serve alongside. Foster an environment of trust, openness, and

collaboration. Seek to understand the needs of others and be responsive to their concerns and aspirations.

8. Lead with Love and Compassion:
- Let love and compassion be the guiding principles of your leadership. Lead by example, demonstrating Christ's love in your words and actions. Show genuine care and concern for the well-being of those under your leadership.

9. Continual Growth and Learning:
- Commit to lifelong learning and growth as a spiritual leader. Stay updated on current trends and challenges in the church and society. Seek feedback, evaluate your leadership, and make necessary adjustments for improvement.

10. Rely on the Holy Spirit:
- Depend on the power and guidance of the Holy Spirit as you step into spiritual leadership. Allow Him to work through you, empowering you to lead with wisdom, discernment, and effectiveness.

---

Stepping into spiritual leadership is both a privilege and a responsibility. By understanding the mantle of authority, embodying the qualities of a spiritual leader, and taking practical steps to develop and grow, you can fulfill the call to lead others in their spiritual journeys. May you embrace the mantle of authority with humility, love, and a deep reliance on God's guidance, impacting lives and advancing God's kingdom on earth.

## Deliverance Prayer

1. Heavenly Father, I come before you in the name of Jesus, surrendering myself to your divine authority and leadership. I declare that I am stepping into the mantle of spiritual leadership with humility, wisdom, and the empowerment of the Holy Spirit.

2. I take authority over every spiritual opposition that seeks to hinder or undermine my effectiveness as a spiritual leader. I declare that no weapon formed against me shall prosper, and every tongue that rises against me in judgment shall be condemned.

3. I release the power of the Holy Spirit to guide me in every decision, every interaction, and every aspect of my spiritual leadership. I rely on His wisdom, discernment, and guidance to lead with integrity and effectiveness.

4. I bind and cast out every spirit of pride, ego, and self-centeredness that would hinder my ability to serve and lead others with humility and love. I humble myself before you and commit to leading as a servant-leader, following the example of Jesus Christ.

5. I declare that I am equipped with the necessary spiritual gifts and abilities to fulfill my calling as a spiritual leader. I embrace the mantle of authority and the responsibility that comes with it, knowing that you have equipped me for this purpose.

6. I take authority over every spirit of fear, doubt, and insecurity that would seek to undermine my confidence and effectiveness as a spiritual leader. I declare that I am bold, courageous, and confident in the Lord.

7. I release the power of unity and harmony among those I lead. I bind and cast out every spirit of division, strife, and discord, declaring that we will walk in love and unity, supporting and encouraging one another in our spiritual journeys.

8. I pray for divine connections and relationships with fellow spiritual leaders and mentors who will provide guidance, support, and accountability. Surround me with wise counsel and godly examples as I grow in my spiritual leadership.

9. I declare that I will lead by example, demonstrating godly character, integrity, and authenticity in all that I do. I commit to living a life worthy of emulation, shining your light and truth to those I lead.

10. I release the power of effective communication and discernment in my leadership. Give me the ability to communicate your truth clearly, to discern the needs and concerns of those I lead, and to address them with wisdom and compassion.

11. I bind and cast out every spirit of complacency and mediocrity that would hinder my commitment to excellence in my spiritual leadership. I declare that I will continually grow, develop, and pursue excellence in all that I do.

12. I pray for divine wisdom and insight as I navigate the challenges and complexities of spiritual leadership. Grant me supernatural discernment to make decisions that align with Your will and bring glory to your name.

13. I take authority over every spirit of discouragement and weariness that would seek to hinder my passion and enthusiasm for spiritual leadership. I declare that I am strengthened and refreshed by the power of the Holy Spirit.

14. I release the power of supernatural provision and resources to fulfill the vision and purposes you have placed within my heart as a spiritual leader. Open doors, provide opportunities, and supply every need according to your riches in glory.

15. I bind and cast out every spirit of control and manipulation that would seek to infiltrate my leadership. I declare that I lead with humility, allowing the Holy Spirit to guide and direct me, and respecting the autonomy and free will of those I lead.

16. I declare that I am anointed to bring transformation and revival in the lives of those I lead. I release the power of the Holy Spirit to bring healing, deliverance, and spiritual growth in the lives of individuals and in the community under my leadership.

17. I bind and cast out every spirit of stagnation and complacency that would hinder the growth and impact of the ministry under my leadership. I declare that we will move forward in faith, with a spirit of innovation, and a willingness to embrace change for your kingdom's advancement.

18. I release the power of supernatural favor and influence in my spiritual leadership. Open doors of opportunity, grant divine connections, and position me strategically to impact lives and advance your kingdom.

19. I declare that I will be a faithful steward of the mantle of authority entrusted to me. I will use my spiritual leadership to honor you, serve others, and make a lasting impact for your glory.

20. I declare that as I step into the mantle of spiritual leadership, I am not alone. You are with me, empowering me, guiding me, and equipping me for every task. I rely on your strength and your anointing to fulfill my calling as a spiritual leader. In Jesus' mighty name, amen.

## Chapter 32

# Jezebel's Spirit of Rebellion:
# Restoring Obedience to God

Jezebel's spirit of rebellion has infiltrated every sphere of society, leading people astray from God's commandments and promoting a culture of disobedience. In this chapter, we will explore the nature of Jezebel's spirit of rebellion, its destructive effects, and how we can restore obedience to God in our lives and communities.

Understanding Jezebel's Spirit of Rebellion:

1. The Origin of Jezebel's Spirit:
   - Jezebel's spirit of rebellion finds its roots in the fall of Lucifer, who rebelled against God's authority. This spirit seeks to usurp God's authority and promotes disobedience to His Word.

2. Tactics of Jezebel's Spirit:
   - Jezebel's spirit of rebellion uses various tactics to deceive and seduce people into disobedience. It appeals to pride, self-will, and the desire for autonomy, leading individuals to reject God's authority and His moral standards.

3. Jezebel's Influence in Society:
- Jezebel's spirit of rebellion has permeated society, promoting moral relativism, secular humanism, and a disregard for God's commandments. It influences laws, policies, and cultural norms that oppose God's truth and promote disobedience.

4. The Destructive Effects of Rebellion:
- Rebellion against God's authority brings about spiritual, emotional, and relational destruction. It leads to brokenness, division, and a separation from God's blessings and protection.

Restoring Obedience to God:

1. Recognizing the Spirit of Rebellion:
- Develop discernment to recognize the spirit of rebellion and its subtle influences in our lives and society. Ask the Holy Spirit to reveal areas of rebellion and disobedience that need to be addressed.

2. Submitting to God's Authority:
- Surrender our lives completely to God's authority, acknowledging His lordship over every aspect of our lives. Submit to His Word, His commands, and His leading, trusting His wisdom and perfect plan.

3. Repenting and Turning Away from Rebellion:

- Repent of any rebellion and disobedience in our lives, seeking God's forgiveness and turning away from sinful patterns. Choose to align our thoughts, attitudes, and actions with God's truth.

4. Renewing our Minds with God's Word:
- Immerse ourselves in God's Word, allowing it to shape our thinking and guide our decisions. Meditate on His commands, promises, and principles, allowing His truth to renew our minds and transform our lives.

5. Cultivating a Heart of Humility and Submission:
- Embrace humility and develop a heart of submission to God and His appointed authorities. Yield to the leading of the Holy Spirit, seeking His guidance and relying on His strength to live a life of obedience.

6. Embracing the Fear of the Lord:
- Cultivate a reverential fear of the Lord, recognizing His holiness, righteousness, and sovereignty. Let the fear of the Lord be a guiding force in our lives, leading us to walk in obedience and reverence for Him.

7. Building a Foundation of Prayer:
- Develop a consistent and fervent prayer life, seeking God's guidance, strength, and empowerment to walk in obedience. Pray

for the spirit of rebellion to be exposed and replaced with a spirit of obedience.

8. Seeking Accountability and Spiritual Community:
-   Surround ourselves with a community of believers who will encourage, support, and hold us accountable in our journey of obedience. Seek mentors and spiritual leaders who can provide guidance and counsel.

9. Walking in the Power of the Holy Spirit:
-   Rely on the power of the Holy Spirit to empower us to live a life of obedience. Allow the Holy Spirit to work in us, transforming our hearts, aligning our will with God's, and giving us the strength to resist the spirit of rebellion.

10. Modeling Obedience to Others:
-   Be a role model of obedience to God's commands, living a life that reflects His truth and righteousness. Let our actions, words, and attitudes testify to the transformative power of walking in obedience to God.

11. Praying for Transformation in Society:
-   Intercede for the transformation of society, praying for the spirit of rebellion to be exposed and replaced with a spirit of obedience. Pray for leaders, influencers, and institutions to align with God's truth and promote obedience to His commands.

Jezebel's spirit of rebellion may be pervasive in our society, but we have the power, through Christ, to resist its influence and restore obedience to God. By recognizing the tactics of rebellion, submitting to God's authority, and cultivating a heart of humility and obedience, we can be agents of change and restoration. Let us commit ourselves to restoring obedience to God in our lives, communities, and the world, bringing glory to His name and experiencing His blessings and transformation.

## Deliverance Prayer

1. Heavenly Father, I come before you in the name of Jesus, taking authority over Jezebel's spirit of rebellion that seeks to undermine obedience to your Word and your authority. I declare that the power of rebellion is broken, and obedience to you is restored in my life and in the lives of those around me.

2. I renounce and reject every form of rebellion and disobedience in my life. I repent for the times I have rebelled against your authority and your commands. I choose to submit myself wholly to you, surrendering my will and aligning myself with your perfect will.

3. I break every generational curse and stronghold of rebellion in my bloodline. I declare that the cycle of rebellion is broken, and a legacy of obedience is established for future generations.

4. I bind and cast out the spirit of rebellion that operates in my thoughts, emotions, and actions. I declare that every influence of this spirit is rendered powerless in my life by the blood of Jesus.

5. I release the power of the Holy Spirit to transform my heart and mind, renewing my thoughts and aligning them with your truth. I declare that I have the mind of Christ, and I will think and respond in obedience to your Word.

6. I pray for a spirit of humility and submission to permeate my being. Help me to yield to your authority, trusting that your plans and ways are higher and better than my own.

7. I declare that I am a doer of your Word, not just a hearer. Empower me, Lord, to walk in obedience and to live out your commands with joy and passion.

8. I bind and cast out every spirit of pride and self-will that would lead me astray from your will. I humble myself before you, acknowledging that apart from you, I can do nothing.

9. I declare that I will not conform to the patterns of this world but will be transformed by the renewing of my mind. I choose to resist the influence of rebellion in society and to stand firm in your truth.

10. I pray for a revival of obedience in the Church and in society. May your Spirit move mightily, convicting hearts, and drawing people back to a place of obedience to your Word.

11. I release the power of your Word to penetrate every area of my life and bring about obedience. Let your Word be a lamp to my feet and a light to my path, guiding me in all righteousness.

12. I pray for leaders, influencers, and institutions in society to be touched by your Spirit, that they may turn from rebellion and lead with integrity and obedience to your commands.

13. I bind and cast out the spirit of rebellion from my relationships and spheres of influence. I declare that unity, love, and obedience to you will prevail in all my interactions.

14. I declare that I am an overcomer through Christ, and I will not be swayed by the spirit of rebellion. I stand firm on your promises, knowing that your grace is sufficient to keep me in obedience.

15. I pray for deliverance and restoration for those trapped in the cycle of rebellion. I intercede for their hearts to be softened, their eyes

to be opened to your truth, and for them to experience the freedom that comes through obedience to you.

16. I release the power of forgiveness, choosing to forgive those who have influenced me or others in rebellion. I pray for their repentance and transformation, that they may experience the joy and blessings of obedience.

17. I declare that your love compels me to obey you. Help me to walk in love, demonstrating your truth and grace to those around me, even in the face of opposition or persecution.

18. I pray for spiritual leaders to rise up with courage and conviction, boldly proclaiming your truth and leading by example in obedience. Strengthen them, Lord, and protect them from the attacks of the enemy.

19. I declare that obedience brings blessings and favor. I expect to see the manifestation of your goodness and provision as I walk in obedience to your Word.

20. I seal these declarations in the name of Jesus, declaring that Jezebel's spirit of rebellion is defeated, and obedience to God is restored. I will live a life of obedience, honoring you in all that I do. In Jesus' mighty name, amen.

## Chapter 33

# Supernatural Strategies:
# Winning the Battle against Jezebel

The battle against Jezebel and her deceptive spirit requires supernatural strategies rooted in the power of God. In this chapter, we will explore key principles and practical strategies to overcome Jezebel's influence and walk in victory. Through the guidance of the Holy Spirit and the application of these supernatural strategies, we can win the battle against Jezebel and experience the fullness of God's purposes in our lives and communities.

Understanding Jezebel's Tactics:

1. The Nature of Jezebel's Spirit:
    - Jezebel's spirit is characterized by manipulation, control, and seduction. It operates through deception, witchcraft, and intimidation, seeking to undermine God's authority and derail His plans.

2. Identifying Jezebel's Tactics:
    - Jezebel employs various tactics to establish her influence and maintain control. These tactics include seduction, false prophecy,

slander, fear, and division. Understanding these tactics is essential in countering her strategies.

3. Recognizing Jezebel's Influence:
-   Jezebel's influence can be found in various spheres of life, including families, churches, organizations, and even nations. Identifying her presence and influence is crucial to effectively combat her destructive work.

Supernatural Strategies to Overcome Jezebel:

1. Clothe Yourself in the Armor of God:
-   Put on the full armor of God, including the belt of truth, the breastplate of righteousness, the shoes of the gospel of peace, the shield of faith, the helmet of salvation, and the sword of the Spirit (the Word of God). This spiritual armor equips and empowers us to stand against Jezebel's schemes.

2. Seek Intimacy with God:
-   Cultivate a deep and intimate relationship with God through prayer, worship, and the study of His Word. Seek His presence and guidance, allowing Him to reveal Jezebel's tactics and provide supernatural strategies for victory.

3. Discernment through the Holy Spirit:

- Develop spiritual discernment by relying on the guidance of the Holy Spirit. Ask Him to reveal the presence of Jezebel's spirit, expose her tactics, and provide discernment in making decisions and taking action.

4. Pray for Jezebel's Exposure and Defeat:
- Engage in fervent prayer, specifically targeting Jezebel's exposure and defeat. Pray for God's light to shine on her works, for her strategies to be unveiled, and for His power to render her powerless.

5. Renounce and Break Jezebel Soul Ties:
- Identify and renounce any soul ties or unhealthy attachments to Jezebel influences. Break free from her control and influence through prayer and renunciation, inviting the healing and restoration of God.

6. Prophetic Intercession:
- Engage in prophetic intercession, standing in the gap on behalf of individuals, families, churches, and nations under Jezebel's influence. Declare God's truth, prophesy His plans, and release His power to break her hold.

7. Unity and Accountability:
- Foster unity and accountability within the body of Christ. Jezebel thrives in an environment of division and secrecy. Encourage

transparency, healthy relationships, and mutual accountability to counter her divisive strategies.

8. Walking in Holiness and Purity:
- Maintain a lifestyle of holiness and purity, seeking to cleanse and purify every area of your life from Jezebel's influence. Renounce any compromise with her ways and align yourself with God's standards of righteousness.

9. Guarding Your Mind and Heart:
- Guard your mind and heart against Jezebel's deceptive influences. Meditate on God's truth, fill your mind with His Word, and discern the subtle lies and manipulations of Jezebel's spirit.

10. Cultivating Spiritual Authority:
- Recognize and embrace your spiritual authority in Christ. Understand that you have been given authority over all powers of darkness, including Jezebel's spirit. Exercise this authority in prayer, declaration, and action.

11. Exposing Jezebel's Lies with Truth:
- Counter Jezebel's lies with the truth of God's Word. Study and meditate on passages that reveal God's character, His promises, and His commands. Use the truth to expose Jezebel's deceptions and bring freedom to those under her influence.

12. Releasing the Fire of God:
    - Invoke the fire of God to consume Jezebel's works and release His purifying and refining power. Pray for the fire of the Holy Spirit to burn away every trace of Jezebel's influence, leaving behind a pure and holy foundation.

13. Walking in the Fruit of the Spirit:
    - Cultivate the fruit of the Spirit in your life, such as love, joy, peace, patience, kindness, goodness, faithfulness, gentleness, and self-control. These attributes counter Jezebel's divisive and manipulative tactics.

14. Operating in the Gifts of the Holy Spirit:
    - Activate and operate in the gifts of the Holy Spirit to counter Jezebel's deception. Discernment, prophecy, and the word of knowledge are particularly powerful in exposing and countering her strategies.

15. Establishing Spiritual Boundaries:
    - Set clear spiritual boundaries to protect yourself and others from Jezebel's influence. Identify and confront any attempts to manipulate, control, or seduce. Firmly establish and enforce healthy boundaries based on God's truth and love.

16. Building Strong Foundations on God's Word:

- Strengthen your spiritual foundation by building your life upon the solid rock of God's Word. Develop a deep understanding of His truth, promises, and principles, so you can withstand Jezebel's attacks.

17. Surround Yourself with Discerning and Spirit-filled Believers:
- Seek fellowship and community with discerning and spirit-filled believers who can provide support, accountability, and prayer. Together, stand against Jezebel's spirit and support one another in the battle.

18. Walking in Love and Forgiveness:
- Counter Jezebel's divisive tactics by walking in love and forgiveness. Extend grace and forgiveness to those who have been influenced by her spirit, praying for their deliverance and restoration.

19. Guarding Your Anointing:
- Protect and guard the anointing and calling that God has placed upon your life. Jezebel seeks to extinguish and steal the anointing of God. Stay vigilant, seek the Holy Spirit's guidance, and reject any compromise that threatens your anointing.

20. Celebrating and Encouraging Authenticity:
- Foster an environment that celebrates authenticity and transparency. Encourage vulnerability, openness, and humility

among believers, creating a culture that exposes Jezebel's counterfeit and fosters true spiritual growth.

---

Winning the battle against Jezebel requires supernatural strategies rooted in God's Word and empowered by the Holy Spirit. By understanding her tactics, engaging in spiritual warfare, and aligning ourselves with God's truth, we can overcome her influence and walk in victory. May we rise up as empowered believers, equipped with supernatural strategies, and experience the fullness of God's purposes in our lives and communities, free from the control of Jezebel's spirit.

## Deliverance Prayer

1. Heavenly Father, in the name of Jesus, I take authority over Jezebel's spirit of manipulation, control, and rebellion. I declare that her influence is broken, and I stand firm in the supernatural strategies you have given me to win the battle against her.

2. I renounce and reject every lie, deception, and manipulation of Jezebel's spirit. I declare that I am covered by the blood of Jesus, and I am empowered to walk in victory and freedom.

3. I bind and cast out every spirit of fear, intimidation, and division that Jezebel uses to undermine unity and disrupt relationships. I

release the power of God's love and unity to restore harmony and peace.

4. I pray for divine discernment and supernatural insight to recognize Jezebel's tactics and strategies. Open my spiritual eyes to see through her deception and give me wisdom to counter her every move.

5. I release the power of the Holy Spirit to guide me in every decision, every interaction, and every battle against Jezebel. Fill me with your discernment, wisdom, and revelation to overcome her schemes.

6. I declare that I am clothed in the armor of God, and I take my stand against Jezebel and her spirits of darkness. I wield the sword of the Spirit, which is the Word of God, to expose and defeat her lies.

7. I pray for a fresh infilling of the Holy Spirit's fire to consume every stronghold and bondage created by Jezebel's spirit. Let the fire of God purify and refine my heart, mind, and spirit.

8. I break every soul tie and connection to Jezebel's spirit, whether through personal experiences, generational influence, or external sources. I renounce and sever all ties that have allowed her access into my life.

9. I release the power of forgiveness and extend it to those who have been influenced by Jezebel's spirit. I pray for their deliverance and restoration, that they may experience the freedom and abundant life found in Christ.

10. I pray for a supernatural release of the gifts of the Holy Spirit, particularly discernment, prophecy, and the word of knowledge, to expose and counter Jezebel's strategies. Let your Spirit flow through me to bring clarity and revelation.

11. I decree and declare that I am an overcomer through Christ. I reject the spirit of defeat and discouragement that Jezebel seeks to impose. I walk in the victory and authority that Jesus has won for me.

12. I pray for divine connections with other believers who are also fighting against Jezebel's influence. Surround me with a community of like-minded warriors who will stand with me in prayer, support, and encouragement.

13. I release the power of God's truth to dispel every lie and deception of Jezebel's spirit. Let your Word penetrate the hearts and minds of those under her influence, bringing them to a place of repentance and freedom.

14. I bind and cast out every spirit of rebellion, witchcraft, and control that Jezebel operates through. I break their power and influence in the lives of individuals, families, churches, and nations.

15. I pray for a fresh outpouring of your love and grace to heal the wounds and hurts caused by Jezebel's spirit. Bring restoration and wholeness to those who have been impacted by her tactics.

16. I release the power of worship and praise to dismantle Jezebel's strongholds. Let the sound of worship rise as a weapon against her, causing her plans to crumble and her influence to fade away.

17. I declare that my mind is guarded and renewed by the truth of God's Word. I resist every thought and suggestion that aligns with Jezebel spirit, and I choose to meditate on whatever is true, honorable, just, pure, lovely, and praiseworthy.

18. I pray for supernatural breakthrough in areas of my life that have been hindered by Jezebel's influence. Let your power and anointing break every chain and open doors of opportunity and advancement.

19. I release the power of God's healing and restoration to those who have been wounded by Jezebel's spirit. Let your love bring wholeness, freedom, and a renewed sense of identity and purpose.

20. I declare that the victory is already won through Jesus Christ. I stand firm in faith, knowing that Jezebel's spirit is defeated and that I walk in the authority and power of Christ to overcome every obstacle and opposition. In Jesus' mighty name, amen.

## Chapter 34

# Jezebel's Effect on Mental Health:
# Restoring Soundness of Mind

Jezebel's spirit not only seeks to control and manipulate in the natural realm but also has a profound impact on mental health. In this chapter, we will delve into the detrimental effects of Jezebel's spirit on mental well-being, explore the tactics she employs to attack the mind, and discover strategies to restore soundness of mind and experience emotional healing. Through the power of God's truth and healing, we can overcome Jezebel's influence and walk in the freedom and peace that God desires for our mental health.

Understanding Jezebel's Effect on Mental Health:

1. The Manipulative Tactics of Jezebel:
   - Jezebel's spirit uses various manipulative tactics to undermine mental health. She employs deception, gaslighting, and emotional manipulation to instill fear, doubt, and confusion, leading to anxiety, depression, and other mental health issues.

2. The Attack on Identity and Self-Worth:

- Jezebel attacks the very core of a person's identity and self-worth. By distorting truth and planting seeds of insecurity and inferiority, she aims to weaken mental and emotional resilience, leading to issues like low self-esteem and self-doubt.

3. Jezebel's Seeds of Fear and Anxiety:
- Jezebel's spirit sows seeds of fear and anxiety, creating a constant state of worry and apprehension. This can manifest as generalized anxiety disorder, panic attacks, or other anxiety-related disorders, hindering mental well-being and peace.

4. Emotional Manipulation and Control:
- Jezebel's spirit excels in emotional manipulation and control, leading to emotional instability, mood swings, and a loss of emotional balance. This can contribute to conditions such as bipolar disorder, borderline personality disorder, or emotional dysregulation.

Restoring Soundness of Mind:

1. Embracing God's Truth and Identity:
- Counter Jezebel's attacks on identity and self-worth by embracing God's truth about who we are in Him. Meditate on Scripture that affirms our identity as beloved children of God, fearfully and wonderfully made.

2. Renewing the Mind with God's Word:

- Combat the distorted thinking patterns instigated by Jezebel's spirit through the regular intake of God's Word. Replace lies and negative thoughts with the truth of God's promises, transforming our minds and bringing clarity and peace.

3. Seeking Healing from Emotional Wounds:

- Seek healing from emotional wounds inflicted by Jezebel's spirit through prayer, counseling, and inner healing ministries. Allow the Holy Spirit to bring restoration, bringing deep emotional healing and release from past hurts.

4. Casting Out the Spirit of Fear:

- Take authority over the spirit of fear that Jezebel operates through. Declare God's promises of peace, love, and a sound mind, rebuking the spirit of fear and commanding it to leave in the name of Jesus.

5. Pursuing Emotional Well-being:

- Engage in practices that promote emotional well-being, such as self-care, healthy boundaries, and seeking professional support when needed. Take time for rest, relaxation, and engaging in activities that bring joy and fulfillment.

6. Cultivating a Spirit of Love and Forgiveness:

- Counter the divisive and manipulative nature of Jezebel's spirit by cultivating a spirit of love and forgiveness. Release any bitterness or resentment towards those who have been influenced by Jezebel, allowing God's love to flow freely.

7. Developing Resilience through Faith:
   - Develop resilience through a strong foundation of faith in God. Trust in His goodness, His faithfulness, and His plans for your life. Allow your faith to anchor you during challenging times, knowing that God is with you and for you.

8. Surrounding Yourself with a Supportive Community:
   - Seek out a supportive community of believers who can provide encouragement, accountability, and prayer support. Share your struggles, seek wise counsel, and allow others to come alongside you in your journey towards mental well-being.

9. Surrendering Control to God:
   - Release the need for control and surrender your life, thoughts, and emotions to God. Recognize that He is the ultimate source of peace, stability, and soundness of mind. Trust Him to guide and lead you on the path of healing and wholeness.

10. Praying for Inner Healing and Deliverance:
    - Engage in specific prayers for inner healing and deliverance from the effects of Jezebel's spirit on your mental health. Invite the Holy

Spirit to expose and uproot any lies, traumas, or wounds that have been inflicted, replacing them with God's truth and restoration.

11. Embracing the Power of the Holy Spirit:
-   Invite the Holy Spirit to work in and through your life, empowering you to overcome Jezebel's influence on your mental health. Allow His presence to bring comfort, peace, and healing to your mind, renewing your thoughts and emotions.

12. Seeking Professional Help:
-   Recognize the importance of seeking professional help when needed. Consult with mental health professionals who align with your faith and can provide guidance, therapy, or medication if necessary. Allow them to partner with you on your journey towards mental well-being.

---

Jezebel's spirit takes aim at our mental health, seeking to sow seeds of fear, confusion, and emotional turmoil. However, through the power of God's truth, healing, and the Holy Spirit, we can overcome her influence and experience restoration and soundness of mind. By embracing God's identity for us, renewing our minds with His Word, seeking healing, and cultivating healthy practices, we can walk in mental well-being and live in the peace and freedom that God intends for us.

## Deliverance Prayer

1. Heavenly Father, I come before you in the name of Jesus, taking authority over Jezebel's spirit and its effects on mental health. I declare that through your power, I can experience restoration and soundness of mind.

2. I renounce and reject every lie, distortion, and manipulation of Jezebel's spirit that has affected my thoughts and emotions. I choose to align my mind with your truth and reject any negative influence that seeks to steal my peace and well-being.

3. I break every stronghold of fear, anxiety, and confusion that Jezebel's spirit has attempted to establish in my mind. I declare that I am no longer a slave to these emotions, but I am free in Christ Jesus to walk in peace and soundness of mind.

4. I declare that my identity is rooted in you, Lord. I am fearfully and wonderfully made, chosen, and loved by you. I reject any thoughts or beliefs that undermine my self-worth and embrace the truth of your unconditional love for me.

5. I release the power of your Word to renew my mind. I ask that you replace every negative thought pattern and replace them with your thoughts of truth, love, and peace. Let your Word penetrate deep into my soul, transforming my thinking and renewing my mind.

6. I pray for healing and restoration from any emotional wounds inflicted by Jezebel's spirit. Pour out your healing balm upon my heart and mind, bringing inner healing and releasing me from the pain and trauma of the past.

7. I bind and cast out every spirit of confusion, doubt, and despair that Jezebel's spirit has attempted to plant in my mind. I release the power of your Holy Spirit to bring clarity, faith, and hope to my thoughts and emotions.

8. I choose to forgive those who have been influenced by Jezebel's spirit, releasing any bitterness or resentment. I declare that forgiveness is a key to my emotional healing and freedom. I choose to walk in love and extend grace to others.

9. I pray for a fresh infilling of your Holy Spirit, who is the Comforter and Counselor. Fill me afresh with your presence and peace, guiding my thoughts and emotions into alignment with your will.

10. I declare that I have the mind of Christ. I am filled with wisdom, understanding, and discernment. I am able to make sound decisions and overcome any mental battles through the power of the Holy Spirit within me.

11. I release the power of your peace that surpasses all understanding to guard my mind and heart in Christ Jesus. I reject any thoughts of anxiety, worry, and fear, and I choose to dwell in your peace that brings stability and soundness of mind.

12. I take authority over every spirit of depression and sadness that Jezebel's spirit may have brought upon my mind. I command them to leave in the name of Jesus, and I declare that joy and gladness fill my heart and mind.

13. I declare that I am an overcomer. I have the power to overcome any negative thought patterns, destructive habits, or emotional struggles. I am more than a conqueror through Christ Jesus who strengthens me.

14. I bind and break every generational curse or negative thought pattern that Jezebel's spirit has tried to perpetuate in my family. I release the power of your healing and restoration to flow through the generations, bringing freedom and soundness of mind.

15. I pray for divine connections and relationships that edify and uplift my mental well-being. Surround me with godly friends and mentors who speak life, truth, and encouragement into my mind and spirit.

16. I declare that my mind is a dwelling place for your peace, joy, and soundness. I reject any invasion of negative thoughts, toxic influences, or spiritual attacks. I declare that my mind is protected by the blood of Jesus.

17. I release the power of worship and praise to fill my mind and atmosphere, pushing back the darkness and bringing light, joy, and freedom. I choose to worship you in spirit and in truth, aligning my thoughts with your goodness and faithfulness.

18. I pray for divine strategies and insights to navigate any mental battles I may face. Empower me to discern the tactics of Jezebel's spirit and to counter them with your truth and wisdom.

19. I release the power of gratitude and thanksgiving to shift my perspective and uplift my mental well-being. Help me to focus on your goodness, blessings, and faithfulness, cultivating a grateful heart that overflows with joy and peace.

20. I declare that I am victorious in Christ. I will not be shaken by the attacks of Jezebel's spirit on my mental health. I stand firm in the truth of your Word and the power of your Spirit, experiencing restoration, soundness of mind, and emotional healing. In Jesus' name, amen.

## Chapter 35

# Crushing Jezebel's Intimidation:
# Walking in Holy Boldness

Jezebel's spirit operates through intimidation, seeking to silence and hinder God's people from walking in their true identity and purpose. In this chapter, we will explore the tactics of Jezebel's intimidation, the impact it has on our lives, and how we can overcome it by walking in holy boldness. Through the power of the Holy Spirit and a deep understanding of our authority in Christ, we can crush Jezebel's intimidation and step into the fullness of God's calling for our lives.

Understanding Jezebel's Intimidation:

1. The Spirit of Fear and Intimidation:
   - Jezebel's spirit uses fear and intimidation as primary weapons to silence and control individuals. Through threats, manipulation, and the creation of a toxic environment, she seeks to keep God's people from stepping into their true calling and purpose.

2. Undermining Confidence and Self-Worth:
   - Jezebel's intimidation tactics aim to undermine confidence and self-worth. By attacking personal identity and worthiness, she

attempts to keep individuals in a state of self-doubt, rendering them ineffective and unable to fulfill their God-given destiny.

3. Creating Division and Isolation:

- Jezebel's spirit uses intimidation to create division and isolate individuals from their support systems. By sowing seeds of doubt and mistrust, she seeks to weaken relationships, hinder collaboration, and hinder the collective strength of the Body of Christ.

4. Suppressing Holy Boldness:

- Jezebel's intimidation aims to suppress the holy boldness and courage that comes from the Holy Spirit. By instilling fear and doubt, she hinders believers from stepping out in faith, speaking truth, and confronting unrighteousness.

Walking in Holy Boldness:

1. Embracing the Spirit of Power, Love, and a Sound Mind:

- Counter Jezebel's intimidation by embracing the spirit of power, love, and a sound mind that God has given us. Trust in the power of the Holy Spirit working within you and reject the spirit of fear and intimidation.

2. Knowing Your Identity in Christ:

- Ground yourself in the truth of who you are in Christ. Recognize that you are a child of God, redeemed by the blood of Jesus, and empowered by the Holy Spirit. This knowledge will strengthen your confidence and help you overcome intimidation.

3. Cultivating Intimacy with God:
   - Deepen your relationship with God through prayer, worship, and studying His Word. Seek His presence and guidance, allowing Him to fill you with His peace, wisdom, and strength.

4. Standing on the Promises of God:
   - Meditate on the promises of God's Word and declare them over your life. Stand firm on His faithfulness, His provision, and His protection. Remind yourself of His promises in times of intimidation, knowing that He is with you and for you.

5. Filling Your Mind with Truth:
   - Counter the lies and intimidation of Jezebel by filling your mind with the truth of God's Word. Meditate on Scriptures that affirm your identity, purpose, and the victory you have in Christ. Replace negative thoughts with the truth of God's promises.

6. Surrounding Yourself with Supportive Believers:
   - Seek fellowship and accountability with believers who encourage and support your walk with God. Build relationships with those

who speak truth and life into your journey, uplifting and strengthening your holy boldness.

7. Praying for Courage and Boldness:
- Seek the Holy Spirit's empowerment through prayer. Pray for courage, boldness, and the release of the spiritual gifts necessary to combat Jezebel's intimidation. Pray for divine opportunities to step out in faith and confront unrighteousness.

8. Confronting Jezebel's Tactics:
- With the leading of the Holy Spirit, confront Jezebel's tactics of intimidation with truth, love, and righteousness. Speak up against injustice, expose her lies, and stand for what is right, even in the face of opposition.

9. Rejecting the Spirit of Compromise:
- Refuse to compromise your convictions and principles due to intimidation. Stay rooted in the truth of God's Word and stand firm in righteousness, regardless of the pressures or threats that may come your way.

10. Releasing Forgiveness and Letting Go of Offenses:
- Release forgiveness towards those who have been used by Jezebel's spirit to intimidate or harm you. Forgiveness releases the power of God's love, healing your heart and setting you free from bitterness and resentment.

11. Activating Spiritual Warfare:
    - Engage in spiritual warfare against Jezebel's intimidation through prayer, intercession, and the use of spiritual weapons. Use the authority given to you by Jesus to bind and rebuke Jezebel's spirit and declare victory over intimidation.

12. Building Spiritual Discernment:
    - Develop spiritual discernment to recognize the tactics and presence of Jezebel's spirit. Ask the Holy Spirit to sharpen your discernment, enabling you to identify and address intimidation in its various forms.

13. Trusting in God's Provision and Protection:
    - Trust that God is your provider and protector. Even in the face of intimidation, trust that He will guide you, provide for you, and keep you safe. Rest in His faithfulness and know that He is fighting for you.

14. Releasing Prophetic Declarations:
    - Speak forth prophetic declarations against Jezebel's intimidation. Proclaim God's truth, His victory, and the dismantling of Jezebel's tactics. Release declarations of holy boldness, confidence, and victory in the face of intimidation.

15. Walking in Love and Compassion:

- Counter Jezebel's spirit by walking in love and compassion towards others. Show kindness, grace, and forgiveness, reflecting the character of Christ. Love has the power to break down walls and dispel the spirit of intimidation.

16. Pursuing Personal Growth and Development:
    - Continually pursue personal growth and development, equipping yourself with knowledge, skills, and spiritual maturity. Cultivate a teachable spirit and seek opportunities to grow in areas that strengthen your holy boldness.

17. Remaining Steadfast and Persevering:
    - Stand firm in your faith and persevere in the face of intimidation. Do not waver or be discouraged. Trust that God's plans for you are greater than any intimidation tactics of Jezebel and remain steadfast in pursuing His purposes.

18. Resting in God's Sovereignty:
    - Rest in the sovereignty of God, knowing that He is in control. Release any need to control or manipulate situations in response to intimidation. Trust that God is working all things together for your good and His glory.

19. Extending Grace and Redemption:
    - Extend grace and redemption to those who have been influenced by Jezebel's spirit. Pray for their deliverance and restoration,

recognizing that they too are victims of her manipulation. Extend the love and forgiveness of Christ to bring healing and transformation.

20. Celebrating Victories and Testimonies:
   - Celebrate every victory, no matter how small, over Jezebel's intimidation. Share testimonies of God's faithfulness and the triumphs of holy boldness. Let these testimonies inspire and encourage others to crush Jezebel's intimidation in their lives.

---

Jezebel's intimidation tactics may be fierce, but we have been empowered by the Holy Spirit to walk in holy boldness. By understanding her strategies, relying on God's truth, and activating the gifts and authority given to us, we can crush Jezebel's intimidation and walk confidently in our God-given calling. Embrace your identity in Christ, surround yourself with supportive believers, and boldly confront the spirit of intimidation. You are an overcomer, and in the power of the Holy Spirit, you will walk in holy boldness, fulfilling your purpose for God's Kingdom.

## Deliverance Prayer

1. Heavenly Father, I come before you in the name of Jesus, taking authority over every form of intimidation and fear that Jezebel's spirit has tried to bring into my life. I declare that I walk in holy boldness and confidence, empowered by your Spirit.

2. I renounce and reject every lie, threat, and manipulation of Jezebel's spirit that has sought to undermine my confidence and hinder my purpose. I declare that I am a child of God, fearfully and wonderfully made, and I walk in the authority and power You have given me.

3. I break every stronghold of fear and intimidation that Jezebel's spirit has attempted to establish in my life. I declare that I am not governed by fear, but I am led by your Spirit, who fills me with courage, boldness, and a sound mind.

4. I declare that I am rooted in my identity in Christ. I am chosen, redeemed, and called for a specific purpose. I will not be swayed or intimidated by the opinions or threats of others, but I will walk confidently in the path you have set before me.

5. I release the power of your Word to strengthen and embolden me. I declare that your Word is a lamp to my feet and a light to my path. I am guided by your truth, and I reject every lie and deception of Jezebel's spirit.

6. I pray for divine discernment to recognize and expose Jezebel's tactics of intimidation. Open my eyes to see the schemes and strategies she employs, and empower me to counter them with your truth and wisdom.

7. I refuse to be divided or isolated by Jezebel's spirit. I declare that I am part of the Body of Christ, connected to other believers who support and encourage me. I stand united with my brothers and sisters, knowing that together we are strong.

8. I release forgiveness towards those who have been influenced by Jezebel's spirit to intimidate or harm me. I choose to walk in love and extend grace, knowing that forgiveness releases me from the bondage of bitterness and resentment.

9. I bind and rebuke the spirit of Jezebel and its intimidation in the name of Jesus. I declare that it has no power or authority over my life. I release the power of the Holy Spirit to dismantle its influence and render it powerless.

10. I pray for divine opportunities to step out in faith and confront unrighteousness. Empower me, Holy Spirit, to speak truth, shine light, and stand up against injustice. Let your holy boldness flow through me, touching lives and transforming situations.

11. I declare that I walk in the spirit of power, love, and a sound mind. I reject every spirit of timidity, fear, and doubt. I embrace your power that works within me, enabling me to overcome every obstacle and intimidation I face.

12. I refuse to compromise my convictions or principles due to intimidation. I stand firm on your truth and righteousness, even when faced with opposition or threats. I trust that you will defend and uphold me as I walk in holy boldness.

13. I release the power of prayer to dismantle Jezebel's intimidation. I intercede for those who have been victimized by her spirit, praying for their deliverance and restoration. I declare freedom and healing in Jesus' name.

14. I activate the spiritual gifts you have given me to combat Jezebel's intimidation. I release the gift of discernment, prophecy, and boldness. I speak forth your truth and declare victory over the spirit of intimidation.

15. I surround myself with supportive believers who uplift and encourage me. I am accountable to those who speak truth into my life. Together, we stand against Jezebel's intimidation, supporting one another in our walk of holy boldness.

16. I reject every thought of defeat, discouragement, and inadequacy. I declare that I am more than a conqueror through Christ Jesus. I am equipped, anointed, and empowered to overcome every form of intimidation that comes my way.

17. I pray for divine encounters with those influenced by Jezebel's spirit. Let your love flow through me, breaking down walls, dispelling fear, and bringing restoration. Use me as an instrument of your peace and healing.

18. I celebrate every victory over Jezebel's intimidation, no matter how small. I testify of your faithfulness and the triumphs of holy boldness in my life. I share my testimonies to inspire and encourage others to walk in the power and authority you have given them.

19. I walk in the assurance that you, Lord, are with me. I trust in your guidance, provision, and protection. I know that no weapon formed against me shall prosper, and I am secure in your unfailing love.

20. I declare that Jezebel's spirit is crushed under the weight of your authority. I walk in holy boldness, knowing that I am more than a conqueror. I will not be intimidated, for I am empowered by your Spirit. In Jesus' mighty name, amen.

## Chapter 36

# The Spirit of Esther:
# Awakening Courage to Confront Jezebel

The story of Queen Esther in the Bible is a powerful example of courage and boldness in the face of Jezebel's influence. In this chapter, we will explore the spirit of Esther and how it can awaken courage within us to confront Jezebel. We will delve into the characteristics of Esther, the challenges she faced, and the lessons we can learn from her story. By embracing the spirit of Esther, we can overcome fear, step into our God-given authority, and confront the spirit of Jezebel with holy boldness.

1. The Courageous Identity of Esther:
   - Esther's story begins with her identity as an orphaned Jewish girl who became queen. She had a humble background, yet she was chosen for such a time as this. We learn that courage can arise from unexpected places, and God equips us with the strength to confront Jezebel's influence.

2. A Hidden Purpose Unveiled:
   - Esther initially kept her Jewish heritage hidden, but Mordecai encouraged her to use her position to bring deliverance to her people. This teaches us that sometimes our purpose is hidden, and

it is through God's guidance and the support of others that our purpose is revealed.

3. The Power of Prayer and Fasting:
   - Before approaching the king to intercede for her people, Esther called for a time of prayer and fasting. This demonstrates the importance of seeking God's guidance, wisdom, and strength through prayer and fasting when confronting Jezebel's influence.

4. Confronting Fear and Embracing Risk:
   - Esther faced a life-threatening situation by approaching the king without being summoned. However, she chose to confront her fear and embrace the risk, declaring, "If I perish, I perish." We learn that confronting Jezebel requires stepping out of our comfort zones and taking risks for the sake of God's Kingdom.

5. Gathering Support and Unity:
   - Esther sought unity and support by calling for a collective fast among her people. She recognized the importance of community and rallied them together to stand against Jezebel's destructive plans. This teaches us the significance of gathering support and unity when confronting Jezebel's influence.

6. The Power of Timing and Divine Appointments:
   - Esther's courage was marked by her understanding of divine timing. She waited for the right moment to approach the king,

trusting in God's perfect timing. This reminds us to be patient, discerning, and aligned with God's timing when confronting Jezebel's influence.

7. Boldly Speaking Truth:
- Esther fearlessly exposed Haman's plot and spoke truth to the king, even at great personal risk. Her courage in speaking up against injustice teaches us the importance of boldly speaking truth, even when it is difficult or unpopular.

8. The Cost of Confrontation:
- Esther faced personal sacrifice and potential danger when she confronted Jezebel's influence. This reminds us that confronting Jezebel may come at a cost, but the impact and freedom it brings to others are worth the sacrifice.

9. The Victory of God's Deliverance:
- Through Esther's courage and intervention, God brought about a great deliverance for His people. This highlights the truth that when we confront Jezebel's influence with holy boldness, God's power and deliverance are at work.

Awakening the Spirit of Esther:

1. Embracing Your Identity:

- Like Esther, embrace your identity as a chosen child of God, uniquely equipped to confront Jezebel's influence. Recognize that you have been called for such a time as this and that God has a purpose for your life.

## 2. Seeking God's Guidance:
- Seek God's guidance through prayer and fasting. Dedicate time to hear His voice, receive His wisdom, and align yourself with His will as you confront Jezebel's influence.

## 3. Overcoming Fear with Faith:
- Confront your fears by putting your trust in God. Draw strength from His promises, knowing that He is with you and empowers you to overcome any obstacle or fear that Jezebel's spirit may try to instill.

## 4. Stepping out of the Comfort Zone:
- Be willing to step out of your comfort zone and take risks for the sake of God's Kingdom. Remember that holy boldness often requires stepping into unfamiliar territory and embracing the unknown.

## 5. Seeking Support and Unity:
- Surround yourself with like-minded believers who support and encourage you. Seek unity and collective prayer as you confront

Jezebel's influence, knowing that there is power in the collective stand against her destructive plans.

6. Discerning God's Timing:
   - Develop a sensitivity to God's timing and guidance. Seek His leading as you confront Jezebel's influence, trusting that He will open doors, orchestrate divine appointments, and align circumstances according to His perfect timing.

7. Speaking Truth with Love:
   - Boldly speak truth with love, just as Esther did. Stand up against injustice, expose deception, and speak out against the lies propagated by Jezebel's spirit. Let your words be guided by the love and wisdom of God.

8. Counting the Cost:
   - Recognize that confronting Jezebel's influence may come at a cost. Be prepared to make sacrifices, trusting that God's purposes are greater than any personal loss or discomfort.

9. Trusting in God's Deliverance:
   - Place your trust in God's deliverance. As you confront Jezebel's influence with holy boldness, believe that God is working behind the scenes, bringing about His victory and deliverance in the lives of those impacted by her spirit.

The spirit of Esther awakens within us the courage and boldness necessary to confront Jezebel's influence. By embracing our identity, seeking God's guidance, overcoming fear, stepping out in faith, and standing in unity with other believers, we can effectively confront Jezebel's spirit with holy boldness. Let us emulate the bravery and wisdom of Queen Esther as we arise as modern-day Esthers, bringing deliverance and freedom to those oppressed by Jezebel's influence.

## Deliverance Prayer

1. Heavenly Father, I come before you in the name of Jesus, empowered by the Spirit of Esther. I declare that I am anointed and equipped to confront Jezebel's influence with holy boldness and courage.

2. I renounce every spirit of fear, timidity, and insecurity that Jezebel's influence has tried to instill in my life. I declare that I walk in the confidence and courage of the Spirit of Esther.

3. I break every stronghold of intimidation and manipulation that Jezebel's spirit has established. I declare that I am free from her tactics, and I walk in the authority and power given to me by Christ.

4.  I declare that I am chosen and appointed by God for such a time as this. I embrace my identity as a vessel of His purpose, standing against Jezebel's destructive plans.

5.  I pray for a fresh infilling of the Holy Spirit, awakening the spirit of Esther within me. Fill me with courage, discernment, and wisdom to confront Jezebel's influence with grace and love.

6.  I bind and rebuke every lying spirit associated with Jezebel's influence. I declare that the truth of God's Word prevails, exposing every deception and manipulation.

7.  I declare that I walk in divine timing, aligned with God's purposes. I trust that He will open doors and orchestrate divine appointments as I confront Jezebel's influence.

8.  I release forgiveness towards those who have been used by Jezebel's spirit to intimidate or harm me. I choose to walk in love and extend grace, knowing that forgiveness releases me from the bondage of bitterness and resentment.

9.  I pray for unity and support from fellow believers as we stand together against Jezebel's influence. Let us encourage one another, pray for one another, and be a source of strength in our confrontation with her spirit.

10. I declare that I am filled with holy boldness to speak truth in the face of Jezebel's lies. I will not be silenced or intimidated, but I will boldly proclaim the truth of God's Word.

11. I pray for divine strategies and discernment as I confront Jezebel's influence. Grant me the wisdom to expose her tactics and the courage to confront her stronghold in every area of my life.

12. I release the power of prayer and fasting to dismantle Jezebel's influence. I intercede for those under her control, praying for their deliverance and restoration.

13. I bind and render powerless every principality, power, and ruler of darkness associated with Jezebel's spirit. I declare their influence is broken in the mighty name of Jesus.

14. I declare that Jezebel's influence will not hinder or derail God's purposes for my life. I am focused, determined, and unwavering in my pursuit of God's calling.

15. I pray for courage and discernment to recognize Jezebel's spirit and its tactics in the world around me. Open my eyes to see her influence and empower me to confront it with boldness.

16. I reject compromise and wavering in the face of Jezebel's influence. I stand firm in my convictions, knowing that God's truth prevails over every lie and deception.

17. I pray for the release of divine favor and open doors as I confront Jezebel's influence. Grant me opportunities to speak truth, expose deception, and bring freedom to those under her sway.

18. I declare that I am a vessel of honor and righteousness, empowered by the Spirit of God. Jezebel's spirit has no authority over me, for I am covered by the blood of Jesus.

19. I release prophetic declarations against Jezebel's influence. I declare that her strongholds are dismantled, her influence is diminished, and her power is broken in the name of Jesus.

20. I celebrate the victory that is already won in Christ. I walk in the confidence that Jezebel's influence is defeated, and I am an overcomer through Him who strengthens me.

## Chapter 37

# Jezebel's Destruction: Rebuilding the Broken Walls

Jezebel spirit is known for its destructive nature, seeking to tear down and undermine the work of God. In this chapter, we will explore the devastating effects of Jezebel's influence and the process of rebuilding the broken walls that she has caused. We will examine the spiritual, emotional, and relational damage caused by Jezebel's spirit and provide insights on how to rebuild and restore what has been broken. Through the power of God's grace, healing, and restoration, we can overcome the devastation of Jezebel's destruction and rebuild strong and fortified walls in our lives.

1. Understanding Jezebel's Destructive Nature:
   - Jezebel's spirit operates with the intent to destroy and undermine the work of God in our lives. It seeks to tear down relationships, distort truth, and hinder spiritual growth. Understanding her tactics and destructive nature is crucial in the process of rebuilding.

2. Assessing the Damage:
   - It is important to assess the extent of the damage caused by Jezebel's influence. This includes examining the areas of our lives

that have been affected, such as our spiritual walk, emotions, relationships, and identity.

3. Seeking God's Healing and Restoration:
   - The first step in rebuilding is seeking God's healing and restoration. We must bring our brokenness before Him, allowing Him to heal our wounds, restore our identity, and renew our strength.

4. Embracing Forgiveness:
   - Forgiveness is a crucial aspect of rebuilding. We must release bitterness, resentment, and anger towards those who have been influenced by Jezebel's spirit. Through forgiveness, we open the door for healing and restoration.

5. Rebuilding Spiritual Foundations:
   - Rebuilding begins with strengthening our spiritual foundations. This involves deepening our relationship with God, immersing ourselves in His Word, and re-establishing a firm foundation in prayer, worship, and fellowship.

6. Restoring Emotional Wholeness:
   - Jezebel's spirit can cause emotional wounds and trauma. Restoring emotional wholeness requires seeking professional help if needed, processing our emotions in a healthy way, and allowing the Holy Spirit to bring healing and restoration.

7. Rebuilding Trust and Healthy Relationships:
-   Jezebel's influence can damage trust and disrupt healthy relationships. Rebuilding trust involves open communication, setting healthy boundaries, and allowing time for relationships to heal. It also requires discernment in choosing healthy connections moving forward.

8. Guarding Against Jezebel's Return:
-   Rebuilding also involves guarding against Jezebel's return. This requires staying vigilant, discerning her tactics, and maintaining a strong spiritual defense. It is important to remain rooted in God's Word and to surround ourselves with godly accountability and support.

9. Walking in Spiritual Authority:
-   Rebuilding after Jezebel's destruction requires walking in our spiritual authority. We must understand our identity as children of God, armed with His power and authority. By walking in this authority, we can resist Jezebel's influence and rebuild with confidence.

10. Cultivating a Culture of Discernment:
-   To prevent further damage, we must cultivate a culture of discernment. This involves being vigilant in recognizing and addressing Jezebel's tactics in our personal lives, relationships,

and church communities. It requires sharpening our spiritual discernment and seeking the guidance of the Holy Spirit.

11. Restoring God's Kingdom Purposes:
- Rebuilding after Jezebel's destruction is ultimately about restoring God's Kingdom purposes. It is about reestablishing our focus on advancing His Kingdom, walking in obedience, and fulfilling our calling with renewed passion and commitment.

12. Embracing the Beauty of Restoration:
- Though Jezebel's destruction is devastating, there is beauty in restoration. God can take the broken pieces of our lives and rebuild something even stronger and more beautiful. As we allow Him to work in us, He transforms our pain into purpose and our brokenness into testimony.

Rebuilding the Broken Walls:

1. Heavenly Father, I come before you, acknowledging the devastation caused by Jezebel's influence in my life. I surrender my brokenness to you and invite your healing and restoration.

2. I confess any bitterness, resentment, or unforgiveness that I have harbored towards those influenced by Jezebel's spirit. I choose to forgive and release them into your hands, knowing that you are the ultimate judge and healer.

3. I invite your Holy Spirit to heal the wounds caused by Jezebel's destruction. Bring your comfort, peace, and wholeness to every area of my life that has been affected.

4. I declare that I am a new creation in Christ Jesus. I renounce the lies and distortions that Jezebel's spirit has spoken over me, and I embrace the truth of your Word and your love for me.

5. I rebuild my spiritual foundations on your Word, prayer, and worship. I commit to deepening my relationship with you and seeking Your guidance in every area of my life.

6. I surrender my emotions to you, knowing that you are the ultimate healer of the brokenhearted. Mend my emotional wounds and restore me to a place of joy, peace, and emotional stability.

7. I seek your wisdom in rebuilding trust and healthy relationships. Help me set healthy boundaries, communicate effectively, and discern healthy connections from toxic ones.

8. I am aware of Jezebel's tactics, and I commit to remaining vigilant. I put on the full armor of God and declare that no weapon formed against me shall prosper.

9. I walk in my spiritual authority as a child of God. I declare that Jezebel's influence has no power over me, for greater is He who is in me than he who is in the world.

10. I cultivate a culture of discernment in my life. Open my eyes to recognize Jezebel's tactics and empower me to address them with wisdom, love, and grace.

11. I surrender my life to your Kingdom purposes. Use me to advance your Kingdom, to be a light in the darkness, and to bring hope and healing to others who have been affected by Jezebel's spirit.

12. I embrace the beauty of restoration. I believe that you are able to rebuild and restore what has been broken, and I trust that you will bring beauty from the ashes.

---

Jezebel's destruction is devastating, but it is not the end of the story. Through God's healing and restoration, we can rebuild the broken walls and emerge stronger and more resilient. By seeking God's wisdom, cultivating discernment, and embracing the process of restoration, we can overcome the effects of Jezebel's influence and walk in the fullness of God's purpose for our lives. Let us rebuild with faith, hope, and the assurance that God is with us every step of the way.

## Deliverance Prayer

1. Heavenly Father, I come before you in the mighty name of Jesus, taking authority over Jezebel's destructive influence in my life. I declare that her power is broken, and I am entering a season of rebuilding and restoration.

2. I renounce every lie, deception, and manipulation that Jezebel's spirit has spoken over me. I declare that I am a child of God, redeemed and set free by the blood of Jesus.

3. I release the power of the Holy Spirit to heal the wounds caused by Jezebel's destruction. Let your healing balm flow through every area of my life, bringing restoration and wholeness.

4. I break every generational curse and pattern of destruction associated with Jezebel's spirit. I declare that the cycle of destruction stops with me, and I walk in the freedom and victory that Christ has secured for me.

5. I declare that I am empowered by the Word of God to rebuild the broken walls. I embrace your promises, your truth, and your guidance as I embark on this journey of restoration.

6. I pray for divine wisdom and discernment as I assess the areas of my life that have been affected by Jezebel's influence. Show me

where to begin the process of rebuilding and give me clarity in setting priorities.

7. I release forgiveness towards those who have been used by Jezebel's spirit to cause destruction in my life. I choose to forgive them, just as Christ has forgiven me, and I release them into Your hands.

8. I declare that the power of Jezebel's spirit is broken over my relationships. I pray for reconciliation, healing, and restoration in my relationships, and I break the stronghold of division and strife.

9. I rebuild my spiritual foundations on the rock of Jesus Christ. I surrender my life afresh to Him, seeking His guidance and allowing Him to rebuild and strengthen my faith.

10. I take authority over every spirit of fear and timidity that Jezebel's influence has instilled in my life. I declare that I walk in the courage and boldness of the Holy Spirit as I rebuild and confront the works of darkness.

11. I pray for divine connections and godly relationships to be established in my life. Surround me with believers who will support, encourage, and edify me as I rebuild and grow in you.

12. I break every stronghold of despair and hopelessness that Jezebel's spirit has tried to impose on me. I declare that I am filled with hope, faith, and confidence in God's ability to restore what has been broken.

13. I release the power of restoration and renewal in my finances, career, and ministry. I declare that as I trust in the Lord, He will rebuild and bless every area of my life that has been affected by Jezebel's destruction.

14. I rebuke every spirit of sabotage and hindrance that Jezebel's spirit has sent against my progress and prosperity. I declare that I am moving forward with divine acceleration and supernatural favor.

15. I rebuild the broken walls of my identity and self-worth. I declare that I am fearfully and wonderfully made, and I embrace my true identity as a child of God.

16. I pray for divine strategies and guidance as I rebuild. Give me creative ideas, supernatural insights, and wisdom to make wise decisions that align with your purposes.

17. I declare that as I rebuild, I am becoming a living testimony of your power and grace. Use my restoration story to bring hope and encouragement to others who have been affected by Jezebel's destruction.

18. I break the power of Jezebel's spirit over my thought life. I take every thought captive to the obedience of Christ and declare that my mind is renewed by the truth of God's Word.

19. I release the power of praise and worship as I rebuild. I declare that in the midst of the rebuilding process, I will worship and praise you, knowing that your presence brings breakthrough and victory.

20. I declare that as I rebuild the broken walls, your glory will be revealed. Let your light shine through me as a testimony of your faithfulness, love, and restoration power.

## Chapter 38

# Discerning Jezebel's Jealousy: Embracing God's Love

Jezebel's spirit is not only destructive and manipulative, but it is also fueled by a deep-seated jealousy. In this chapter, we will explore the underlying jealousy behind Jezebel's actions and learn how to discern and overcome this destructive aspect of her influence. We will delve into the roots of jealousy, its impact on relationships, and the ways in which it hinders our growth and spiritual walk. More importantly, we will discover how to embrace God's love and walk in freedom, breaking free from the chains of Jezebel's jealousy.

1. Understanding Jezebel's Jealousy:
   - Jealousy is at the core of Jezebel's spirit. It stems from her desire for control, power, and attention. Understanding the root of her jealousy is crucial in discerning and dismantling her influence.

2. Unmasking Jealousy in Our Lives:
   - It is essential to examine our own hearts and confront any traces of jealousy within ourselves. Jezebel's spirit seeks to stir up jealousy in others, but by identifying and dealing with it in our own lives, we can break its power.

3. The Destructive Power of Jealousy:
- Jealousy breeds comparison, rivalry, and division. It hinders our ability to celebrate the success and blessings of others and keeps us trapped in a mindset of scarcity and competition.

4. Overcoming Jealousy through God's Love:
- God's love is the antidote to jealousy. By embracing His unconditional love for us and others, we can walk in freedom and release the chains of jealousy that Jezebel's spirit tries to bind us with.

5. Cultivating Contentment and Gratitude:
- Contentment and gratitude are powerful weapons against jealousy. When we learn to appreciate what God has given us and rejoice in the blessings of others, we break free from the grip of jealousy.

6. Finding Identity in Christ:
- Jezebel's spirit attacks our identity, seeking to diminish our self-worth and value. By finding our identity in Christ and understanding our unique purpose and calling, we become immune to the jealousy that Jezebel's spirit tries to instill.

7. Celebrating the Success of Others:
- Instead of being threatened by the success of others, we should learn to celebrate and rejoice with them. Jezebel's spirit tries to

foster competition and comparison, but we can choose to walk in a spirit of unity and encouragement.

8. Guarding Against Envy and Comparison:
   - Envy and comparison go hand in hand with jealousy. We must guard our hearts against these toxic attitudes and focus on the unique journey and calling that God has for each of us.

9. Praying for Those Affected by Jezebel's Jealousy:
   - Jezebel's spirit not only stirs up jealousy in others but also affects those under her influence. We must pray for their liberation, that they may be set free from the chains of jealousy and embrace God's love.

10. Extending Forgiveness and Grace:
   - Jealousy can lead to bitterness and resentment. We must extend forgiveness and grace to those who have been used by Jezebel's spirit to stir up jealousy. In doing so, we release the power of God's love and break the cycle of bitterness.

11. Embracing Humility and Servanthood:
   - Jezebel's spirit thrives on pride and self-promotion. By embracing humility and servanthood, we counteract the jealousy that Jezebel's spirit tries to ignite within us.

12. Pursuing God's Kingdom Above All:

- When we shift our focus from self to God's kingdom, we break free from the chains of jealousy. By seeking first His kingdom and His righteousness, we align ourselves with His purposes and find fulfillment in His love.

13. Fostering Healthy Relationships:
- Jealousy thrives in toxic and unhealthy relationships. We must surround ourselves with healthy connections that encourage, support, and celebrate one another, fostering an environment of love and unity.

14. Renewing Our Mind with God's Word:
- The renewing of our minds with God's Word is crucial in combating jealousy. By meditating on Scripture, we align our thoughts with His truth and allow His Word to transform our perspective.

15. Rejecting Jezebel's Lies:
- Jezebel's spirit whispers lies of comparison, inadequacy, and insufficiency. We must reject these lies and replace them with God's truth, reminding ourselves of our worth and value in Him.

16. Seeking God's Wisdom and Discernment:
- Jezebel's spirit is subtle and cunning. We must seek God's wisdom and discernment to recognize her tactics and the jealousy she tries

to stir within us. By relying on the Holy Spirit, we can navigate through her deceptions.

17. Surrendering Our Desires to God:
   - Jealousy often arises from unmet desires and unfulfilled dreams. We must surrender these desires to God, trusting in His perfect timing and plan for our lives.

18. Walking in Love and Compassion:
   - Love and compassion are powerful weapons against jealousy. By actively loving others and extending compassion, we break down the walls of jealousy and build bridges of unity and understanding.

19. Praying for God's Heart:
   - Jezebel's spirit seeks to divide and destroy, but we can pray for God's heart of love and reconciliation. As we intercede for others, we release the power of God's love to transform hearts and relationships.

20. Embracing a Life of Abundance:
   - Jezebel's spirit operates from a mindset of scarcity and lack. We choose to embrace God's abundant provision and blessings, knowing that His love and grace are more than enough to fulfill every desire of our hearts.

Jezebel's spirit seeks to stir up jealousy and destroy the unity and love among God's people. However, through discernment, embracing God's love, and cultivating gratitude, contentment, and humility, we can overcome Jezebel's destructive influence. Let us choose to walk in freedom, rejecting jealousy, and embracing the abundant life that God has for us. By doing so, we not only break free from the chains of Jezebel's jealousy but also become vessels of God's love, unity, and reconciliation in the world.

## Deliverance Prayer

1. Heavenly Father, I come before you in the name of Jesus, taking authority over Jezebel's spirit of jealousy. I declare that her power is broken, and I choose to embrace your unconditional love.

2. I renounce every trace of jealousy within me, whether conscious or unconscious. I release it into your hands, knowing that your love is greater than any jealousy I may feel.

3. I declare that your love fills every crevice of my being, leaving no room for jealousy to take root. Your love casts out all fear, insecurity, and comparison.

4. I pray for discernment to recognize Jezebel's jealousy in my own heart and in the actions of others. Open my eyes to see beyond the surface and discern the underlying motives and intentions.

5. I choose to celebrate the success, blessings, and achievements of others. I reject the spirit of competition and comparison and embrace a heart of gratitude and joy for the goodness you pour out on others.

6. I release forgiveness towards those who have stirred up jealousy in my life. I choose to extend grace, knowing that we are all susceptible to the destructive influence of Jezebel's spirit.

7. I pray for healing and restoration in relationships that have been affected by jealousy. I declare unity, understanding, and love to reign in every connection, breaking down walls of division and restoring trust.

8. I reject every lie of inadequacy and insufficiency that Jezebel's spirit whispers in my ear. I choose to meditate on your Word and embrace the truth of my identity in Christ.

9. I surrender my desires and dreams to you, trusting in your perfect plan for my life. I release any jealousy that arises from unmet expectations and choose to walk in contentment and peace.

10. I pray for an overflow of your love to fill my heart. Pour out your love so abundantly that it overflows onto others, dispelling

jealousy and fostering an environment of unity and encouragement.

11. I declare that I am secure in your love. I am deeply loved, accepted, and valued by you, and no amount of comparison or jealousy can diminish the truth of your love for me.

12. I rebuke every spirit of envy and covetousness that Jezebel's spirit tries to instill. I declare that my focus is on your Kingdom and your purposes, not on what others possess or achieve.

13. I pray for your wisdom and discernment to navigate relationships and situations where jealousy may arise. Guide me in responding with grace, humility, and compassion, rather than allowing jealousy to dictate my actions.

14. I declare that I walk in the freedom of your love. I am released from the bondage of jealousy, and I choose to embrace the abundant life you have for me.

15. I release blessings and prayers of love over those who have been influenced by Jezebel's spirit of jealousy. May they encounter your love in a profound way and be set free from its destructive grip.

16. I reject comparison and competition in every aspect of my life. I choose to embrace collaboration, encouragement, and unity, knowing that we are all unique and valued members of your body.

17. I pray for a heart of humility and servanthood. Help me to genuinely rejoice with those who rejoice and to support and uplift others without seeking recognition or validation.

18. I break the power of jealousy over my thought life. I take captive every jealous thought and replace it with thoughts of love, gratitude, and affirmation for others.

19. I pray for a revelation of your love that surpasses all understanding. Help me to fully embrace your love and to extend it to others, breaking the cycle of jealousy and fostering a culture of love and acceptance.

20. I declare that your love is transforming me from the inside out. As I embrace your love and reject jealousy, I am being conformed to the image of Christ and walking in the fullness of your purpose for my life.

Chapter 39

# Jezebel's Seductive Manipulation: Guarding Your Heart

Jezebel's spirit operates through seductive manipulation, seeking to control and deceive. In this chapter, we will explore the tactics of Jezebel's seductive manipulation and learn how to guard our hearts against her cunning schemes. We will delve into the subtle ways in which she attempts to gain influence and control, and we will discover practical strategies to protect ourselves from her deceit. By understanding her tactics and fortifying our hearts with truth and discernment, we can navigate through her seductive manipulation and walk in the freedom and wisdom of God.

1. Understanding Jezebel's Seductive Manipulation:
   - Jezebel's spirit is skilled at using seductive tactics to gain control over others. We will explore the ways in which she manipulates, deceives, and entices her victims.

2. Recognizing the Signs of Jezebel's Seductive Manipulation:
   - It is essential to be aware of the warning signs of Jezebel's seductive manipulation. We will examine the subtle cues and behaviors that indicate her presence.

3. The Dangers of Jezebel's Seductive Manipulation:

- Jezebel's seductive manipulation can lead to emotional and spiritual bondage. We will discuss the potential dangers and consequences of falling into her web of deceit.

4. Guarding Your Heart with Discernment:
   - Discernment is key in protecting ourselves from Jezebel's seductive manipulation. We will explore how to cultivate discernment and the importance of relying on the Holy Spirit for guidance.

5. Anchoring Yourself in God's Word:
   - God's Word is a firm foundation against Jezebel's seductive manipulation. We will discover the power of Scripture in exposing her lies and empowering us to stand strong.

6. Cultivating Intimacy with God:
   - A deep, intimate relationship with God is vital in guarding our hearts against Jezebel's seductive manipulation. We will explore practical ways to foster intimacy with Him and develop a sensitivity to His voice.

7. Establishing Boundaries:
   - Setting healthy boundaries is crucial in protecting ourselves from Jezebel's seductive manipulation. We will discuss the importance of clear boundaries and how to enforce them in our relationships.

8. Strengthening Your Identity in Christ:
   - Jezebel's spirit preys on insecurities and seeks to distort our identity. We will discover the importance of knowing our identity in Christ and the power it holds in resisting her seductive tactics.

9. Seeking Accountability and Community:
   - Accountability and community are essential safeguards against Jezebel's seductive manipulation. We will explore the role of trusted relationships in providing support, encouragement, and accountability.

10. Guarding Your Mind and Thoughts:
   - Jezebel's spirit targets our minds, planting seeds of doubt, confusion, and deception. We will discuss practical strategies to guard our minds and renew our thoughts with truth.

11. Praying for Discernment and Protection:
   - Prayer is a powerful tool in guarding our hearts against Jezebel's seductive manipulation. We will learn how to pray for discernment, wisdom, and protection from her schemes.

12. Overcoming the Fear of Rejection and Abandonment:
   - Jezebel's seductive manipulation often exploits our fear of rejection and abandonment. We will explore how to overcome these fears and find our security and validation in God alone.

13. Walking in Transparency and Authenticity:
    - Jezebel's spirit thrives in secrecy and manipulation. We will discover the freedom and protection that come from walking in transparency and authenticity, refusing to play into her games.

14. Recognizing Your Worth and Value:
    - Jezebel's seductive manipulation tries to undermine our self-worth and value. We will delve into the truth of our inherent worth in God's eyes and learn how to resist her attempts to devalue us.

15. Trusting God's Timing and Providence:
    - Jezebel's spirit often tempts us to take matters into our own hands, to manipulate and control outcomes. We will explore the importance of trusting God's timing and surrendering to His providence.

16. Discerning False Promises and Manipulative Tactics:
    - Jezebel's seductive manipulation often comes with false promises and manipulative tactics. We will learn how to discern her deceit and avoid falling into her traps.

17. Guarding Your Emotions:
    - Jezebel's spirit seeks to manipulate our emotions and keep us in a state of turmoil. We will discover how to guard our emotions and find stability in God's peace and truth.

18. Developing Emotional Intelligence:
- Emotional intelligence is a valuable skill in navigating Jezebel's seductive manipulation. We will explore how to cultivate emotional intelligence and discern the motivations behind manipulative behavior.

19. Seeking Healing from Past Wounds and Trauma:
- Jezebel's spirit can exploit past wounds and trauma, using them to manipulate and control. We will delve into the healing process and seek restoration from past hurts, finding freedom from her influence.

20. Walking in Spiritual Authority:
- Jezebel's seductive manipulation crumbles in the face of spiritual authority. We will learn how to walk in the authority given to us by Jesus and resist her attempts to manipulate and deceive.

---

Guarding our hearts against Jezebel's seductive manipulation is a necessary step in our journey of spiritual maturity and freedom. By understanding her tactics, anchoring ourselves in God's Word, and cultivating discernment, we can protect ourselves from her deceitful schemes. Let us be vigilant, walking in transparency, authenticity, and emotional intelligence, relying on God's wisdom and guidance. As we guard our hearts, we will walk in the freedom, truth, and love that God has called us to, escaping the snare of Jezebel's seductive manipulation.

# Deliverance Prayer

1. Heavenly Father, I come before you in the name of Jesus, taking authority over Jezebel's spirit of seductive manipulation. I declare that her power is broken, and I am covered by the blood of Jesus.

2. I renounce and reject every seductive tactic of Jezebel's spirit. I declare that I am wise to her deceitful schemes, and I will not be enticed or manipulated by her seduction.

3. I pray for discernment and wisdom to recognize the signs of Jezebel's seductive manipulation. Open my eyes to see beyond the outward appearance and discern her true motives and intentions.

4. I declare that my heart is guarded with the truth of God's Word. I meditate on your promises and declare them over my life, knowing that your truth sets me free from the lies of Jezebel's seduction.

5. I surrender my heart to you, Lord, and ask you to cleanse it from any trace of susceptibility to Jezebel's seductive manipulation. Fill my heart with your love, grace, and discernment.

6. I declare that I am rooted and grounded in Christ, and my identity is secure in Him. I reject any false sense of validation or

acceptance that Jezebel's seduction may offer and find my worth in Christ alone.

7. I set healthy boundaries in my relationships, guarding my heart against manipulation and deceit. I refuse to be swayed by flattery or false promises but seek genuine connections based on truth and trust.

8. I rebuke the spirit of confusion that Jezebel's seduction tries to bring into my mind. I declare that my thoughts are clear, focused, and aligned with the truth of God's Word.

9. I pray for a spirit of discernment to recognize Jezebel's spirit operating in the lives of others. Help me to walk in love and extend grace, while also maintaining healthy boundaries and protecting myself from her manipulation.

10. I release forgiveness toward those who have been used by Jezebel's spirit to manipulate and deceive. I choose to extend grace and pray for their deliverance and restoration.

11. I resist the temptation to compromise my values, integrity, or faith in the face of Jezebel's seductive manipulation. I stand firm in the truth and choose righteousness over temporary satisfaction.

12. I declare that my emotions are anchored in God's peace and truth. I reject any manipulation of my emotions and choose to rely on the stability of His presence.

13. I release any past wounds or traumas that may make me vulnerable to Jezebel's seductive manipulation. I invite your healing and restoration into those areas, closing the door on her influence.

14. I pray for an increased measure of emotional intelligence to discern the underlying motivations behind manipulative behavior. Help me to respond with wisdom, grace, and assertiveness when faced with manipulation.

15. I declare that I walk in the spiritual authority given to me by Jesus Christ. I take authority over Jezebel's spirit and declare that she has no power or influence over my life.

16. I pray for divine connections and relationships that are aligned with your will. Surround me with trustworthy individuals who operate in truth, love, and accountability, guarding me against Jezebel's seduction.

17. I invite the Holy Spirit to guide and lead me in every decision, interaction, and relationship. Help me to discern His voice and follow His promptings, resisting the manipulation of Jezebel's spirit.

18. I declare that I am strong in the Lord and in the power of His might. I am equipped with the armor of God, and no seductive manipulation of Jezebel's spirit can penetrate or deceive me.

19. I pray for the deliverance and freedom of those who have fallen prey to Jezebel's seductive manipulation. May they be set free from her grasp and come to know the truth and love of Jesus.

20. I declare that my heart is a dwelling place for God's love, truth, and discernment. I am a vessel of His light, shining brightly in a world of darkness, and Jezebel's seductive manipulation has no place in my life.

## Chapter 40

## The Sound of Victory: Worship Warfare against Jezebel

In this chapter, we will explore the power of worship as a weapon in the spiritual warfare against Jezebel's influence. Worship is not merely a musical expression; it is a spiritual weapon that releases the sound of victory in the heavenly realms. We will discover how worship can break through the strongholds of Jezebel's spirit, dismantle her influence, and bring freedom and deliverance to individuals and communities. Through an in-depth exploration of worship warfare strategies, practical insights, and biblical examples, we will learn how to engage in worship that overcomes the seductive tactics of Jezebel and ushers in the triumph of God's Kingdom.

1. The Weapon of Worship:
    - We will establish the foundation of worship as a powerful weapon in spiritual warfare, understanding its significance and role in confronting Jezebel's spirit.

2. Worshiping in Spirit and Truth:
    - Discover the importance of worshiping God in spirit and truth, as we align our hearts and minds with His Word and invite the Holy Spirit to lead us in worship.

3. The Sound of Freedom:
- Learn how the sound of worship releases freedom and breaks the chains of bondage imposed by Jezebel's spirit. Explore the transformative power of worship to bring deliverance and liberation.

4. Prophetic Worship:
- Dive into the realm of prophetic worship and its ability to expose Jezebel's tactics, release God's prophetic declarations, and bring alignment with His Kingdom purposes.

5. Spiritual Atmosphere Shift:
- Uncover how worship creates a spiritual atmosphere that opposes Jezebel's influence, dismantles her strongholds, and invites the presence and authority of God to reign.

6. Singing the Word:
- Discover the impact of singing Scripture and declaring God's Word through worship. Learn how it confounds the plans of Jezebel's spirit and establishes God's truth in our hearts and circumstances.

7. Warfare through Praise:

- Understand the power of praise as a weapon against Jezebel's spirit. Discover how praise disarms the enemy and releases the authority of God, transforming the spiritual landscape.

8. Intimacy with God:
- Deepen your understanding of worship as a vehicle for intimate connection with God. Learn how cultivating intimacy through worship strengthens our resistance to Jezebel's seductive manipulation.

9. Breakthrough Worship:
- Explore the concept of breakthrough worship and how it empowers us to push through barriers, dismantle strongholds, and seize victory over Jezebel's spirit.

10. Corporate Worship:
- Discover the strength and impact of corporate worship in warfare against Jezebel's influence. Learn how unified worship creates a powerful synergy that overwhelms the enemy.

11. Cultivating a Lifestyle of Worship:
- Understand the importance of a lifestyle of worship in maintaining victory over Jezebel's spirit. Learn how to integrate worship into every aspect of your life, cultivating a continual atmosphere of spiritual warfare.

12. Singing in the Night Season:
   - Discover the power of worship in the midst of spiritual darkness and opposition. Learn how worship can shift the atmosphere and bring breakthrough even in the most challenging seasons.

13. Jezebel's Opposition to Worship:
   - Gain insight into how Jezebel's spirit opposes worship and seeks to silence the sound of victory. Learn to identify and overcome the barriers she erects to hinder worship warfare.

14. The Authority of the Name of Jesus:
   - Understand the authority and power inherent in the name of Jesus. Learn how to invoke His name through worship and see Jezebel's spirit retreat in the face of His supremacy.

15. Dancing in Warfare:
   - Explore the role of dance as a powerful expression of worship warfare. Discover how dancing before the Lord releases joy, breaks through resistance, and confounds Jezebel's strategies.

16. Soaking in God's Presence:
   - Delve into the practice of soaking in God's presence through worship. Learn how it opens the heavens, invites divine encounters, and weakens the influence of Jezebel's spirit.

17. Ascending in Worship:

- Understand the concept of ascending in worship, where we go deeper into the heavenly realms, leaving behind the constraints of Jezebel's influence and accessing the authority of heaven.

18. Spiritual Instruments of Warfare:
  - Explore the use of spiritual instruments in worship warfare. Learn how they can amplify the sound of victory, release prophetic declarations, and dismantle Jezebel's strongholds.

19. Worshiping in Unity:
  - Discover the power of unified worship in breaking down Jezebel's divisive tactics. Learn how to cultivate unity, harmony, and agreement in worship, creating a force that Jezebel cannot withstand.

20. Persistent Worship:
  - Understand the value of persistence in worship warfare. Learn how to press through discouragement, opposition, and spiritual resistance, knowing that breakthrough is on the other side.

---

Worship is a potent weapon in the spiritual warfare against Jezebel's seductive manipulation. As we engage in worship that is rooted in truth, fueled by the Holy Spirit, and aligned with God's Word, we release the sound of victory that shatters Jezebel's influence. Let us embrace the call to worship warfare, cultivating a lifestyle of worship, and entering into the fullness of God's presence. With the sound of victory ringing in our hearts and voices, we will see the transformative power of worship breaking chains, setting captives free, and establishing God's Kingdom on earth.

## Deliverance Prayer

1. Heavenly Father, I come before you in the name of Jesus, declaring that worship is a powerful weapon against Jezebel's influence. I take authority over every seductive manipulation of her spirit, and I release the sound of victory through worship.

2. Lord, I thank you for the privilege of worshiping you in spirit and truth. I invite the Holy Spirit to lead me in worship and empower me to release the sound of freedom and deliverance through my praise.

3. I declare that as I worship you, the chains of bondage imposed by Jezebel's spirit are broken. I release the sound of freedom and liberation, declaring the triumph of your Kingdom over her influence.

4. I engage in prophetic worship, declaring your truth and exposing the tactics of Jezebel's spirit. I release prophetic declarations that dismantle her influence and align us with your Kingdom purposes.

5. Lord, I understand that worship creates a spiritual atmosphere that opposes Jezebel's influence. I release the sound of victory, shifting the spiritual atmosphere and inviting your presence and authority to reign.

6. I sing your Word and declare your promises through worship. I release the sound of truth that confounds the plans of Jezebel's spirit and establishes your truth in my life and circumstances.

7. I engage in warfare through praise, knowing that praise disarms the enemy and releases your authority. I release the sound of praise that transforms the spiritual landscape and weakens Jezebel's influence.

8. Lord, as I worship you, I cultivate intimacy with you. I declare that my heart is filled with your love, grace, and discernment, making me resistant to Jezebel's seductive manipulation.

9. I set a spiritual atmosphere of breakthrough through worship. I release the sound of breakthrough that pushes through barriers, dismantles strongholds, and ushers in victory over Jezebel's spirit.

10. I understand the strength and impact of corporate worship in warfare against Jezebel's influence. I join with other believers, releasing a unified sound of worship that overwhelms the enemy and establishes Your authority.

11. Lord, I commit to cultivating a lifestyle of worship. I integrate worship into every aspect of my life, creating a continual atmosphere of spiritual warfare against Jezebel's influence.

12. I declare that even in the midst of spiritual darkness and opposition, I will sing and worship. I release the sound of worship that shifts the atmosphere and brings breakthrough.

13. I resist and overcome any opposition that Jezebel's spirit brings against worship. I declare that the sound of victory through worship cannot be silenced, and I continue to worship with boldness and confidence.

14. I invoke the name of Jesus through worship, knowing that His name carries authority and power. I release the sound of worship that causes Jezebel's spirit to retreat in the face of His supremacy.

15. I engage in dance as a powerful expression of worship warfare. I release the sound of joyful dancing that releases joy, breaks through resistance, and confounds Jezebel's strategies.

16. I soak in your presence through worship, inviting encounters with you that weaken Jezebel's influence and strengthen my spiritual resilience.

17. I ascend in worship, going deeper into the heavenly realms, leaving behind the constraints of Jezebel's influence, and accessing the authority of heaven. I release the sound of worship that brings heavenly breakthrough.

18. I use spiritual instruments in worship warfare, amplifying the sound of victory, releasing prophetic declarations, and dismantling Jezebel's strongholds.

19. Lord, I embrace unified worship, knowing that it breaks down Jezebel's divisive tactics. I release the sound of unified worship that creates a force she cannot withstand.

20. I persist in worship warfare, pressing through discouragement, opposition, and spiritual resistance. I release the sound of persistent worship, knowing that breakthrough is on the other side.

## Chapter 41

# Exposing Jezebel's False Doctrines: Holding Fast to Truth

In this chapter, we will uncover the deceptive nature of Jezebel's false doctrines and explore the importance of holding fast to truth in the face of her seductive manipulation. Jezebel's spirit seeks to distort and pervert the Word of God, leading people astray from the path of righteousness. We will delve into the various false doctrines propagated by Jezebel and equip ourselves with the knowledge and discernment to recognize and refute them. By anchoring ourselves in the truth of God's Word, we can stand firm against Jezebel's deceitful teachings and safeguard our faith.

1. The Danger of Deception:
   - We will examine the grave consequences of falling prey to Jezebel's false doctrines and understand the urgency of holding fast to truth.

2. Jezebel's Manipulation of Scripture:
   - Discover how Jezebel distorts and manipulates Scripture to support her deceptive teachings. Learn to discern her misuse of God's Word and avoid being led astray.

3. The Spirit of Error:

-   Gain insight into the spirit of error that operates through Jezebel's false doctrines. Understand its deceptive nature and the need for discernment in identifying and rejecting it.

4. The True Foundation of Faith:
-   Explore the importance of building our faith on the solid foundation of God's Word. Learn how to discern and reject the false doctrines propagated by Jezebel, anchoring ourselves in the truth.

5. Prosperity Gospel: Unmasking the Deception:
-   Expose the distortions and false promises of the prosperity gospel, which Jezebel often promotes. Learn to discern the true biblical principles of abundance and prosperity.

6. False Teachings on Spiritual Authority:
-   Uncover the false teachings on spiritual authority propagated by Jezebel's spirit. Understand the true nature of spiritual authority and how it should be exercised in alignment with God's Word.

7. Manipulation of Grace:
-   Discover how Jezebel manipulates the concept of grace to justify sinful behavior and compromise. Learn to embrace the true biblical understanding of grace as a transformative and empowering force.

8. Jezebel's Distortion of Gender Roles:
- Examine how Jezebel distorts and perverts God's design for gender roles, promoting an agenda contrary to biblical principles. Embrace the truth of God's plan for men and women.

9. False Teachings on Holiness and Sanctification:
- Unmask the false teachings on holiness and sanctification that Jezebel promotes. Embrace the biblical call to live a holy and set-apart life, empowered by the Holy Spirit.

10. Discerning False Prophets and Teachers:
- Develop the ability to discern false prophets and teachers who propagate Jezebel's false doctrines. Learn the characteristics and warning signs that reveal their true nature.

11. Cultivating Discernment:
- Understand the importance of cultivating discernment to recognize and refute Jezebel's false doctrines. Learn practical steps to grow in discernment through prayer, studying God's Word, and seeking the guidance of the Holy Spirit.

12. Embracing Sound Doctrine:
- Explore the significance of sound doctrine in safeguarding our faith against Jezebel's false teachings. Learn to discern and embrace the truth of God's Word as the ultimate standard of faith.

13. The Authority of Scripture:
    - Discover the unchanging authority of Scripture in the face of Jezebel's false doctrines. Embrace the Word of God as the final and infallible source of truth.

14. Cultivating a Berean Spirit:
    - Learn from the Bereans' example in Acts 17, who diligently examined the Scriptures to verify the teachings they received. Develop a spirit of discernment and a commitment to test all teachings against the Word of God.

15. Overcoming Jezebel's Deception through Prayer:
    - Understand the power of prayer in overcoming Jezebel's deception. Learn to pray for wisdom, discernment, and protection from her seductive manipulation.

16. Equipping Others with Truth:
    - Discover the importance of equipping others with the truth to counter Jezebel's false doctrines. Learn to share sound doctrine, engage in respectful dialogue, and disciple others in the truth of God's Word.

17. Standing Firm in Truth amidst Cultural Pressure:
    - Explore the challenges of standing firm in truth amidst cultural pressure and shifting ideologies. Learn to navigate cultural

currents while remaining anchored in the unchanging truth of God's Word.

18. Unity in Truth:
- Embrace the call for unity among believers based on the foundation of truth. Learn to distinguish between essential doctrines and secondary matters, fostering unity in the body of Christ.

19. Rejecting Compromise:
- Develop the resolve to reject compromise with Jezebel's false doctrines. Learn to hold fast to truth and remain steadfast in the face of opposition or temptation to compromise.

20. Growing in Spiritual Maturity:
- Embrace the journey of growing in spiritual maturity as a means of fortifying ourselves against Jezebel's false doctrines. Learn to discern truth, mature in faith, and walk in the fullness of God's revelation.

---

In a world where false doctrines and deceptive teachings abound, we must hold fast to truth and discern Jezebel's false doctrines. By anchoring ourselves in the unchanging Word of God, we can expose and refute her deceptions. Let us remain vigilant, cultivating discernment, and empowering others with truth. With unwavering commitment to sound doctrine, we will overcome Jezebel's false teachings, grow in spiritual maturity, and stand firm in the unshakable truth of God's Word.

## Deliverance Prayer

1. Heavenly Father, I come before you in the name of Jesus, declaring that I stand firm in the truth of your Word. I take authority over every false doctrine propagated by Jezebel's spirit, and I expose her deceptive teachings.

2. Lord, I thank you for the discernment to recognize Jezebel's manipulation of Scripture. I declare that your Word is the ultimate authority, and I reject any distortion or misuse of it.

3. I bind and break the spirit of error that operates through Jezebel's false doctrines. I declare that I have the mind of Christ, and I discern and reject every false teaching that contradicts your Word.

4. I anchor my faith in the true foundation of your Word. I declare that I will not be swayed by Jezebel's deceptive doctrines, but I hold fast to the unchanging truth revealed in your Word.

5. I expose and refute the prosperity gospel promoted by Jezebel's spirit. I declare that true abundance and prosperity come from seeking first your Kingdom and living in alignment with your principles.

6. I reject the false teachings on spiritual authority propagated by Jezebel's spirit. I declare that spiritual authority is exercised in humility, love, and submission to your Word.

7. I discern and resist any manipulation of grace by Jezebel's spirit. I embrace the true biblical understanding of grace as a transformative force that empowers me to live a holy and righteous life.

8. I stand against the distortion of gender roles promoted by Jezebel's spirit. I embrace your design for men and women, rooted in love, mutual respect, and the honoring of each other's unique giftings.

9. I expose and reject the false teachings on holiness and sanctification spread by Jezebel's spirit. I embrace the call to live a holy and set-apart life, empowered by the Holy Spirit.

10. I discern and reject false prophets and teachers who propagate Jezebel's false doctrines. I declare that I will not be led astray by their deceptive teachings, but I will test every spirit against your Word.

11. Lord, I pray for the cultivation of discernment in my life. Grant me wisdom, understanding, and a sensitive ear to discern the difference between truth and falsehood.

12. I embrace sound doctrine as a safeguard for my faith. I declare that I will not be tossed to and fro by every wind of false teaching, but I will remain anchored in the truth of your Word.

13. I declare the authority of Scripture over Jezebel's false doctrines. Your Word is living and active, sharper than any two-edged sword, and I wield it as a weapon against her deceptions.

14. Lord, cultivate in me a Berean spirit that diligently examines the Scriptures to verify the teachings I receive. Help me to discern and reject any teachings that do not align with your Word.

15. I pray for protection from Jezebel's deceptive doctrines. Guard my heart and mind, and surround me with discerning mentors and fellow believers who uphold sound doctrine.

16. Lord, strengthen me to stand firm in truth amidst cultural pressure and shifting ideologies. Grant me the courage to be a voice for truth, even when it goes against the popular narrative.

17. Help me to foster unity in the body of Christ based on the foundation of truth. Grant me grace and wisdom to engage in respectful dialogue and pursue unity without compromising your Word.

18. I reject any compromise with Jezebel's false doctrines. I declare that I will hold fast to truth, even in the face of opposition or temptation to compromise my beliefs.

19. I commit to growing in spiritual maturity, deepening my understanding of your Word, and walking in the fullness of your revelation. Grant me a hunger for truth and a thirst for righteousness.

20. Lord, I pray for the liberation of those deceived by Jezebel's false doctrines. Open their eyes to the truth, break the chains of deception, and lead them into a deeper knowledge of you.

## Chapter 42

## Jezebel's Assault on the Family: Restoring God's Design

In this chapter, we will examine the destructive influence of Jezebel's spirit on the family unit and explore the importance of restoring God's design for the family. Jezebel seeks to undermine the biblical principles of marriage, parenting, and family relationships, leading to brokenness, dysfunction, and spiritual oppression. We will delve into the specific ways Jezebel targets the family, uncover her strategies of deception, and equip ourselves with the knowledge and tools to restore and strengthen God's design. By embracing the truth of God's Word and aligning our families with His purposes, we can overcome Jezebel's assault and experience the restoration and blessings that flow from living in alignment with His design.

1. God's Design for the Family:
    - Explore the foundational principles and purposes of God's design for the family. Understand the roles of marriage, parenting, and familial relationships as established by God.

2. Jezebel's Attack on Marriage:

- Examine how Jezebel targets marriages, seeking to undermine the covenantal bond and distort the roles of husbands and wives. Learn to recognize and counter her tactics.

3. Restoring Biblical Marriage:
- Discover the steps to restore and strengthen marriages in the face of Jezebel's assault. Embrace the principles of love, selflessness, and mutual submission as outlined in Scripture.

4. Parenting God's Way:
- Understand how Jezebel influences parenting, promoting permissiveness, neglect, and ungodly control. Learn to parent according to God's principles of love, discipline, and nurture.

5. Breaking Generational Curses:
- Uncover the generational curses perpetuated by Jezebel's assault on the family. Learn how to identify and break these cycles through repentance, forgiveness, and spiritual warfare.

6. Healing Family Wounds:
- Address the wounds and brokenness caused by Jezebel's attack on the family. Discover the healing power of forgiveness, restoration, and seeking God's truth.

7. Embracing Fatherhood:

- Examine the importance of fatherhood in the family unit and the strategies Jezebel employs to undermine it. Discover the blessings and transformative impact of fathers embracing their God-given roles.

8. Nurturing Motherhood:
- Understand how Jezebel distorts and devalues motherhood, promoting worldly ideals and neglecting the nurturing and guiding role of mothers. Rediscover the sacredness and impact of motherhood according to God's design.

9. Building Strong Foundations:
- Learn how to build strong foundations in the family that withstand Jezebel's assault. Explore the importance of prayer, studying God's Word, and cultivating an environment of love, grace, and truth.

10. Discipling the Next Generation:
- Recognize the critical role of discipleship in raising children who can withstand Jezebel's influence. Discover practical strategies to pass on faith, values, and biblical truth to the next generation.

11. Guarding Against Jezebel's Influence:
- Equip yourself with discernment and wisdom to guard your family against Jezebel's influence. Learn to recognize her subtle tactics, resist her deception, and establish spiritual boundaries.

12. Overcoming Division and Conflict:
    - Address the division and conflict that Jezebel's assault can cause within families. Discover the power of forgiveness, reconciliation, and the pursuit of unity in overcoming these challenges.

13. Creating a Culture of Honor:
    - Foster a culture of honor within your family, where love, respect, and appreciation are valued. Counter Jezebel's assault by affirming and empowering each family member.

14. Cultivating Spiritual Intimacy:
    - Explore the significance of spiritual intimacy within the family unit. Learn how to create an environment where each family member can grow in their relationship with God and support one another's spiritual journey.

15. Restoring Family Altars:
    - Rediscover the power of family worship and devotion. Learn to establish and cultivate family altars, where the presence of God is invited, and His Word is central.

16. Engaging in Spiritual Warfare for the Family:
    - Equip yourself with spiritual warfare strategies to protect your family from Jezebel's assault. Pray for divine covering, spiritual

discernment, and the power of the Holy Spirit to combat her attacks.

17. Seeking Wise Counsel:
   - Recognize the importance of seeking wise counsel and support in navigating the challenges posed by Jezebel's assault on the family. Surround yourself with godly mentors and seek professional help when needed.

18. Extending God's Love Beyond the Family:
   - Understand the significance of extending God's love beyond your immediate family. Explore opportunities to bless and impact other families, fostering a sense of community and kingdom-mindedness.

19. Restoring Hope and Redemption:
   - Discover the hope and redemption available to families affected by Jezebel's assault. Experience the transforming power of God's love and restoration as you surrender your family to Him.

20. Living as a Counter-Cultural Family:
   - Embrace the call to live as a counter-cultural family, committed to God's design amidst a world influenced by Jezebel's assault. Stand as a testimony of His grace, love, and truth.

## Deliverance Prayer

1. Heavenly Father, I come before you in the name of Jesus, taking authority over Jezebel's assault on the family. I declare that your design for the family will be restored and upheld in my life and in the lives of those I intercede for.

2. I bind and break every influence of Jezebel's spirit that seeks to undermine marriages and distort the roles of husbands and wives. I declare restoration, love, and unity in every marriage affected by her assault.

3. I pray for the healing and restoration of parent-child relationships that have been impacted by Jezebel's attack. I declare that parents will embrace their God-given roles, raising children in the nurture and admonition of the Lord.

4. I break every generational curse perpetuated by Jezebel's assault on the family. I declare freedom and restoration from the cycles of brokenness, dysfunction, and spiritual oppression.

5. I pray for healing and restoration in families that have been wounded by Jezebel's influence. I declare your love and forgiveness to flow, bringing reconciliation, healing, and wholeness.

6. I bind and break every strategy of Jezebel that seeks to undermine fatherhood. I pray for fathers to rise up in their God-given roles, embracing their responsibility to lead, protect, and nurture their families.

7. I declare that motherhood will be honored and valued according to your design. I break every lie that devalues and distorts the role of mothers. I pray for mothers to walk in wisdom, love, and godly influence.

8. I pray for strong foundations to be built in families, anchored in prayer, your Word, and the pursuit of righteousness. I declare that families will be rooted in your love, grace, and truth.

9. I bind and rebuke the spirit of division and conflict that Jezebel uses to disrupt families. I pray for unity, forgiveness, and a spirit of reconciliation to prevail within every family.

10. I declare that the culture of honor will be established in families, where love, respect, and appreciation are practiced. I break every spirit of disrespect and dishonor, replacing it with a spirit of humility and gratitude.

11. I pray for spiritual intimacy to flourish in families. I declare that each family member will grow in their relationship with you and support one another's spiritual journey.

12. I engage in spiritual warfare to protect my family from Jezebel's assault. I plead the blood of Jesus over my family, declaring divine covering, discernment, and victory over every scheme of the enemy.

13. I seek wise counsel and support to navigate the challenges posed by Jezebel's assault. I pray for godly mentors and counselors to speak wisdom and provide guidance as we seek to restore and uphold your design for the family.

14. I extend your love beyond my family, blessing and impacting other families with your grace and truth. I pray for opportunities to be a source of encouragement, support, and godly influence to those around me.

15. I declare hope and redemption for families affected by Jezebel's assault. I release the power of your love and restoration to transform every broken area and bring forth your purposes.

16. I commit to living as a counter-cultural family, standing firm in your design amidst a world influenced by Jezebel's assault. I declare that we will be a testimony of Your grace, love, and truth.

17. I pray for the strengthening and protection of families within the body of Christ. I declare that families will be a source of strength, unity, and Kingdom impact in the church and the world.

18. I break the power of Jezebel's assault on the family over my bloodline and generational heritage. I release the healing and transforming power of the Holy Spirit to restore and align my family with your purposes.

19. I thank you, Lord, for the authority you have given me to overcome Jezebel's assault on the family. I declare that your design will be fully restored, and your blessings will flow abundantly in my family and the families around me.

20. In Jesus' name, I decree and declare the restoration and strengthening of families according to your perfect design. Amen.

Chapter 43

# Overcoming Jezebel's Jealousy:
# Walking in Divine Identity

In this chapter, we will explore the destructive influence of Jezebel's jealousy and the power of overcoming it by embracing our divine identity in Christ. Jealousy is one of the key weapons Jezebel uses to manipulate, control, and destroy relationships. By understanding the roots of jealousy, the tactics Jezebel employs, and the truth of our identity in Christ, we can break free from its grip and walk in the fullness of who God created us to be. We will delve into the effects of jealousy, uncover strategies to overcome it, and empower ourselves to live confidently in our divine identity.

1. The Roots of Jealousy:
   - Examine the origins and nature of jealousy, understanding how it aligns with Jezebel's spirit. Recognize the destructive consequences of jealousy in our lives and relationships.

2. Jezebel's Jealousy Tactics:
   - Uncover the specific ways Jezebel uses jealousy to manipulate and control others. Learn to recognize her subtle tactics and protect yourself from her influence.

3. Embracing Divine Identity:

- Discover the truth of your divine identity in Christ. Understand that you are fearfully and wonderfully made, chosen, loved, and valued by God.

4. Overcoming the Comparison Trap:

- Break free from the comparison trap fueled by Jezebel's jealousy. Learn to appreciate and celebrate your uniqueness and the specific calling God has placed on your life.

5. Rejecting the Spirit of Competition:

- Release the spirit of competition and embrace a spirit of collaboration and unity. Understand that we are part of the body of Christ, each with a unique role and purpose.

6. Renewing the Mind:

- Renew your mind with the truth of God's Word. Replace negative thoughts and comparisons with the truth of your identity in Christ.

7. Gratitude and Contentment:

- Cultivate an attitude of gratitude and contentment. Appreciate the blessings and gifts God has given you, and guard against the temptation of jealousy.

8. Celebrating Others' Success:

- Learn to genuinely celebrate the success and achievements of others. Release any jealousy or envy and choose to support and encourage others in their journey.

9. Walking in Confidence:
- Build your confidence in who God created you to be. Embrace your strengths, gifts, and talents, knowing that you have a unique purpose and contribution to make.

10. Guarding Against Comparison in the Age of Social Media:
- Navigate the challenges of comparison in the age of social media. Learn to use social media as a tool for inspiration and connection, rather than a platform for comparison and jealousy.

11. Overcoming Jealousy in Relationships:
- Address jealousy in relationships and learn healthy ways to overcome it. Cultivate trust, open communication, and a secure foundation in God's love.

12. Jealousy in Ministry and Leadership:
- Recognize and address jealousy in ministry and leadership contexts. Embrace a spirit of collaboration, servant leadership, and the recognition that God's Kingdom is not limited by human achievement.

13. Embracing God's Abundance:

- Shift your mindset from scarcity to abundance. Recognize that God's blessings are not limited and that He has a unique plan and purpose for each person.

14. Focusing on God's Approval:
   - Seek God's approval above the approval of others. Rest in the knowledge that you are deeply loved and accepted by Him, regardless of what others may think or say.

15. Prayer and Surrender:
   - Surrender any jealousy or comparison to God in prayer. Invite the Holy Spirit to transform your heart and renew your mind, aligning it with God's truth and perspective.

16. Surrounding Yourself with Encouragers:
   - Surround yourself with individuals who uplift, encourage, and celebrate your journey. Seek out relationships that foster growth, accountability, and support.

17. Developing a Kingdom Mindset:
   - Develop a Kingdom mindset that focuses on serving others and advancing God's purposes rather than personal gain or recognition. Understand that true greatness comes from humble service.

18. Releasing Jealousy through Forgiveness:

- Release any bitterness, resentment, or jealousy through forgiveness. Choose to forgive those who may have triggered feelings of jealousy, knowing that forgiveness sets you free.

19. Cultivating a Heart of Love:
   - Cultivate a heart of love that extends grace and kindness to others. Embrace the truth that love rejoices with the success of others and seeks their well-being.

20. Walking in Freedom:
   - Walk in the freedom that comes from overcoming Jezebel's jealousy. Embrace your divine identity and live confidently in the truth of who you are in Christ.

---

I thank you, Lord, for the power to overcome Jezebel's jealousy. I declare that I am secure in my divine identity, loved by you, and empowered to walk confidently in who you created me to be. I release any jealousy or comparison, choosing instead to celebrate and support others on their journey. I pray that your truth and love would fill my heart and overflow into every aspect of my life. In Jesus' name, amen.

## Deliverance Prayer

1. Heavenly Father, in the name of Jesus, I take authority over Jezebel's spirit of jealousy that seeks to rob me of my divine

identity. I declare that I am fearfully and wonderfully made, chosen, and loved by you.

2. I bind and break every influence of Jezebel's jealousy in my life and relationships. I renounce and reject any comparison, envy, or insecurity that stems from her tactics. I choose to walk in the truth of my identity in Christ.

3. I declare that I am free from the comparison trap. I release any jealousy or envy that arises from comparing myself to others. I choose to appreciate and celebrate the unique gifts and callings you have placed on their lives.

4. I break every spirit of competition that Jezebel tries to stir within me. I choose collaboration, unity, and the recognition that we are all part of the body of Christ, each with a unique role and purpose.

5. I renew my mind with the truth of your Word. I replace negative thoughts and comparisons with thoughts that reflect my identity in Christ. I declare that I am accepted, approved, and equipped by you.

6. I cultivate gratitude and contentment in my heart. I choose to focus on the blessings you have bestowed upon me and the abundant life you have provided. I guard against the temptation of jealousy and discontentment.

7. I celebrate the success and achievements of others genuinely. I choose to support and encourage them in their journey, knowing that their victories do not diminish my own. I rejoice in the success of others as we advance your Kingdom together.

8. I walk in confidence, knowing that I am equipped by your Spirit and empowered to fulfill my purpose. I embrace my strengths, gifts, and talents, using them to glorify you and impact the world around me.

9. I guard against comparison in the age of social media. I use social media as a platform for inspiration, encouragement, and connection, rather than a place of comparison and jealousy. I set healthy boundaries and focus on using it as a tool for Kingdom impact.

10. I overcome jealousy in my relationships. I cultivate trust, open communication, and a secure foundation in your love. I choose to celebrate and support the success of those around me, fostering healthy and thriving relationships.

11. I release any jealousy or comparison in ministry and leadership contexts. I embrace a spirit of collaboration, servant leadership, and the recognition that your Kingdom is not limited by human

achievement. I walk in humility, seeking your guidance and direction.

12. I embrace your abundance, knowing that your blessings are limitless. I reject a scarcity mindset and choose to trust in your provision. I believe that you have a unique plan and purpose for me, and I walk in the confidence that you will fulfill it.

13. I focus on your approval above the approval of others. I seek to please you and align my life with your will. I rest in the knowledge that I am deeply loved and accepted by you, regardless of the opinions of others.

14. I surrender any jealousy or comparison to you in prayer. I invite the Holy Spirit to transform my heart and renew my mind, aligning it with your truth and perspective. I release any negative emotions and receive your peace and joy.

15. I surround myself with encouragers and like-minded believers who uplift, support, and celebrate my journey. I cultivate relationships that foster growth, accountability, and Kingdom impact. I choose to be an encourager and supporter to others as well.

16. I develop a Kingdom mindset that focuses on serving others and advancing your purposes. I reject self-centered ambition and embrace a heart of humility, love, and servant leadership.

17. I release any bitterness, resentment, or jealousy through forgiveness. I choose to forgive those who may have triggered feelings of jealousy, knowing that forgiveness sets me free and releases your healing in my life.

18. I cultivate a heart of love that extends grace, kindness, and compassion to others. I choose to celebrate their successes and well-being. I walk in love, reflecting your character and love in all I do.

19. I walk in the freedom that comes from overcoming Jezebel's jealousy. I embrace my divine identity and live confidently in the truth of who I am in Christ. I declare that jealousy has no power over me, and I am victorious in Him.

20. I thank you, Lord, for the victory I have in Christ. I declare that I am an overcomer, walking in divine identity and freedom from Jezebel's jealousy. I surrender myself to your plans and purposes, knowing that you will lead me into an abundant life that glorifies you. In Jesus' name, amen.

## Chapter 44

# Jezebel's Control in the Workplace: Releasing God's Authority

In this chapter, we will delve into the topic of Jezebel's control in the workplace and how to release God's authority in such environments. Jezebel's spirit seeks to exert control, manipulate, and dominate in various spheres of life, including the workplace. Whether it manifests through toxic leadership, unhealthy power dynamics, or manipulative behaviors, Jezebel's control can hinder productivity, stifle creativity, and create a toxic work environment. However, as believers, we have been given divine authority to release God's kingdom principles and establish an atmosphere of freedom, collaboration, and godly leadership. In this chapter, we will explore strategies to identify and overcome Jezebel's control in the workplace, empower ourselves with God's authority, and create a healthy and thriving work environment.

1. Understanding Jezebel's Control:
   - Examine the characteristics and tactics of Jezebel's control in the workplace. Gain insights into her manipulative strategies, power plays, and desire for domination.

2. Identifying Jezebel's Behaviors:

- Learn to recognize the signs of Jezebel control in the workplace, such as manipulation, intimidation, micromanagement, and toxic power dynamics. Develop discernment to identify her influence.

3. The Impact of Jezebel's Control:
   - Understand the detrimental effects of Jezebel's control on individuals and the overall work environment. Explore the emotional, mental, and spiritual toll it can take on employees and the organization as a whole.

4. Embracing God's Authority:
   - Discover the authority we have as believers in Christ to overcome Jezebel's control. Understand that we are called to operate in a different kingdom and release God's principles in the workplace.

5. Breaking Free from Jezebel's Grip:
   - Equip yourself with strategies to break free from Jezebel's control. Develop healthy boundaries, assertiveness, and resilience to resist her manipulations and establish a healthier work environment.

6. Cultivating a Culture of Trust and Collaboration:
   - Foster trust, open communication, and collaboration in the workplace. Create an atmosphere where individuals are valued, ideas are respected, and teamwork is encouraged.

7. Walking in Integrity and Authenticity:

- Embrace a lifestyle of integrity and authenticity in the workplace. Lead by example and inspire others to operate with transparency and sincerity.

8. Discerning and Confronting Jezebelic Leaders:
- Develop discernment to identify Jezebelic leaders and their destructive influence. Learn how to address and confront their behaviors in a wise and assertive manner, seeking resolution and change.

9. Releasing God's Wisdom and Guidance:
- Seek God's wisdom and guidance in decision-making, problem-solving, and conflict resolution in the workplace. Invite the Holy Spirit to lead and guide your actions, bringing about godly solutions.

10. Praying for Transformation:
- Engage in fervent prayer for transformation in the workplace. Pray for Jezebel's influence to be broken, for hearts to be softened, and for a shift towards godly leadership and healthy dynamics.

11. Exercising Servant Leadership:
- Embrace the model of servant leadership exemplified by Jesus. Lead with humility, compassion, and a heart to serve others, fostering a culture of support, empowerment, and growth.

12. Encouraging Authentic Relationships:
    - Foster authentic relationships in the workplace, where individuals can be themselves, express their opinions, and build genuine connections. Encourage a culture of empathy, respect, and understanding.

13. Developing Emotional Intelligence:
    - Cultivate emotional intelligence in the workplace, fostering self-awareness, empathy, and effective communication. Develop the ability to navigate emotions and build positive relationships.

14. Establishing Clear Boundaries:
    - Set clear boundaries to protect yourself from Jezebel's control. Define your roles, responsibilities, and limitations, ensuring that you maintain a healthy work-life balance and protect your well-being.

15. Encouraging Employee Empowerment:
    - Empower employees to take ownership of their work, make decisions, and contribute to the organization's success. Create opportunities for growth, skill development, and personal fulfillment.

16. Implementing Conflict Resolution Strategies:

- Implement effective conflict resolution strategies in the workplace. Encourage open dialogue, active listening, and a focus on resolution rather than blame or personal attacks.

17. Promoting a Culture of Appreciation and Recognition:
- Foster a culture of appreciation and recognition, where individuals' contributions are valued and celebrated. Acknowledge and reward achievements, fostering a positive and uplifting work environment.

18. Seeking Wise Counsel and Mentoring:
- Seek wise counsel and mentoring from trusted individuals in the workplace. Surround yourself with experienced leaders who can provide guidance, support, and accountability.

19. Overcoming Fear and Intimidation:
- Overcome the fear and intimidation that Jezebel's control can create. Lean on the strength of the Lord and walk in the assurance that He is with you, empowering you to navigate challenging situations.

20. Walking in God's Peace and Rest:
- Rest in God's peace amidst the storms of workplace control. Trust in His sovereignty and believe that He is working all things together for your good. Allow His peace to guard your heart and mind.

## Deliverance Prayer

1. Heavenly Father, in the name of Jesus, I take authority over Jezebel's spirit of control in the workplace. I declare that your authority is supreme, and I release your kingdom principles to govern every aspect of my workplace.

2. I bind and break every influence of Jezebel's control in my workplace. I cancel her assignments, schemes, and manipulations. I release the power of your Word to dismantle her strongholds and establish your authority in its place.

3. I decree and declare that my workplace is a zone of freedom, collaboration, and godly leadership. I release a culture of trust, respect, and healthy dynamics among colleagues and superiors.

4. I release your wisdom and discernment to identify Jezebelic behaviors in the workplace. Give me insight and understanding to recognize her tactics and strategies. Empower me to confront and address them with wisdom, grace, and assertiveness.

5. I walk in the authority you have given me to break free from Jezebel's control. I refuse to be manipulated, intimidated, or

dominated. I declare that I am empowered by your Spirit to navigate any challenging situations with confidence and grace.

6. I release a spirit of collaboration and teamwork in my workplace. I declare that individual gifts and talents are valued and utilized for the greater good of the organization. I bind any spirit of competition or division and release a spirit of unity and harmony.

7. I pray for the transformation of Jezebelic leaders in my workplace. Soften their hearts, convict them of their manipulative behaviors, and lead them to walk in godly leadership. Bring about a change in their mindset and actions for the well-being of all.

8. I seek your wisdom and guidance in every decision-making process. Help me to align my actions with your will and establish a culture that reflects your values. I release your favor and creativity in finding solutions and strategies that honor you.

9. I pray for a spirit of servant leadership to permeate my workplace. Help me to lead by example, demonstrating humility, compassion, and a heart to serve others. Empower me to be a source of encouragement and support to those around me.

10. I release forgiveness towards those who have operated under Jezebel's control. I choose to let go of any resentment, bitterness,

or offense. I release your healing and restoration in relationships and declare that reconciliation and unity prevail.

11. I pray for the empowerment and equipping of all employees in my workplace. Help them to discover their unique giftings and talents, and use them for the advancement of the organization. Release your favor, promotion, and success upon them.

12. I declare that fear and intimidation have no place in my workplace. I walk in the confidence and peace that come from knowing you are with me. I release your boldness and courage to speak truth, challenge injustice, and stand firm against Jezebel's control.

13. I release your supernatural wisdom and discernment to navigate office politics and power dynamics. Help me to navigate relationships with grace and integrity, always seeking your guidance in every interaction.

14. I release a culture of appreciation and recognition in my workplace. Help us to acknowledge and celebrate the accomplishments and contributions of everyone. I bind any spirit of envy or jealousy and release a spirit of encouragement and support.

15. I release your divine order and structure in my workplace. Help us to operate with excellence, efficiency, and integrity. I bind any

chaos, confusion, or disunity and release your peace, clarity, and unity.

16. I pray for divine connections and relationships that will bring positive influence and godly counsel in my workplace. Surround me with wise mentors and colleagues who will support and guide me in my professional journey.

17. I release your supernatural provision and abundance in my workplace. I declare that financial resources, opportunities, and favor flow abundantly. I bind any spirit of lack or poverty and release a spirit of prosperity and increase.

18. I pray for your divine protection over my workplace. Guard us against any form of harm, deception, or evil intent. Surround us with your angels and create an atmosphere of safety and security.

19. I release your anointing and creativity upon me in my workplace. Help me to bring forth innovative ideas, strategies, and solutions. I bind any spirit of stagnation or limitation and release a spirit of growth and advancement.

20. I declare that my workplace is a testimony of your kingdom on earth. I release your light, love, and truth to impact the lives of those around me. May your presence be felt, and your glory be revealed in all that we do. In Jesus' name, amen.

## Chapter 45

# Jezebel's Fear of the Prophetic: Releasing the Voice of God

In this chapter, we will explore Jezebel's fear of the prophetic and how we can overcome her attempts to silence the voice of God. Jezebel seeks to suppress and control the prophetic gifting and the voice of God in our lives and in the Church. However, as believers, we are called to release and embrace the prophetic, for it carries the power to bring transformation, direction, and alignment with God's purposes. In this chapter, we will delve into the tactics Jezebel employs to hinder the prophetic, understand the importance of the prophetic voice, and discover strategies to overcome Jezebel's fear and release the voice of God in our lives, churches, and communities.

1. Understanding Jezebel's Fear of the Prophetic:
   - Gain insights into Jezebel's fear of the prophetic and her attempts to suppress it. Understand her tactics of intimidation, deception, and manipulation to silence the voice of God.

2. The Power and Purpose of the Prophetic:

- Explore the power and purpose of the prophetic in the life of believers and the Church. Understand how the prophetic brings revelation, encouragement, correction, and direction.

3. Recognizing Jezebelic Attacks on the Prophetic:
   - Learn to discern Jezebelic attacks on the prophetic. Identify the signs of intimidation, discouragement, and manipulation aimed at silencing prophetic voices.

4. Cultivating a Prophetic Atmosphere:
   - Create an atmosphere that cultivates and honors the prophetic in your life and in your church. Embrace a culture of expectation, faith, and openness to hearing God's voice.

5. Nurturing Prophetic Gifts:
   - Encourage and nurture prophetic gifts in individuals. Provide opportunities for training, mentoring, and activation in the prophetic. Help believers develop confidence and clarity in hearing and sharing God's messages.

6. Spiritual Discernment:
   - Develop spiritual discernment to distinguish between genuine prophetic voices and false ones. Seek the Holy Spirit's guidance to avoid deception and manipulation.

7. Overcoming Fear of Man:

- Confront the fear of man that may hinder the release of the prophetic. Trust in God's approval and stand boldly in obedience to His voice, regardless of others' opinions or reactions.

8. Prayer and Intercession:
- Engage in fervent prayer and intercession to break Jezebel's fear and release the voice of God. Pray for boldness, clarity, and accuracy in prophetic utterances.

9. Submission to Spiritual Authority:
- Submit to spiritual authority and accountability in the prophetic. Seek guidance and feedback from trusted leaders and mentors to grow in maturity and accuracy.

10. Embracing Humility and Teachability:
- Cultivate a spirit of humility and teachability in the prophetic journey. Recognize that the prophetic gift is a stewardship from God and continuously seek growth, correction, and refinement.

11. Speaking God's Truth with Love:
- Release the prophetic voice with a balance of love and truth. Speak God's heart with compassion, grace, and wisdom, challenging and encouraging others to align with His purposes.

12. Discerning and Addressing Jezebelic Attacks:

- Discern Jezebelic attacks against the prophetic and address them with wisdom and authority. Stand firm in the truth, exposing and rebuking the spirit of control and manipulation.

13. Building Prophetic Communities:
- Connect with other prophetic believers to build supportive communities. Engage in fellowship, accountability, and mutual edification to strengthen the prophetic giftings and resist Jezebel's attempts to isolate and discourage.

14. Prophetic Intercession and Warfare:
- Engage in prophetic intercession and warfare against Jezebel's fear. Release prophetic declarations and prayers that dismantle her strongholds and release the voice of God with power and authority.

15. Walking in the Fear of the Lord:
- Embrace the fear of the Lord as the foundation for operating in the prophetic. Seek holiness, reverence, and obedience to God, allowing His presence to guide and empower the prophetic voice.

16. Embodying the Prophetic Message:
- Live a life that aligns with the prophetic message you carry. Let your character, actions, and lifestyle testify to the truth and authenticity of God's word spoken through you.

17. Perseverance in the Face of Opposition:
   - Stand firm and persevere in releasing the prophetic despite opposition and resistance. Trust in God's faithfulness and His ability to overcome Jezebel's attempts to silence His voice.

18. Prophetic Alignment with God's Word:
   - Ensure that the prophetic messages align with the truth of God's Word. Test every prophetic utterance against the Scriptures and submit to the authority of God's written Word.

19. Releasing Prophetic Creativity:
   - Embrace the creativity and innovation that often accompany the prophetic. Release prophetic expressions through various art forms, music, writing, and other creative outlets to impact hearts and minds.

20. Prophetic Impact and Transformation:
   - Anticipate and celebrate the impact and transformation that the release of the prophetic voice can bring. Trust that as God's messages are proclaimed, lives, churches, and communities will be changed for His glory.

---

In conclusion, Jezebel's fear of the prophetic can only be overcome by embracing the power and purpose of the prophetic voice. As believers, we have been entrusted with the privilege of hearing and sharing God's messages. By cultivating a prophetic atmosphere, nurturing prophetic gifts, and walking in humility and obedience, we can break free from Jezebel's fear and release the voice of God in our lives and in the world around us. Let us stand bold and unyielding in the face of opposition, trusting that the prophetic will bring transformation, edification, and alignment with God's purposes. May the prophetic voices arise and be heard, bringing forth revival, restoration, and the manifestation of God's kingdom on earth.

## Deliverance Prayer

1. Heavenly Father, in the mighty name of Jesus, I come against the spirit of Jezebel's fear of the prophetic. I declare that the voice of God will be released with power, authority, and clarity in my life, in my church, and in the world around me.

2. I break every stronghold of fear that Jezebel has attempted to establish in my heart and mind concerning the prophetic. I renounce and reject any lies or deception that have hindered the release of God's voice through me.

3. I bind and cast out the spirit of intimidation and manipulation that Jezebel employs to silence the prophetic. I release the spirit of boldness and courage to declare God's truth without fear or hesitation.

4. I decree and declare that the fear of man will no longer have a hold on me when it comes to releasing the prophetic. I surrender to the fear of the Lord and His approval alone, knowing that His voice is the one I am accountable to.

5. I release a spirit of discernment and sensitivity to the Holy Spirit's leading in the prophetic. I pray for a sharpened ability to hear God's voice clearly and accurately, distinguishing it from any false or counterfeit voices.

6. I break off any past disappointments, discouragements, or negative experiences that have caused me to doubt or suppress the prophetic within me. I release healing and restoration to my prophetic gifting.

7. I pray for divine connections and partnerships with other prophetic voices. May we encourage and sharpen one another, strengthening the prophetic anointing and creating a greater impact for your kingdom.

8. I bind any spirit of division or competition among prophetic voices and release a spirit of unity, collaboration, and mutual support. Let us celebrate and honor one another's giftings, recognizing that we are part of a greater tapestry.

9. I release the fire of God's love and passion within me, igniting a fervent desire to prophesy and declare His word. Let my words be filled with His love, compassion, and grace, drawing hearts closer to Him.

10. I decree and declare that Jezebel's fear of the prophetic will not hinder the advancement of God's kingdom. I release a greater awakening to the prophetic in my church, community, and the nations, with a hunger and thirst for the voice of God.

11. I pray for the breaking of Jezebel's influence over leaders and authorities who have suppressed or rejected the prophetic. Soften their hearts, open their ears, and give them a hunger for the true prophetic voice.

12. I release a prophetic anointing upon pastors, teachers, evangelists, and leaders in every sphere of influence. May they boldly proclaim Your word, speaking prophetically into the lives of those they lead, guiding and shepherding them according to your purposes.

13. I pray for the restoration of the prophetic in churches and ministries that have been stifled or silenced by Jezebel's fear. Let a fresh wind of the Holy Spirit blow, reawakening the prophetic gifts and creating an atmosphere where Your voice is heard and heeded.

14. I break every assignment of Jezebel to distort, pervert, or counterfeit the prophetic. I release a spirit of discernment to accurately discern between true and false prophetic voices, protecting Your people from deception.

15. I release the fire of God's presence in my life, purifying my heart, mind, and motives. Remove any impurities or selfish ambitions that may hinder the flow of your prophetic voice through me.

16. I pray for divine encounters and supernatural experiences that heighten my sensitivity to the Spirit and increase my capacity to receive and release prophetic words, dreams, visions, and revelations.

17. I bind every spirit of doubt, fear, and insecurity that would try to hinder my confidence in the prophetic. I release a spirit of faith, trust, and boldness to step out in obedience and speak forth your word with unwavering conviction.

18. I decree and declare that Jezebel's fear of the prophetic will be dismantled in the lives of believers around the world. Let a mighty army of prophetic voices arise, declaring your truth, bringing transformation, and advancing Your kingdom.

19. I pray for divine strategies and wisdom to steward the prophetic anointing with integrity and humility. Keep me grounded in your Word, accountable to spiritual authority, and led by your Spirit in all prophetic endeavors.

20. I release a prophetic mantle upon my life, an anointing to hear, see, and speak forth your word with power and authority. I surrender to your will and purpose for my life, using the prophetic as a tool to glorify your name and bring others into a deeper relationship with you. In Jesus' mighty name, amen.

## Chapter 46

# Jezebel's False Accusations: Overcoming Spiritual Attacks

In this chapter, we will explore the tactics of Jezebel's false accusations and how we can overcome the spiritual attacks that accompany them. Jezebel is known for her manipulative and deceitful nature, using false accusations as a weapon to undermine, discredit, and destroy the reputation and influence of God's people. However, as believers, we have the power and authority to stand firm in the face of these attacks and walk in the truth and victory that Christ has provided for us. In this chapter, we will delve into the nature of Jezebel's false accusations, understand their impact, and discover strategies to overcome and rise above these attacks.

1. Understanding Jezebel's False Accusations:
   - Gain insights into Jezebel's tactics of false accusations. Understand her motives, methods, and the devastating impact these accusations can have on individuals and communities.

2. The Power of Truth and Integrity:
   - Embrace the power of truth and integrity in the face of false accusations. Learn how to maintain a strong foundation of character and conduct that will refute the lies of Jezebel.

3. Recognizing False Accusations:
   - Develop discernment to recognize false accusations from Jezebel. Learn to identify the spirit of accusation, manipulation, and deception behind these attacks.

4. Overcoming Fear and Anxiety:
   - Confront the fear and anxiety that false accusations can trigger. Lean on God's strength and trust in His justice to bring vindication and deliverance.

5. Walking in Forgiveness and Grace:
   - Choose forgiveness and extend grace to those who falsely accuse. Understand that their actions are rooted in spiritual warfare and release them into God's hands.

6. Seeking God's Wisdom and Guidance:
   - Seek God's wisdom and guidance in responding to false accusations. Allow His Spirit to lead you in your actions, responses, and decisions.

7. Responding with Love and Gentleness:
   - Respond to false accusations with love and gentleness, following the example of Christ. Refuse to engage in the spirit of strife, but instead demonstrate the fruit of the Spirit in all interactions.

8. Prayer for Protection and Deliverance:

- Engage in fervent prayer for protection and deliverance from false accusations. Seek God's divine intervention and ask Him to expose the truth and bring justice.

9. Guarding Your Heart and Mind:

- Guard your heart and mind against the negative effects of false accusations. Fill your thoughts with God's truth, meditating on His promises, and rejecting the lies of Jezebel.

10. Surrounding Yourself with Support:

- Surround yourself with a community of believers who can provide support, encouragement, and wise counsel during times of false accusations. Lean on their strength and let them remind you of your identity in Christ.

11. Turning to God's Word for Strength:

- Find strength and encouragement in God's Word when facing false accusations. Discover biblical examples of individuals who overcame false accusations and drew closer to God through the process.

12. Cultivating Humility and Patience:

- Cultivate humility and patience in the face of false accusations. Allow God to work in His timing, trusting that He will vindicate and uplift the righteous in due course.

13. Embracing Spiritual Warfare:
   - Recognize that false accusations are part of spiritual warfare. Engage in spiritual warfare strategies, such as prayer, fasting, and declaring God's truth, to counteract the attacks of Jezebel.

14. Speaking Life and Blessing:
   - Speak life and blessing over yourself and those who falsely accuse you. Refuse to respond in kind but instead release words of healing, restoration, and transformation.

15. Developing Resilience and Endurance:
   - Develop resilience and endurance in the face of false accusations. Trust in God's faithfulness, knowing that He will sustain you and use every trial for His glory.

16. Trusting in God's Vindication:
   - Trust in God's ultimate vindication. Place your confidence in His justice, knowing that He will expose the lies, bring the truth to light, and restore your honor.

17. Learning from the Process:
   - Allow the experience of false accusations to become a learning opportunity. Reflect on the lessons God is teaching you, deepening your faith, character, and trust in Him.

18. Turning the Tables on Jezebel:

    - Turn the tables on Jezebel by refusing to be silenced or discouraged. Allow the attacks to fuel your determination to walk in righteousness and fulfill your God-given purpose.

19. Embracing God's Identity and Calling:

    - Embrace your identity and calling in Christ, understanding that false accusations do not define you. Rest in the knowledge that you are a child of God, loved and empowered by Him.

20. Rising Above the Accusations:

    - Rise above the false accusations of Jezebel. Embrace your identity as an overcomer and a victor in Christ. Walk in the freedom and victory that He has secured for you.

---

In conclusion, Jezebel's false accusations are powerful weapons she uses to attack and hinder God's people. However, as believers, we have the power and authority to overcome these attacks through the truth, love, and grace of Christ. By understanding Jezebel's tactics, walking in integrity and forgiveness, seeking God's wisdom, and surrounding ourselves with a supportive community, we can rise above false accusations and continue to walk in the purpose and calling God has for us. Let us stand strong, knowing that in Christ, we are more than conquerors, and nothing can separate us from His love and truth.

# Deliverance Prayer

1. Heavenly Father, I come before you in the name of Jesus, taking authority over every false accusation of Jezebel that has been spoken against me. I declare that these accusations will not prosper, and their power will be broken by the blood of Jesus.

2. I renounce and reject every lie and false accusation that Jezebel has leveled against me. I refuse to accept the labels and narratives that she has tried to impose on me. I declare that my identity is found in Christ alone.

3. I bind and cast out the spirit of accusation, slander, and deception that Jezebel operates in. I release the power of the Holy Spirit to expose the truth and bring forth justice in every situation.

4. I pray for discernment and wisdom to recognize the spirit of Jezebel behind false accusations. Give me clarity to see beyond the surface and discern the hidden motives and agendas behind these attacks.

5. I release forgiveness towards those who have falsely accused me. I choose to walk in love and extend grace, knowing that Jezebel seeks to divide and destroy relationships. I release the power of reconciliation and restoration.

6.  I declare that the truth of God's Word will prevail over every false accusation. I stand on the promises of Scripture, knowing that God is my defender and vindicator. His truth will be my shield and my refuge.

7.  I release the power of God's light into every dark corner where Jezebel's false accusations have taken root. Let the light of truth expose every lie and bring freedom and healing to those affected by these accusations.

8.  I pray for supernatural protection over my reputation, my relationships, and my calling. I declare that no weapon formed against me shall prosper, and every tongue that rises against me in judgment will be refuted.

9.  I release a spirit of resilience and perseverance in the face of false accusations. Strengthen me to endure, knowing that the trials I face will produce perseverance, character, and hope in me.

10. I decree and declare that Jezebel's false accusations will not define me or hinder my destiny. I walk in the confidence that I am chosen and called by God, and His plans for me will prevail.

11. I pray for those who have been influenced by Jezebel's false accusations to have their eyes opened to the truth. Let them see

beyond the deception and experience the power of God's love and grace.

12. I release a spirit of restoration and redemption over every area of my life that has been affected by false accusations. I declare that God will restore what the enemy has stolen and bring beauty from ashes.

13. I speak blessings and favor over those who have falsely accused me. I choose to bless and not curse, knowing that love and kindness have the power to overcome hatred and malice.

14. I pray for divine connections and alliances with others who have experienced false accusations. Let us encourage and support one another, standing together in unity against the schemes of Jezebel.

15. I release the power of God's healing and restoration to those who have been deeply wounded by false accusations. Bring comfort to their hearts and restore their sense of worth and purpose.

16. I pray for divine wisdom and strategies to navigate through the aftermath of false accusations. Guide me in making wise decisions and taking appropriate steps to bring resolution and healing.

17. I release the fire of the Holy Spirit to consume every false accusation and every negative word spoken against me. Let the

fire of God purify and cleanse, bringing forth truth, justice, and righteousness.

18. I pray for an outpouring of God's peace and assurance in the midst of false accusations. Let His presence surround me and calm my heart, knowing that He is my refuge and strength.

19. I declare that I am an overcomer through Christ who strengthens me. I will not be shaken or discouraged by false accusations, but I will rise above and walk in victory.

20. I surrender every false accusation and its effects to the Lord. I trust in His divine timing and perfect justice. I rest in His love, knowing that He is working all things together for my good. In Jesus' name, amen.

# Chapter 47

# The Roar of Intercession:
# Overthrowing Jezebel's Kingdom

In this chapter, we will explore the power of intercession in overthrowing Jezebel's kingdom. Jezebel is a spiritual stronghold that operates through manipulation, control, and deception, seeking to establish her dominion over individuals, families, churches, and even nations. However, we have been given the authority and privilege to engage in intercessory prayer, partnering with God to dismantle Jezebel's influence and bring forth His kingdom. In this chapter, we will delve into the nature of intercession, understand its significance in spiritual warfare against Jezebel, and equip ourselves with practical strategies to effectively pray and overthrow her kingdom.

1. The Role of Intercession in Spiritual Warfare:
   - Gain a deeper understanding of the role of intercession in spiritual warfare and its specific relevance in overthrowing Jezebel's kingdom. Explore biblical examples of intercessors who brought down strongholds through their prayers.

2. The Nature and Strategies of Jezebel:

- Explore the nature and strategies of Jezebel, understanding her tactics of manipulation, control, and deception. Recognize the areas where she seeks to establish her kingdom and identify her strongholds.

3. The Authority of the Believer:
- Understand the authority and power we have as believers to engage in intercession and overthrow Jezebel's kingdom. Discover the spiritual weapons and resources available to us through Christ.

4. Partnering with God in Intercession:
- Develop a deeper relationship with God through intercession, aligning our hearts with His purposes and receiving His strategies and insights. Learn to listen to His voice and cooperate with Him in prayer.

5. Praying with Authority:
- Learn to pray with boldness and authority, declaring God's Word, promises, and truth over the strongholds of Jezebel. Release the power of God's Word through intercession, knowing that it will not return void.

6. Identifying and Targeting Jezebel's Strongholds:
- Discern the specific areas where Jezebel has established her strongholds and strategically target them in intercession. Pray for the exposure, dismantling, and redemption of these strongholds.

7. Praying for Deliverance and Freedom:

- Intercede for the deliverance and freedom of individuals who have been ensnared by Jezebel's influence. Pray for their eyes to be opened, chains to be broken, and hearts to be restored to God's truth and love.

8. Releasing Prophetic Intercession:

- Embrace the role of prophetic intercession in overthrowing Jezebel's kingdom. Pray with the heart and mind of God, releasing His prophetic word and declarations to break down the strongholds of Jezebel.

9. Praying for the Church:

- Intercede for the Church, both locally and globally, to be awakened to Jezebel's influence and equipped to resist her tactics. Pray for leaders to walk in discernment, wisdom, and boldness to confront Jezebel and establish God's kingdom.

10. Praying for Families and Relationships:

- Lift up families and relationships in intercession, knowing that Jezebel seeks to destroy the foundation of godly relationships. Pray for healing, restoration, and the establishment of godly boundaries and dynamics.

11. Praying for Revival and Transformation:

- Engage in intercession for revival and transformation in communities, cities, and nations. Pray for Jezebel's influence to be uprooted and replaced with the power and presence of God, bringing salvation and restoration.

12. Praying for Government and Authorities:
- Intercede for government leaders and authorities, recognizing Jezebel's infiltration into political systems. Pray for godly leaders to arise, for justice and righteousness to prevail, and for Jezebel's influence to be exposed and overthrown.

13. Praying for Personal Protection:
- Cover yourself and your loved ones in intercession, asking God for protection and spiritual covering against Jezebel's attacks. Pray for the full armor of God to be activated in your life, equipping you to stand strong in the midst of spiritual warfare.

14. Praying for Jezebel's Salvation:
- Extend intercession for the salvation of those operating under Jezebel's influence. Pray for their hearts to be softened, their eyes to be opened, and their lives to be transformed by the power of the Gospel.

15. Praying for Unity and Spiritual Warfare Partnerships:
- Intercede for unity among believers, recognizing the power of corporate intercession in overthrowing Jezebel's kingdom. Pray

for divine connections and partnerships in spiritual warfare, where believers can join together in prayer and strategic intercession.

16. Praying for Continued Discernment and Sensitivity:
- Seek God's guidance in intercession, asking for continued discernment and sensitivity to the leading of the Holy Spirit. Pray for spiritual eyes to be opened and spiritual ears to hear the strategies and instructions of God in overthrowing Jezebel's kingdom.

17. Praying with Perseverance and Faith:
- Cultivate perseverance and faith in intercession, knowing that the battle against Jezebel is ongoing. Pray with persistence, not growing weary, but pressing forward in prayer and standing firm in the victory that Christ has already won.

18. Praying for a Shift in Spiritual Atmospheres:
- Engage in intercession for a shift in spiritual atmospheres, displacing the influence of Jezebel with the presence and power of God. Pray for the release of angels to wage warfare on behalf of the saints, enforcing God's kingdom rule.

19. Praying for Healing and Restoration:
- Lift up those who have been wounded, hurt, and oppressed by Jezebel's influence in intercession. Pray for healing, restoration,

and the release of God's comfort, love, and wholeness in their lives.

20. Praying for the Reign of God's Kingdom:
    - Declare and intercede for the reign of God's kingdom to manifest on earth, overthrowing Jezebel's kingdom. Pray for the establishment of righteousness, justice, and the transformation of lives, communities, and nations.

---

In conclusion, intercession is a powerful weapon in overthrowing Jezebel's kingdom. Through strategic and fervent prayer, we can partner with God to dismantle her strongholds, set captives free, and establish God's kingdom on earth. As we align our hearts with His, listen to His voice, and declare His truth, we will witness the power of intercession in overcoming Jezebel's influence. Let us arise as intercessors, roaring in prayer, and ushering in the victory of Christ over the works of darkness.

## Deliverance Prayer

1. Heavenly Father, I come before you in the name of Jesus, taking authority over Jezebel's kingdom of manipulation, control, and deception. I declare that through the power of intercession, we will overthrow and dismantle every stronghold she has established.

2. I bind and break the influence of Jezebel over individuals, families, churches, and nations. I declare that her strategies and tactics will be exposed and rendered ineffective by the light of your truth.

3. I release the roar of intercession, declaring that every prayer uttered in alignment with your will and empowered by your Spirit carries authority to bring down Jezebel's kingdom. Let the sound of our prayers shake the foundations of her stronghold.

4. I pray for a fresh anointing of intercession to fall upon your people. Ignite a passion for prayer and empower us to pray with fervor, persistence, and faith. Let us be relentless in our pursuit of breakthrough and the overthrow of Jezebel's influence.

5. I pray for divine strategies and insights in intercession, Holy Spirit. Show us the specific areas where Jezebel has established her strongholds so that we can target them with precision and effectiveness.

6. I release the power of God's Word through intercession. Let every declaration and prayer spoken in accordance with your Word be like a sword that cuts through Jezebel's lies and releases freedom and truth.

7. I pray for unity among intercessors, Father. Unite us in purpose and vision, as we stand together in agreement, tearing down Jezebel's kingdom brick by brick. Let our collective prayers resound as a symphony of victory.

8. I declare that the gates of hell will not prevail against the intercessors. We will not be intimidated or discouraged by Jezebel's attacks. Instead, we rise up in boldness and authority, knowing that you have equipped us to overcome.

9. I release a spirit of discernment and revelation to your intercessors. Open our eyes to see beyond the natural realm and perceive the spiritual battles taking place. Illuminate the schemes and strategies of Jezebel, empowering us to pray effectively.

10. I pray for divine protection over your intercessors, Father. Cover us with your armor and surround us with your angelic hosts. Guard our hearts and minds, shielding us from the enemy's attacks as we engage in spiritual warfare.

11. I decree and declare that Jezebel's kingdom is being dismantled and overthrown through the power of intercession. Let her influence crumble, her control weaken, and her deceptions be exposed. your kingdom will prevail!

12. I intercede for those who have been oppressed and ensnared by Jezebel's influence. I pray for their deliverance, healing, and restoration. Break the chains that bind them and set them free to walk in the fullness of your truth and love.

13. I release the fire of God to consume every altar and shrine erected by Jezebel. Let her false gods and idols be destroyed, and let the fire of your Holy Spirit purify and cleanse every place where her influence has been felt.

14. I pray for revival to ignite in the hearts of your people as we engage in intercession. Pour out your Spirit and awaken a hunger for righteousness, truth, and justice. Let our prayers be the catalyst for a mighty move of your Spirit.

15. I decree that the voice of intercession will drown out the voice of Jezebel. Let the sound of our prayers echo in the heavens, shaking the spiritual realm and ushering in breakthrough, healing, and transformation.

16. I release a spirit of boldness and courage upon your intercessors. Let us not shrink back in fear or intimidation but rise up as warriors, standing firm against Jezebel's attacks and advancing your kingdom through our prayers.

17. I pray for restoration and reconciliation in relationships that have been fractured by Jezebel's influence. Heal wounds, remove division, and restore unity. Let your love flow through us, bringing healing and reconciliation to families, churches, and communities.

18. I declare that Jezebel's false prophecies and counterfeit voices will be silenced. Let the voice of truth and the prophetic words spoken in alignment with your heart be heard and received. Expose the lies and bring forth your divine revelation.

19. I pray for a supernatural release of signs, wonders, and miracles as we intercede against Jezebel's kingdom. Let the power of your Spirit demonstrate your authority and bring undeniable evidence of your victory over darkness.

20. I seal these declarations and prayers in the precious name of Jesus. May they be like arrows shot into the heart of Jezebel's kingdom, piercing through her defenses and establishing your dominion. Let the roar of intercession resound until every stronghold is broken, and your kingdom reigns supreme. Amen.

# Chapter 48

# Jezebel's Grip on the Entertainment Industry: Transforming Culture

In this chapter, we will delve into the grip of Jezebel on the entertainment industry and the need for transformation in our culture. The entertainment industry holds immense influence over society, shaping values, beliefs, and behaviors. However, it has become a breeding ground for Jezebel's spirit of manipulation, immorality, and spiritual darkness. As followers of Christ, we are called to bring transformation and redemption to every sphere of society, including the entertainment industry. In this chapter, we will explore the impact of Jezebel in entertainment, understand the spiritual battles that take place, and discover how we can actively engage in transforming the culture through prayer, discernment, and creative excellence.

1. The Influence of the Entertainment Industry:
   - Understand the significant influence that the entertainment industry holds over culture, shaping worldviews, attitudes, and behaviors. Recognize the potential for both positive impact and spiritual darkness within this sphere.

2. Jezebel's Manipulation and Control:

- Examine how Jezebel's spirit operates within the entertainment industry, manipulating and controlling narratives, values, and creative expressions. Identify the tactics employed to further her agenda and suppress the light of truth.

3. Discerning Jezebel's Presence:
- Develop discernment to recognize Jezebel's influence in entertainment, including subtle deceptions, moral compromises, and the glorification of self and sin. Learn to discern the spirit behind the content we consume and engage with.

4. The Power of Prayer for Transformation:
- Explore the power of prayer in transforming the entertainment industry. Discover how prayer can shift spiritual atmospheres, break strongholds, and release God's redemptive purposes within this influential sphere.

5. Praying for Creative Excellence:
- Intercede for artists, filmmakers, musicians, writers, and all creative professionals within the entertainment industry. Pray for the release of God's creativity, anointing, and wisdom to bring forth excellence and reflect His truth and beauty.

6. Praying for Divine Appointments:
- Lift up actors, directors, producers, and other influential individuals in the entertainment industry. Pray for divine

encounters, divine appointments, and divine interventions that will draw them closer to God and open doors for His truth to be proclaimed.

7. Praying for Holy Spirit-led Discernment:
- Seek the Holy Spirit's guidance in discerning what content to engage with and support. Pray for discernment to identify and reject entertainment that promotes Jezebel's agenda while embracing and supporting media that aligns with God's truth.

8. Praying for Truth to Prevail:
- Intercede for a widespread hunger for truth within the entertainment industry. Pray for actors, writers, and content creators to boldly speak and portray God's truth, challenging cultural norms and fostering a hunger for righteousness.

9. Praying for Moral Purity and Integrity:
- Pray for a revival of moral purity and integrity within the entertainment industry. Lift up those who have been ensnared by Jezebel's influence, praying for their deliverance, repentance, and restoration.

10. Praying for Creative Redemptive Storytelling:
- Intercede for the release of redemptive storytelling within the entertainment industry. Pray for the creation of content that

reflects the transformative power of God's love, offers hope, and inspires positive change in individuals and society.

11. Praying for Godly Influencers:
- Lift up influencers, celebrities, and social media personalities in the entertainment industry. Pray for their salvation, spiritual awakening, and transformation. Ask God to raise up godly role models who will shine His light amidst the darkness.

12. Praying for a Shift in Cultural Paradigms:
- Engage in intercession for a paradigm shift in cultural values and norms perpetuated by the entertainment industry. Pray for a revival of biblical values, kingdom principles, and a hunger for righteousness to permeate every aspect of culture.

13. Praying for Exposé and Transformation:
- Intercede for the exposure of hidden agendas, secret societies, and occult practices within the entertainment industry. Pray for the truth to be revealed, leading to repentance, deliverance, and the transformation of individuals and systems.

14. Praying for Protection from Spiritual Attacks:
- Cover believers in the entertainment industry with prayers of protection from spiritual attacks, temptations, and compromises. Ask God to surround them with a community of support,

accountability, and encouragement as they navigate this challenging industry.

15. Praying for Collaboration and Unity:
    - Lift up prayers for collaboration and unity among believers within the entertainment industry. Pray for divine connections and strategic partnerships that will amplify their impact and bring about transformation on a larger scale.

16. Praying for Audience Transformation:
    - Intercede for the transformation of the audience consuming entertainment content. Pray that hearts and minds would be opened to receive truth, experience conviction, and encounter the life-transforming power of Jesus Christ.

17. Praying for Financial Resources and Kingdom Investments:
    - Pray for financial resources to flow into the hands of believers in the entertainment industry who are committed to producing content that honors God and promotes His kingdom values. Pray for kingdom-minded investors to recognize the importance of supporting such endeavors.

18. Praying for Opportunities to Share the Gospel:
    - Lift up prayers for divine opportunities for believers in the entertainment industry to boldly share the Gospel. Pray for hearts

to be receptive, seeds to be planted, and lives to be transformed through the message of salvation.

19. Praying for Redemptive Influence on Society:
   - Intercede for the redemptive influence of the entertainment industry on society. Pray for the media to reflect God's heart, confront injustice, promote unity, and inspire positive change that leads to the transformation of communities and nations.

20. Praying for Revival in the Entertainment Industry:
   - Cry out to God for a mighty revival within the entertainment industry. Pray for a widespread outpouring of His Spirit, transforming hearts, minds, and creative expressions. Ask for a revival that will redefine entertainment, making it a vehicle for His glory and kingdom purposes.

---

As believers, we have a mandate to impact every sphere of society with the transformative power of the Gospel. The entertainment industry is no exception. Through focused intercession, discernment, and active engagement, we can bring about a culture shift, overthrowing Jezebel's grip, and transforming this influential sphere. Let us rise up in prayer, declaring God's truth, and releasing His redemptive power in the world of entertainment. May the light of Christ shine brightly through the creative expressions and voices that influence our culture.

# Deliverance Prayer

1. Heavenly Father, in the name of Jesus, I come before you to declare and decree the transformation of the entertainment industry. I take authority over Jezebel's grip and influence, and I declare that your kingdom will prevail in this sphere.

2. I bind and break every spirit of manipulation, immorality, and darkness operating within the entertainment industry. I release the power of your truth to expose and dismantle every deceptive agenda that seeks to corrupt hearts and minds.

3. I declare that the entertainment industry will become a platform for righteousness, creativity, and the proclamation of your truth. I pray for a revival that will sweep through this sphere, transforming culture and bringing glory to your name.

4. I intercede for artists, actors, musicians, filmmakers, and all those involved in the entertainment industry. I pray that they will encounter your love, grace, and truth. May their hearts be awakened to your purpose, and may they use their talents to glorify you.

5. I pray for a divine shaking within the entertainment industry, Father. Shake the foundations of compromise and darkness. Let

your light penetrate every corner, exposing and dismantling Jezebel's influence.

6. I decree and declare that godly content will rise to prominence within the entertainment industry. I pray for a shift in demand, where audiences hunger for uplifting, morally sound, and inspiring content that reflects your values.

7. I release the power of discernment and conviction upon those who consume entertainment. Open their eyes to recognize the influence of Jezebel's spirit and empower them to make choices that align with your truth.

8. I pray for creative excellence to permeate the entertainment industry. I ask for an outpouring of your anointing upon artists and creators, enabling them to produce content that captivates hearts, uplifts souls, and brings honor to your name.

9. I intercede for believers within the entertainment industry, Father. Strengthen them with your Spirit, fortify their faith, and grant them divine favor and opportunities to shine as beacons of your light amidst the darkness.

10. I release a spirit of boldness and courage upon your children in the entertainment industry. Let them rise up as influencers and agents

of change, unafraid to stand for righteousness and challenge the status quo.

11. I pray for divine connections and collaborations among believers in the entertainment industry. Unite them in purpose, vision, and kingdom-mindedness. Let their collective impact be greater than what they could achieve individually.

12. I pray for the salvation of those who perpetuate Jezebel's agenda within the entertainment industry. I ask that you encounter them with your love, grace, and truth, bringing them to a place of repentance and transformation.

13. I declare that the entertainment industry will be a channel for the release of your redemptive power. Let stories of hope, restoration, and transformation permeate the screen and touch the lives of viewers.

14. I pray for the breaking of ungodly alliances and partnerships within the entertainment industry. Let your truth expose every hidden agenda and bring about a separation from ungodly influences.

15. I pray for divine favor and influence over decision-makers and gatekeepers in the entertainment industry. Open doors for content

that reflects your values, and close doors to that which promotes darkness and corruption.

16. I release a spirit of creativity and innovation within the entertainment industry. Let fresh ideas, originality, and authenticity flourish, impacting hearts, and transforming culture.

17. I pray for a resurgence of family-friendly and uplifting content within the entertainment industry. Let it bring healing, joy, and unity to families and communities, edifying the human spirit and glorifying your name.

18. I bind and break the spirit of fear that has hindered believers from fully engaging in the entertainment industry. Release a boldness and confidence in your children to walk in their calling and make a lasting impact.

19. I declare that the entertainment industry will be a platform for diversity and inclusion, celebrating the beauty of all cultures and backgrounds. Let unity and understanding replace division and discrimination.

20. I release a spirit of revival and transformation upon the entertainment industry. Let the sound of worship, praise, and declaration rise from this sphere, resounding with the power of your presence and ushering in a new era of godly influence and cultural transformation.

## Chapter 49

# Triumph over Jezebel:
# Stepping into Freedom and Restoration

In this final chapter, we will explore the journey of triumph over Jezebel's influence, stepping into a place of freedom and restoration. Throughout this book, we have gained insights into the deceptive nature of the Jezebel spirit, its tactics, and its impact on various areas of our lives and society. Now, it is time to move beyond mere knowledge and understanding and embrace the victory that Christ has secured for us. In this chapter, we will discover how to break free from Jezebel's grip, experience restoration in our lives, and walk in the fullness of our God-given identity and destiny.

1. Recognizing the Signs of Jezebel's Influence:
    - Recap the signs and characteristics of Jezebel's influence that we have explored throughout the book. Reflect on personal experiences and identify areas where her presence may still linger.

2. Embracing the Truth of God's Word:
    - Explore the power of God's Word in dismantling Jezebel's lies and restoring truth to our lives. Discover key scriptures that declare our identity, authority, and freedom in Christ.

3. Breaking Free from Jezebel's Manipulation:

- Dive deeper into the strategies for breaking free from Jezebel's manipulation. Uncover the power of forgiveness, boundaries, and healthy relationships in reclaiming our autonomy and breaking the chains of control.

4. Healing from the Wounds of Jezebel:

- Address the wounds and hurts inflicted by Jezebel's influence. Understand the importance of inner healing, restoration, and forgiveness in the journey toward wholeness.

5. Restoring Healthy Relationships:

- Examine the impact of Jezebel on relationships and discover practical steps for restoring healthy connections. Learn how to set healthy boundaries, cultivate healthy communication, and walk in love and grace.

6. Renewing the Mind:

- Explore the process of renewing the mind and uprooting the lies implanted by Jezebel. Discover the power of declaring God's truth, meditating on His Word, and partnering with the Holy Spirit in the transformation of our thought patterns.

7. Rediscovering God's Design for Authority:

- Uncover God's original design for authority and leadership and contrast it with Jezebel's counterfeit. Learn to embrace healthy leadership, honor God-ordained authority, and walk in the fullness of our own God-given authority.

8. Cultivating a Spirit of Discernment:
   - Develop a spirit of discernment to identify and resist Jezebel's influence in various areas of life. Discover how to rely on the Holy Spirit, sharpen our spiritual senses, and discern between God's voice and the enemy's deceptions.

9. Stepping into Your God-given Identity:
   - Embrace the journey of discovering and stepping into your God-given identity. Recognize the unique gifts, talents, and calling that God has placed within you, and reject the limitations and falsehoods imposed by Jezebel.

10. Embracing the Fullness of God's Love:
   - Experience the overwhelming love of God that breaks the power of Jezebel's spirit. Encounter the depth of His love, acceptance, and affirmation, and allow it to redefine your self-worth and identity.

11. Walking in Spiritual Freedom:
   - Step into the freedom that Christ has secured for you. Declare your independence from Jezebel's influence and embrace the liberty to live a life surrendered to God's purposes and guided by the Holy Spirit.

12. Pursuing Spiritual Wholeness and Holiness:
   - Dive deeper into the journey of spiritual wholeness and holiness. Explore the importance of inner healing, deliverance, and consecration in breaking free from Jezebel's grip and aligning your life with God's perfect will.

13. Activating Your Spiritual Authority:
   - Activate your spiritual authority in Christ to confront and overcome Jezebel's influence. Learn to exercise your authority through prayer, declaration, and standing firmly on the promises of God's Word.

14. Engaging in Strategic Spiritual Warfare:
   - Equip yourself with strategic spiritual warfare tactics to combat Jezebel's influence. Discover the power of intercession, fasting, spiritual weapons, and standing in unity with other believers.

15. Pressing Forward in Victory:
   - Encourage readers to press forward in their journey of triumph over Jezebel. Emphasize the importance of perseverance, faith, and reliance on God's strength as they continue to walk in freedom and restoration.

16. Embracing a Culture of Freedom:

- Challenge readers to become catalysts for a culture of freedom, restoration, and revival. Encourage them to share their testimonies, engage in mentoring relationships, and extend grace and love to those still under Jezebel's influence.

---

In this final chapter, we have discovered the path to triumph over Jezebel's influence, stepping into a place of freedom, restoration, and walking in the fullness of our God-given identity. As we have journeyed through the depths of Jezebel's tactics and the impact on our lives, we have also encountered the transforming power of God's love, truth, and redemption. Now, armed with knowledge, revelation, and practical strategies, we are empowered to break free from Jezebel's grip and live victoriously in Christ. Let us embrace the journey ahead, stepping into our true identity and purpose, and impact the world around us with the transforming power of God's love.

## Deliverance Prayer

1. Heavenly Father, in the name of Jesus, I declare and decree my triumph over Jezebel's influence. I take authority over every stronghold, manipulation, and deception, and I walk in the freedom and restoration you have promised.

2. I break every chain of control and manipulation that Jezebel has attempted to place upon my life. I declare my independence from her influence and embrace the fullness of your truth and love.

3. I renounce and reject every lie that Jezebel has spoken over me. I declare that I am fearfully and wonderfully made, created in your image, and destined for greatness according to your purpose.

4. I release forgiveness to those who have been influenced by Jezebel's spirit. I choose to walk in love and extend grace, knowing that your love has the power to heal and restore every broken relationship.

5. I declare that my mind is renewed by your Word, and I uproot every thought pattern influenced by Jezebel's lies. I align my thoughts with your truth, and I embrace the freedom and clarity that come from thinking according to your perspective.

6. I embrace my God-given identity and destiny. I declare that I am a child of God, empowered by the Holy Spirit, and equipped to fulfill the purpose and calling you have placed upon my life.

7. I activate my spiritual authority in Christ to confront and overcome Jezebel's influence. I bind and rebuke every spirit of control, manipulation, and intimidation, and I release the power of your truth and love to dismantle her strongholds.

8. I engage in strategic spiritual warfare against Jezebel's influence. I stand firm in prayer, intercession, and the declaration of your Word. I use the weapons of my warfare to pull down every stronghold and advance your kingdom.

9. I declare that I am an overcomer through the blood of Jesus. I reject the spirit of fear, and I embrace the spirit of power, love, and a sound mind. I walk in boldness and confidence, knowing that you have equipped me to triumph over every attack of Jezebel.

10. I pursue spiritual wholeness and holiness. I surrender every area of my life to you, and I allow your Spirit to cleanse, heal, and restore me from the inside out. I am made new in Christ, free from the influence of Jezebel.

11. I press forward in victory, knowing that you are with me. I will not be discouraged or defeated by Jezebel's tactics. I walk in faith, perseverance, and the assurance that you who began a good work in me will bring it to completion.

12. I embrace a culture of freedom, restoration, and revival. I share my testimony of triumph over Jezebel's influence, and I extend grace, love, and support to those still under her grip. I become a vessel of hope and healing, pointing others to the freedom found in Christ.

13. I release a spirit of discernment to recognize and expose Jezebel's tactics in my surroundings. I pray for the wisdom to navigate relationships and situations with godly discernment, always aligning myself with your truth and purpose.

14. I declare that Jezebel's influence in my life is null and void. I sever every ungodly tie and influence she may have had, and I surrender myself completely to your will and plan for my life.

15. I embrace the restoration of all that Jezebel has stolen or damaged. I declare that you are the God of restoration, and I trust in your ability to bring beauty from ashes and turn every situation around for my good and your glory.

16. I pray for others who are still under the influence of Jezebel's spirit. I intercede on their behalf, asking for their eyes to be opened, their hearts to be softened, and their lives to be transformed by your love and truth.

17. I walk in the power of the Holy Spirit, knowing that greater is He who is in me than he who is in the world. I am filled with your presence and anointing, and I am empowered to walk in victory over Jezebel's influence.

18. I commit to a lifestyle of continual growth, learning, and seeking your face. I will not become complacent or stagnant but will press on to deeper levels of intimacy with you, knowing that in your presence, Jezebel's power is broken.

19. I declare that my life is a testimony of triumph over Jezebel. I will shine as a light in the darkness, pointing others to the freedom and restoration found in Christ. I will use my voice and influence to bring glory to your name.

20. I give thanks and praise to you, Lord, for the victory and freedom I have in you. I declare that I am more than a conqueror through Christ Jesus, and I will walk in the fullness of my identity and purpose, bringing honor and glory to your name. Amen.

# Appreciation

Thank you for purchasing and reading my book. I am extremely grateful and hope you found value in reading it. Please consider sharing it with friends and family and leaving a review online.

Your feedback and support are always appreciated and allow me to continue doing what I love.

Please go to www.amazon.com/dp/B0C9SBBH6L
if you'd like to leave a review.

**Deliverance & Spiritual Warfare**

Monitoring Spirits exposed and defeated

Jezebel Spirit exposed and defeated

Praise and worship: Potent weapons of warfare

Prophetic warfare: Unleashing supernatural power in warfare

Rise above the curse: An empowering guide to overcome witchcraft attacks

The time is now: A guide to overcoming marital delay

Earth moving prayers: Pray until miracles happen

I must win this battle: Expanded edition

Essential prayers

Open heavens: Unlocking divine blessings and breakthroughs

This battle ends now

Breaking the unbreakable

Reversing evil handwriting

I must win this battle - French Edition

I must win this battle - Spanish Edition

Ammunition for spiritual warfare

Reversing the Irreversible

Let there be a change

Total Deliverance: Volume 1

21 days prayer for total breakthroughs

**14 Days Prayer & Fasting Series**

14 Days prayer to break evil patterns.

14 days prayer against delay and stagnation

14 days prayer for a new beginning

14 days prayer for deliverance from demonic attacks

14 days prayer for total healing

14 days prayer for deliverance from rejection and hatred

14 days prayer for healing the foundations
14 days prayer for breaking curses and evil covenants
14 days prayer for uncommon miracles
14 days prayer for restoration and total recovery
14 days prayer: It's time for a change
14 days prayer for deliverance from witchcraft attacks
14 days prayer for accelerated promotion
14 days prayer for deliverance from generational problems
14 days prayer for supernatural supply
14 days prayer to God's will for your life
14 days prayer for Mountaintop Experience
14 days prayer for home, family and marriage restoration
14 days prayer to overcome stubborn situations
14 days prayer for financial breakthroughs


**Personal Finances**
The art of utility bills negotiation
From strapped to successful: Unlocking Financial Freedom beyond
Paycheck to paycheck

**Bible Study**
The King is coming
Seven judgments of the Bible
The miracle of Jesus Christ
The book of Exodus
Lost and found: The house of Israel
The parables of Jesus Christ

**Christian Fantasy**
The merchant's legacy: A tale of faith and family

**Family Counseling**
Healing whispers: Biblical comfort and healing for men after miscarriage